THIS

WAY

UP

THIS
WAY
UP

SHIRLEY JENNINGS

Copyright © 2024 Shirley Jennings.

Paperback ISBN: 978-1-915490-22-3

A catalogue record for this book is available from the British Library.

No part of this publication may be reproduced, stored in a retrieval system, or transmitted in any form or by any means, electronic, mechanical, photocopying, recording, or otherwise, without written permission of the publisher.

All rights reserved including the right of reproduction in whole or in part in any form. The moral right of the author has been asserted.

www.blkdogpublishing.com

Have you ever done something totally random? Made a spur of the moment decision that was completely out of character?

I did.

I flew an aeroplane and somehow became a pilot. That wasn't supposed to happen. People like me don't fly aeroplanes.

Then I discovered gyroplanes – it was all James Bond's fault. People like me didn't fly gyroplanes either.

Now the timid introvert that I am drives the length of France to fly with a special group of friends at the Gyro Club Toulouse, down by the Pyrenees. Six hundred miles alone on the wrong side of the road, in a language I can barely speak.

It's been a voyage of discovery and new horizons in every sense. This is the tale of a Rotormouse.

Foreword

If someone had told me four decades ago that come the year 2020, a casual appraisal of my life would inspire an account of the highlights (and what those highlights would prove to be!), I would've chuckled at such a crazy notion. Deeply introverted and socially inadequate with confidence levels of precisely zero, what could I ever achieve? Yet as ridiculous as it may seem, the quiet and unassured creature that I am *did* do something extraordinary, a fact that I've always been reluctant to acknowledge as the 'firsts' were merely coincidental. I don't do what I do because I wanted be first – I do what I do because it speaks to my soul like nothing else can. What's extraordinary is this timid pint-sized mouse falling head-over-heels for what many perceive to be a renegade and suicidal activity, but au contraire, I'm a most unlikely renegade, without a death wish.

Early in 2019, eight years of struggle culminated in the publication of *Spinning on the Wind,* which in turn marked the approaching end of the Brookland Rotorcraft project. Repeated appeals to promote my disastrously flawed paperback on social media fell on deaf ears. I don't do the Snapface, Twittergram or Chatbook thing and have no desire to be followed, liked or shared. 'But you must have an online presence!' they persisted, hence the reluctant creation of my website, which found me dredging up past events in order to pad it out a bit. This, combined with the unprecedented global lockdown of 2020 (weirdly appropriate for such a year of hindsight), led me to ponder the episodes that have shaped my life, sitting here in reflection thinking...

I can't believe I did that!

*

I don't know exactly when it began. Sometime around the late seventies or early eighties, I remember being captivated by a television documentary about an affable old gentleman whizzing around his garden in strange little home-made 'helicopters'. I thought it looked like fun and life carried on as usual, completely unaware that a seed had been sown. I had no intention of becoming a pilot. People like me don't become pilots. Flying is the domain of confident types who articulate with ease and possess considerably more intelligence than I, but fortune works in mysterious ways and thus I came upon it by accident – a flying accident you might say. Half a lifetime ago, warships were my passion.

Growing up in an area of historic seafaring tradition greatly influenced my desire to join the Royal Navy, even though mere females were strictly land-based in those days. The summer of 1977 saw several thousand bewildered sixteen-year-olds released from secondary education straight into the sombre embrace of the dole queue, and one particularly bewildered sixteen-year-old among them was me. How I hated that weekly trek to sign on at Plymouth Civic Centre. Raw kids fresh from the classroom joined the jaded ranks of long-term unemployed in a hopeless quest for work that wasn't there. A grim line of depression queuing around the block swathed in a choking cloud of nicotine.

Devonport Dockyard offered a few dozen apprenticeships, but like the hundreds of other hopeful teenagers who took the entrance exam, I didn't stand a chance. No one else wanted me either. Inexperienced kids were ten-a-penny and no use to anyone, but I didn't mind. Time was now my own and thanks to the hated ritual of the dole queue, a fortune of three pounds a week in my pocket meant freedom. My parents presented me with an elderly moped, my first step on the road to adult independence. Blessed with a modest selection of first or second gears, its automatic transmission was a poor match for the steep Devonian hills up which we crawled, but I loved it, zipping along at a carefree twenty miles an hour – well it felt like zipping. Life was good and the coming February meant that I would at last be old enough to apply for the Navy.

The dying embers of that blissful summer were, upon reflection, to herald the approaching twilight of my childhood. That hallowed existence of mine came to an abrupt and unwelcome conclusion as my parents uprooted, returning the family to our native and horribly land-locked county of Berkshire. It was awful. The same hapless dole queue awaited, a faithful replica of despondency to be found in every major British town during the 1970s. Hemmed in by dreary suburbia, I longed for the open sea and spacious freedom of the Devon countryside. February couldn't come soon enough for my liking. Confidence is not my strong point but as the long-awaited month crept closer, a small seed of belief was beginning to take root in my mind. My aunt mentioned vacancies in the factory where she worked, a soul-destroying monotony of mass-produced metalwork; *but it will only be temporary* I thought, and a thousand times better than the dole queue. So it was that I entered the mechanical cacophony of the grease-stained shop floor, a culture shock to put it mildly.

The work was incredibly boring and repetitive, with none of the Health and Safety concerns of today. Protective equipment was minimal and only the men were provided with boiler suits and steel-capped boots. Female employees made do with dust coats and stiff rubber gloves that were invariably man-sized, but the sharp metal components shredded them with ease. The access way to the factory floor was dubbed 'Firework Alley', lined on either side by rows of spot-welding machines that spewed jets of hot embers, raining fiery sparks that burned tiny holes in clothes, scalps and skin. My workstation was an asbestos-lined box that shed a fine tickling dust which made me sneeze. That's how it was back then, we just got on with it.

Everyone told me that if I wanted something badly enough then it was sure to happen – I wanted to join the Navy and get the hell out of there! Christmas slipped by. Amidst the raucous heat and grime of the press shop, January turned into February, and I could finally begin my escape plan. Initial doubts at the recruitment centre were quelled by the ease of the entrance exam, after which I was summoned to London for a medical and an interview. Verbal communication has always been my Achilles heel, but I hoped for the best and returned home to await the verdict. Back in the confines of the factory, nondescript days of ceaseless industrial noise blended into forgettable weeks of sweltering heat caked in a greasy filth. Time dragged on. Well-meaning folk encouraged me that the wait was a good sign, it was bound to be all right. Rejection came in its own good time. A brief but polite missive arrived, thanking me for my interest and wishing me well in some other profession, and deep down I probably wasn't that surprised. I put on a brave face. It was only a setback and after waiting the mandatory year between applications, I would try again. But twelve months of tedium later, I failed to regain that elusive bout of confidence. To rebuild all my hopes on that fragile scaffold of optimism only to have them come crashing back down again, I couldn't do it. I chickened out. The temporary factory job turned into a seven-year stretch, and I was in a rut.

Model making was a favourite hobby in which I could escape the dull reality that my life had become. By now I'd built pretty much every warship kit that I could afford, the results of which filled a cabinet and all available shelving in my room. It seemed a logical step to tackle some larger versions of the tiny flying machines that lined the decks of my aircraft carriers, the added bonus being that I could hang them from the ceiling! And so it began. Blissfully ignorant of the affliction I was contracting, squadrons of fighters and bombers started to outnumber the prized fleets in my room, as aviation books and videos squeezed in alongside naval literature on the shelf. In those innocent days before twisted minds turned passenger jets into missiles, I roamed freely around the expanse of Heathrow Airport and on the roof of the Queens Building in particular, spending hours just watching and waiting for a glimpse of Concorde. I became hooked on air shows, driving many miles in pilgrimage to the sight and sounds of those rare vintage aircraft I had created in miniature. There was more to this than mere diversity, yet I remained unaware of the radical shift in focus, let alone where it would ultimately lead. Not in a million years could I have guessed where it would ultimately lead!

My twenty-first birthday crept up on me. I was horrified: *I'm too young to be this old!* But an amazing gift awaited my coming of age. Out on the busy apron at Heathrow Airport, I stood at the foot of the steps staring in disbelief at the slender white fuselage towering above me, lost in the perfection of sleek lines and shapely curve of that unique delta wing. The babble of my fellow passengers faded out of existence and the most beautiful aircraft ever designed waited for me alone. Concorde G-BOAC was all mine. What a momentous way to take wing for the very first time. Fastened inside the snug tubular cabin of the world's fastest and most emotive passenger jet, the gentle background hum swelled to a thunderous roar that rose in volume with a sense of tremendous energy gathering itself beneath us. The aircraft seemed poised in anticipation as she trembled on tiptoe. The thrust was incredible! Four Olympus engines unleashed their fury with an almighty shove in the back that pinned us breathless against our seats, fired down the runway like an arrow from a bow as Alpha Charlie reared up and powered steeply in to the heavens. WOW! Craning to peer through the thick glass of the impossibly small windows, I gaped out on a dazzling panorama unfolding below. Travelling faster than sound according to the famous Mach meter on the bulkhead, at 60,000 feet we seemed to be suspended on the very edge of space. The sunlit globe of the Earth curved gently on the horizon, capped dramatically by a dark void beyond the atmosphere. Far below, an ocean of blue steel sparkled with silver and gold, flanked by quilts of brilliant white cloud like the purest of snows. The planet was radiant. I was completely in awe.

In retrospect, the implications of my first flight were to remain hidden for the time being, I still had a ground-dweller's mentality. My brief experience of Concorde had been beyond anything I could've imagined - she was magnificent! - and I'm forever grateful to my parents for such a marvellous gift. To witness the hitherto unimagined beauty of the heavens had been a rich and unexpected bonus, yet I harboured no thought of returning to the skies, the possibility just never occurred to me.

This Way Up

At least, not for another three years it wouldn't...

IN THE BEGINNING

19 May 1985 – and so it begins

By 1985, life had improved enormously. No longer caged by factory tedium (voluntary redundancy provided welcome release), I was now happily settled in a small workshop learning the art of corporate badge and sign making. It was interesting, required some skill and therefore it was fun. Model making activities had been curtailed somewhat having reached critical mass on the storage front, despite dangling surplus aircraft from the ceiling to gather dust, which they managed to attract in impressive quantities. Although the fixation with air shows, aviation books and videos remained, a definite hole had appeared in my leisure time, so was it coincidence or something more profound that led me to Earls Court that year?

Ambling half-heartedly among the crowded stands of the Ideal Home Exhibition, I suddenly caught a glimpse of a small aeroplane. It was most surreal. My expectations of finding anything of interest had been practically zero, yet here amid the vast displays of domestic gadgetry and housewares was a real live aircraft! I squeezed through the throng to get a better look. It was a different species to my usual military machines: a civilian light aircraft. Small aeroplanes often buzzed over our village from local airfields, but I paid them little attention, vaguely aware that the ugly ones with their wings on top were a breed called Cessna. But this one was oddly appealing. Although divested of its wings, the remaining stubs hinted that the low wing design definitely looked right, much nicer than the flying bus shelters.

Providence opened a gap in the crowd and I slipped through to peer in to the cockpit. Apart from a few extra controls, I could have been looking at the interior of a posh modern car. Two pairs of comfortable seats with ordinary safety belts filled the cabin, a twin set of control yokes and chunky foot pedals arranged for the occupants up front. A large dashboard filled with strange dials in neat order fitted snugly against a spaciously curved windscreen. This was the first time I had seen inside a light aircraft, yet (perhaps because of my models) I was enchanted by its familiarity. I'm one of those soppy people who talk to inanimate objects and bestow pet names on my vehicles. Maybe the curse of the introvert is a contributing factor, but for whatever reason, I've always felt a natural empathy with machinery, despite not being particularly mechanically minded. It's an intangible awareness that some have a spirit of their own, in a mechanical sense rather than the biological. Okay, it sounds weird and I probably am, but that's how it goes. I've lived with me a long time – just roll with it!

Despite my passion for aviation, the thought of actually learning to fly hadn't crossed my mind. There was no life-long ambition to fulfil or anything like that, it wasn't on my radar at all. Pilots were a cut above ordinary mortals like me. I could no more become an aviator than delve into nuclear physics – so how as I stood beside that truncated little aeroplane did I know that this was inevitable? Even before the salesman homed in on me, sensing commission, there wasn't a shred of doubt that my hard-earned cash would be exchanged for a trial flight voucher. It wasn't like me at all, but that simple transaction lit the fuse on the greatest adventure of my life. Back at work, my colleagues laughed at what I had done and questioned my sanity, but that was nothing new. Another birthday was imminent so it seemed appropriate to take wing on the same day, and should the predictions of doom by my irreverent pals come to fruition, it'd be a pleasing touch of irony to shuffle off this mortal coil on the exact date that I had shrugged it on. Either way I'd be trying on a new pair of wings! But the best laid plans of mice and would-be aviators and all that – my first lesson was meteorology. It was raining. We couldn't fly.

Surprised by an unexpected level of disappointment, I fretted my way through an exceptionally long working week until Sunday finally crawled around again. The weather was much improved so with camera-wielding family in tow, we headed for Blackbushe Airport along a route that would become very familiar over the next couple of years. I even remember asking my dad to use up the film in my camera as this would only be a one-off experience, unsuspecting child that I was. So that's how on 19 May 1985, I first took the controls of a light aircraft: a Grumman Cheetah, or AA5A to be exact, sister to the friendly little machine that had snared me in the exhibition hall. There were three of them parked on the grass by the fence: one with orange and brown stripes, and a pair with identical red and blue markings on their white skins. I would come to know the twins, G-FANG and G-PAWS very well in the future. The trio of Cheetahs was considerably outnumbered by a flock of the flying bus shelters belonging to a rival school across the way, but they held no appeal for me whatsoever. Had one of those been on display at Earls Court, this story might have been very different.

Inside I met David, the instructor tasked to accompany me. We completed a few formalities then I followed him out to the brown-striped machine, G-MELD. Together we walked around her inspecting fuel and oil levels, waggling control surfaces and generally looking for defects until David was satisfied that all was in order. With my brother Graham installed in the back seat and tied down, it was my turn to climb up on the wing root and step into the cockpit. I loved it at once. In front of me were eight large dials with a row of rocker switches laid out below: a stack of radio and navigation equipment divided the panel in two, with a collection of smaller gauges and dials housed on the far side. A central console ran between the seats, housing fuel gauges and tank selector, along with trim wheel and a small tab to activate the electrically driven flaps. Twin control yokes sprouted from the panel above our knees, while our feet rested on identical pairs of combined brake and rudder pedals.

Locking the canopy in place over our heads, David pointed out each instrument and dial, explaining their functions as he prepared to start the engine. The little aircraft began to hum into life around us, responding to various switches and levers as David worked through the check list. Seat belts fastened, headsets plugged into the intercom and we were all set. Feet on the brake pedals, ignition switch on: the two-bladed propeller jerked through a couple of turns and vanished in a blur as the engine caught and shuddered into life. G-MELD trembled and nosed forward as the slipstream whipped over her wings, standing on tiptoe – just like Concorde but with considerably less oomph! We waited a moment for the engine to warm up, and after checking all the gauges were reading correctly, David keyed the microphone and spoke to the tower. The controller replied with something unintelligible inside my headphones, and away we went.

As instructed, I held the yoke in my left hand to follow David's actions, taking the throttle lever with my right. Releasing the brakes, I cautiously pushed open the throttle just enough to get us rolling and steered the aeroplane on to the tarmac with the pedals. At twenty-two feet in length, the Cheetah was a good deal longer than any car I had driven and although the cockpit was a familiar size, the wings stretching out on either side spanned thirty feet from tip to tip. Always nervous of driving larger vehicles, I was strangely undaunted by G-MELD's vital statistics and felt completely at home. We arrived safely at the holding point where David took over to do the run up checks, talking me through the check list as he advanced the throttle and did things with some switches. I followed as best I could, completely fascinated if not exactly comprehending. Satisfied that everything was as it should be, David spoke again to the tower and the voice in my ears replied with a string of letters and numbers, which evidently contained permission to proceed.

David released the brakes and steered us out on to the runway, aiming the nose wheel along the centre line. Looking ahead through the blur of the propeller was like sitting in the middle of an empty motorway, a smooth tarmac super highway stretched out before us. This was it. My senses were on overload, barely aware of David's commentary as he opened the throttle. For someone whose only flying experience was the ultimate supersonic airliner, I was now at the opposite end of the scale and naturally it couldn't have been more different. Comparisons with the family car again came to mind as G-MELD began to accelerate down the runway, all very gentle and even sedate. I tried to follow the rising needles of the airspeed indicator, engine rpm and temperature gauges, while glancing at the pointer of the direction indicator slaved to match our compass heading - this was impossible! But David seemed totally unconcerned as he eased back on the yoke and several mysterious forces combined to lift us into the air as the engine cowling filled the windscreen, blocking the view ahead. It felt like driving up a moderately steep slope as I glanced out to the left and was surprised to see treetops already disappearing beneath the wings. There was no fanfare, it was all very casual. We were flying, and I loved it.

SPROUTING WINGS

Romeo Romeo – wherefore art thou...

It's said in the aviation world that a pilot doesn't forget their first solo, but conforming to type doesn't really work for me. The milestone had been a long time coming. Having reached an acceptable standard around mid-autumn, suitable weather conditions were few and far between and rarely coincided with my lesson. So alongside Peter, my long-suffering instructor, I continued to practice the art of returning a light aircraft to earth in one piece. My last lesson of 1985 was booked for Sunday, 22 December, a day that arrived complete with howling wind and torrential rain lashing against the windows. I fretted all morning as the time for my afternoon slot drew closer. The wrathful elements had somewhat abated by lunchtime, but the heavy overcast didn't look at all promising, so I was surprised by the ops desk telling me to come up when I phoned to see if another scrub was on the cards. Things were improving slowly as the weather front passed through, and the wind was due to moderate and shift favourably. Well, that was something: I might get a bit more dual time to finish off the year.

A couple of machines were already in the air when I arrived at a very soggy Blackbushe an hour later, with no expectation of flying alone that day. The clouds were beginning to lift and although there was still a stiff breeze, it was behaving as forecast and steadily aligning itself down the runway. G-FANG was my allotted mount, thoughtfully parked in the middle of a very large puddle. My feet were soaked by the time the external checks were complete, but the sun was already breaking through and matters had improved considerably. Peter hopped in beside me and off we went into the circuit.

He put me through all the drills - engine failure, glide approach, flapless - taking control on climb out from a practice overshoot to zoom ahead of the other traffic in a tight low-level circuit that put us at the front of the queue to land. That was fun! I couldn't believe how quickly the day had changed from such a wildly inclement morning to a very pleasant and flyable afternoon. Finally the weather gods had smiled on me, but it still came as a shock when Peter radioed 'November Golf, full stop' as we touched down from our rapid short circuit, braking hard and turning FANG's nose back toward the parking area. Apparently, this was it and immediately the doubts set in. I see from the notes I scribbled the following day that Peter gave me a long pep talk, double-checked the magnetos and radio before leaving me as sole captain of my ship - or a little Grumman Cheetah that suddenly seemed a whole lot bigger.

Thankfully, Paul was on duty in the tower and not old Reg, who was a bit deaf and rarely failed to tell me that my stressful transmissions were 'unreadable'. I taxied FANG to the holding point where we idled awaiting clearance, presumably giving Peter time to get up in the tower, along with another instructor whose student was behind me in a Cessna, also on their first solo. Yes, that memorable first solo that no pilot can forget. To quote my notes: *Took off all right, then I must've done a circuit and landed. It went so fast, I don't know what happened. Tibor asked me how I felt, I said I didn't know!* So that was that.

FANG was still in one piece and could be used again, so presumably it was a great landing as the old adage goes. Peter presented me with my wings, and I still have them today, even if I can't remember how I got them.

*

Having fulfilled my requisite share of circuit bashing, subsequent upper air work and navigation exercises, it was time to leave the nest and venture further afield on my own. I wasn't looking forward to this at all. The first trip out was a simple overhead to Thruxton then turn around back to Blackbushe, pretty much a straight line that did nothing to improve my confidence. Next up was a dogleg to land at Bembridge on the Isle of Wight, crossing a busy control zone and having to talk to Southampton air traffic. I was so stressed by the radio and fear of doing something wrong in controlled airspace that I completely failed to appreciate my successful landing of the faithful FANG at Bembridge, or any of the stunning coastal views while crossing the Solent and returning her safely to the Bushe.

Marc was manning the ops desk when I signed in, and he congratulated me on completing a milestone flight (first solo landing away), asking if I had enjoyed it. *No* was the answer to that one. I was just relieved that it was over and to have brought FANG back in one piece - enjoyment hadn't come in to it! Marc looked concerned and asked if I would wait for him at the table while he finished updating the tech logs, joining me a few minutes later with two cups of coffee. He said he was sorry that I hadn't enjoyed myself, and asked if anything had gone wrong. What a nice guy; I wasn't one of his students and he didn't need to do that. I briefly explained my radio phobia and general feeling of inadequacy when left in sole charge of an expensive piece of equipment, not forgetting the potential for causing havoc in busy airspace. Marc gave me a bit of pep talk and said what an achievement I had made that day - even if I didn't really believe it! Then he told me a tale that has stayed with me ever since.

During the Second World War, a young American fighter

pilot was also afraid to fly (albeit with far greater reason) so to help calm his nerves and to keep him company, he imagined that a blue dove sat with him in the cockpit. And therein lies the reason why my gyroplane has a blue bird painted on her nose. Some are convinced that it's Woody Woodpecker and there is a passing resemblance, to be fair, but inspiration actually came from a USAF squadron patch and it's just the way it turned out. Our blue bird perches on a rainbow instead of a gauntlet as I wanted something more ephemeral to represent to the sky, so no, it's not Woody Woodpecker and definitely has nothing to do with gay rights either! It stems from that first solo fright to Bembridge all those years ago. I was really touched by Marc's concern that day, and the time he took to straighten me out. Thanks Marc. And hell yeah – I *did* do that.

*

The most *purrfect* flight that I ever did in an aeroplane happened to be my qualifying cross-country. Having already flown a dual trip to Staverton with Peter, I had some idea of what to expect, but Kidlington was new territory and the qualifying flight would be my first visit – if I could find it. I'd been waiting for over a month for suitable weather and had to thank my boss for giving me free rein to leave work whenever the opportunity presented itself. The triangular route had long been plotted on my chart, so all I had to do was add the appropriate winds, adjust the timings and we would be good to go. When I finally got the call, it was literally drop everything and scoot up to the airfield as fast as my moped would carry me, stopping briefly at home on the way to grab my flight bag. On arrival at the Bushe, I was pleased to have been allocated G-PAWS, having done my first solo in her twin it would be nice to complete the set.

I updated my calculations for Staverton to Kidlington and back, while chaos reigned at the ops desk. Unlike her sisters, PAWS wasn't fitted with long range tanks and so lacked the capacity to complete the trip without refuelling away, which (for reasons I can't remember) wasn't an option. I would have to wait for G-PURR to come back and take her instead. Nice little aircraft that she was in her rather garish new paint scheme of orange and yellow stripes, my radio woes were compounded by having to call 'Romeo Romeo' over the airwaves, I always felt such a berk! She was on frequency in the circuit returning from a lesson, and the tower relayed a message to leave her at the pumps for fuelling ready to go straight back out. This confusion had seriously eaten in to my schedule and there was no more time to lose if I was to complete the qualifying flight before official night (thirty minutes after sunset), otherwise it wouldn't count and I would have to go back and do it again.

The chief instructor came out with me to the pumps where PURR was having her tanks topped up, telling me to get settled in the cockpit as soon as the caps were back on while he did the external checks. It was a record turn-around but we were now against the clock. I don't remember much about the flight itself except that everything in the air was spot on to the minute with all landmarks appearing on cue exactly as I had calculated, which was a miracle in itself. Conflicting traffic caused a short delay while waiting to take off from Staverton, putting us behind schedule for arrival at Kidlington. A message from the school was waiting for me at Kidlington ops, telling me to make tracks for Blackbushe asap so as not to be caught out by official night. PURR was running beautifully and we poured on the coals to make up time, even managing to enjoy myself along the way despite the radio calls. Blackbushe appeared on the nose right where it should be, and it was a relief to hear Paul's familiar voice in reply to my joining call. We were back in home territory if not quite home yet. The airport was deserted this late in the day apart from one other aircraft on frequency, but we weren't conflicting and I was too busy concentrating as time was getting tight. Paul cleared Romeo Romeo to land and apparently her wheels touched down five seconds before official night. YES!

I was so chuffed as I parked her on the grass and ran through the shutdown checks. Everything had gone to the letter, which wasn't like me at all. Barry, a fellow student, came out to greet me, all excited. He had been up in the tower with Paul and told me what a close-run thing it'd been. Then he asked if I had seen the Spitfire. *Eh?!* The other aircraft on frequency was the late Charles Church with one of his Spitfires – they escorted me downwind, related Barry. OMG. I'd flown in formation with a Spitfire and didn't even see it!

*

The impossibly tiny space allowed for recording generalities in personal log books means the vast majority of flights fade from memory over the years, and flicking through the pages now, very few entries leap out at me to spark recollection. My favourite exercises were spiral glides, stalls and steep turns, which really gave a sense of the extra dimension we were playing in and made it real. Tipping the aircraft on its side and pivoting round on the wing tip, fighting against the increasing press of gravity to keep the nose carving around the horizon until the satisfying jolt of busting through our own prop wash verified the completion of a perfect circle.

I hated flying under the hood, which meant wearing a contraption like half a bucket beneath my headset to prevent me seeing outside of the cockpit, or that was the intention anyway. I felt like a dog fitted with one of those plastic lampshade collars after a visit to the vet, bashing in to obstacles at every turn. The uncomfortable bucket had minimal adjustment to accommodate the smaller than average pilot, consequently it kept slipping down over my eyes, often taking my headset with it. Another of my favourite exercises was unusual attitude recovery. My instructor would put the aircraft into some random off-kilter position which I then had to correct by interpreting instruments alone to get us back on the straight and level. As this normally involved some moderate increase in G-force, the accursed bucket would inevitably end up in my lap along with my headset, so to do a proper instrument flight in real instrument conditions without the dang bucket was a treat indeed.

Early in my student days with a mere five hours of flight time in the log book, a warm front had settled in for the weekend bringing a thick blanket of low cloud that leaked a persistent and depressing drizzle over the surrounding counties. Damp and miserable pretty much summed it up. I had no hope of flying but headed up to the Bushe just to see the Cheetahs and maybe scrounge some ground school. The parking areas were full of tied down aeroplanes dripping despondently in the murk, but there was something of a party going on inside. The instructors had been grounded all day and boredom set in with mischief afoot, so when Peter suddenly declared that we were going flying, his colleagues immediately howled a barrage of abuse. Everyone thought he was joking as I was herded into the briefing room for a quick instrument refresher before being dispatched to preflight G-HASL. Suspecting an instructor's prank that would summon me back to the crew room once thoroughly drenched for their entertainment, I didn't believe for one moment that wheels would leave the ground.

It was that deceptively soft invasive rain that permeates everything, and I was dripping as I scrambled back into the cockpit to complete the internal checks, wondering how long they were going to leave me out there. I was sure the joke was on me, but it wasn't the one I expected. Peter bounced up the wing and dropped into the seat beside me, showering us with water as he slammed the canopy in to place – we were actually *doing* this thing! Nothing else moved on that silent sodden airfield, our navigation lights flashing cheerfully in the gloom as we splashed through the puddles towards the holding point. Paul was in the tower, chiding us over the radio for disturbing the peace and asking where we would like them to send the flowers. The poor conditions didn't worry me at all. This was new and exciting.

We took off in a spray of surface water and disappeared inside a turbulent wet sponge, bucking and twisting as the clouds vented their displeasure at the intrusion. Prop wash blasted streams of water over the windscreen, and ghostly vapour trails whispered off the wings, our nav lights reflecting back in muted colours. This was really flying blind. I fought to keep HASL steady in the climb, scanning the instruments in sequence and loving the opportunity to do it properly without balancing a bucket on my head, but of course that was only half the story. While I enjoyed myself flying the aircraft, Peter was handling the crucial task of radio navigation and keeping track of exactly where we were, a side of the equation that would forever remain beyond my grasp.

It grew lighter ahead as we climbed through a dense fog into a thinning mist, and suddenly the clouds spat us out into a world of dazzling brilliance. What a contrast. It reminded me of my Concorde flight, but instead of powering on up to the heavens I was told to level off and skim the top of this pristine whiteness that looked exactly like a snow-covered plateau. Pockets of mist floated up as if to grab the wheels and pluck us back into the depths, the sun reflecting through the canopy projected a perfect glory on to the snow. This was awesome! A brief glimpse of perfection was more than I could've dreamed of on such a filthy day, but this was exercise nineteen and soon I was pushing the nose down to slide beneath the surface like a submarine. Enveloped once more in a featureless world of dismal wetness, Peter let me play for a while with some unusual attitude recoveries which felt more extreme than usual, but perhaps he too was enjoying a break from normal training parameters. Moisture dripped from the canopy as we threw HASL around in our gloomy twilight zone between heaven and earth, trusting the instruments to realign her from Peter's enthusiastic attempts to confound me.

I had no idea of our location, my focus purely on handling the aeroplane and steering the headings provided. Lowering one third of flap and applying carb heat, we rocked and bounced down a gentle slope that ended abruptly as we broke through the murk at a mere 200 feet. Paul had thoughtfully left a light on. A dark river of shining tarmac lay ahead, illuminated by twin rows of blazing runway lights reflecting in the surface water. Peter scored a bullseye, bringing us home smack on the centre line of a very short final and already well committed to landing – not that I had realised! Concentrating on the instruments I completely failed to appreciate the bigger picture that low power, full flap and steadily diminishing height were so obviously painting, but somehow recovered enough presence of mind to make a half decent splash down. What a thrill, even Peter was smiling! An unusual and most unexpected flying lesson. To discover that gorgeous sunlit infinity was within my reach (accompanied by a suitably qualified pilot, of course) and not the exclusive domain of commercial airliners completely changed my perspective, and grey skies would no longer seem so dismal.

*

A month before my first solo with just eleven hours in the log book, I was lucky to get an actual night flight. Normally we only flew in visual flight conditions, meaning in sight of the surface, navigating by ground features such as towns, roads, and railway lines. To fly outside the hours of official daytime (thirty minutes before sunrise to thirty minutes after sunset) requires a night rating or special dispensation. G-FANG had developed a problem late in the afternoon and required attention from the maintenance facility at Denham airfield, all of which coincided with my slot time. It was decreed that Gary would go on ahead with the poorly FANG, while Peter accompanied me to Denham in G-PAWS to bring him back, so we would be flying home in the dark.

It was still relatively light as we took off in pursuit, so I struggled beneath the bucket until released to peer out on an ill-defined world, the horizon now lost in a dull fusion of earth and sky. Snug in the cockpit bathed in the soft glow of the instrument panel, we were suspended in a cocoon lulled by the pulsing beat of the engine. PAWS was rock steady, an occasional twitch through the controls the only hint of motion as she reacted to the airflow, but again I had the easy bit, keeping us the right way up while Peter attended to the black art of radio navigation. We could hear Gary on frequency talking to Denham, but I struggled to find the airfield. Everything looked flat as visual references merged beneath a camouflage of dusk, and all definition was gone. Peter coached me into a circuit that I couldn't see as I prepared to set us down, eyes glued to heading, airspeed and altimeter. Sinking through an increasingly murky void, trusting the equation of attitude and airspeed to bring us safely down to earth, I eased back on the yoke feeling for the ground with our wheels as PAWS whispered in gently, waiting for contact – and there it was.

Time was of the essence, so Peter took control and taxied rapidly across the grass to stop beside FANG, throttling back to idle as Gary appeared and leapt on to the wing root. The canopy slammed shut and we were off again, driving PAWS up an invisible ramp towards oblivion - this was a proper night flight now! Beyond our left wingtip spread the vast metropolis of Greater London, a bewildering mass of luminescence, and to our right lay a hidden landscape dotted with thousands of tiny lights shining like pinholes through a blackout curtain. Dense clusters of distant illumination expelled lines of glowing embers through the pools of darkness between suburbia. Miniature headlights flowed along invisible tracks and brake lights flared like rubies. Peter identified the larger towns to give me a reference point, indicating Slough, Windsor and Maidenhead, and I found myself adjusting to the strange lack of definition in this nocturnal scene, picking out roads and junctions from tangled threads of light to create some sense of order. I didn't fancy having to cope with an emergency landing though - how would you find a field if the engine stopped? Happily there were no nasty surprises and the welcoming lights of Blackbushe runway shone brightly amid the black void of Yateley common, like an aircraft carrier at sea. No problem finding the airfield this time and we arrived safely without further ado, feeling very grown up as I guided PAWS down the approach lights to land, just like a real pilot.

Praise generally makes me uncomfortable as I rarely feel that it's warranted, but an unintentional compliment is truly authentic. A week later, doing the introductions at an informal student/instructor gathering at the school, Gary referred to our night excursion, informing everyone that I had completed the course and was about to qualify for my licence. He was genuinely shocked when Peter corrected him by saying I had yet to fly solo! Gary's honest reaction was a compliment that I could gratefully accept.

*

In 1985, the Blackbushe School of Flying introduced a Student of the Year trophy: a large wooden shield filled with an array of small silver shields to be engraved annually with each recipient's name. That inaugural year bears the name of my pal, Barry Scott, a deserved winner - and implausibly tied for first place -

me. Or more likely as Peter remarked, they couldn't think of anyone to give it to. Barry was far more capable than me. He wuz robbed.

*

Almost two years had passed since that 'one-off' never to be repeated trial lesson, and flying had become all consuming. The sound of a passing aero engine sent me dashing to the nearest window to catch a glimpse. I found myself pulling against the steering wheel as we drove up hill, subconsciously trying to raise the nose and climb. Weather forecasts gained a new importance, fretting through Monday to Friday at the daily predictions and willing the clouds away from the coming weekend, I headed for Blackbushe as often as my bank balance would allow. Even when unable to take wing, the allure of the airport was too strong and many hours were spent just watching from the car park as other students flew *my* Cheetahs. It always looked so cool when other people did it, an apparent ease of confidence that was sorely lacking in my case. It never felt cool when I took command of those very same aircraft. I felt like a fraud who wasn't up to the mark, my guilty secret disguised in pilot's paraphernalia, hidden behind flight bag, check list and charts. All the gear and no idea.

By now the exams and a mountain of paperwork were all behind me, and I was able to return a light aircraft to earth fairly consistently and with some semblance of dignity. My focus throughout all of the training was always on the next lesson, the next hurdle or the next exam. Every stage presented a new challenge like an endless series of hills to be climbed, cresting each summit to descend in to the valley ready for the next ascent, but the thought of actually reaching the end didn't cross my mind. All the exercises had been mastered to some degree with the requisite number of hours duly logged, and I even managed an unexpected pass in my General Flight Test, although an assessment of *well above average* seemed overly generous. So it came as a shock to receive a letter from the Civil Aviation Authority informing me there was a Private Pilot's Licence awaiting collection and it had my name on it. Surely there was some mistake? A nobody like me couldn't be a pilot.

But now apparently – I were one.

Er, now what...?

At first, I was reluctant to take passengers and have other people depend on my barely adequate skills – how would I cope with a *real* in-flight emergency? It's a whole other level from practising with a very capable instructor sitting alongside to sort out the mess, but the school encouraged me to get up there and enjoy it, saying it would boost my confidence to be the one in command and show what I could do. It was more what I *couldn't* do that worried me, so I'm grateful that my sixty-two hours in sole charge of a light aircraft were wholly uneventful.

Having flown everyone brave enough to put their lives in my timorous hands, I seemed to have reached an impasse, at a loss for what to do next with my expensive piece of brown card. There was no interest in upgrading to more sophisticated aircraft, mastering the added complications of retractable legs and wobbly props. Speed and aerobatics held no appeal: I wanted to savour the sky, not tear a hole in it. Much as I loved the little Grummans (always my favourite light aircraft), it was a costly exercise to rent one and fly around the patch for an hour once a month just to avoid having to do a dual check with an instructor, which only increased the bill. So that's how I ended up at the historic grass airfield of White Waltham in search of cheaper flying. This was before the presence of Fairey Aviation and their iconic Rotodyne had been erased from the landscape, but unfortunately I knew nothing about it at the time and missed a golden opportunity to absorb some rotary-winged history right on the spot.

It was January of 1988 when I first flew a Piper Cherokee

PA28-140. I was stepping back a decade in light aircraft design and it showed. Despite similar dimensions, the older Cherokee seemed more solid and chunky in comparison with the slinky Cheetah. Cockpit access was via a side door over each wing root, the extra framework causing a clutter of blind spots in addition to the narrow split windscreen, all of which considerably reduced visibility from the pilot's seat. It felt quite dim inside after the spacious sliding canopies that I was used to. A beefy shock absorber of a nose leg made the fuselage sit tail down, requiring three extra seat cushions before I could see out over the instrument panel! Instead of a dainty electronic tab, the manual flap lever was like a large handbrake fitted between the front seats, prodding me in the armpit when full flap was applied. The trim control was set in the roof above the flap lever, operated by a handle from a car window winder. Flying from a grass runway wasn't much different thanks to that beefy shock absorber of a nose leg, which was far more suited to rough ground than the Cheetah's elegant stalk.

So I went from a short flight once a month round the patch at Blackbushe, to a short flight once a month round the patch at White Waltham – it was pretty much the same patch and the lack of thrill in flying was just the same. Once in the air it was easier than driving a car: the aeroplanes flew themselves and all I did was to give them an occasional nudge in the required direction. The Cherokees were all right, but I wasn't connecting with them in the same way and only G-AVLF became a favourite, the rest were mainly anonymous in character. Some aircraft have a good feeling about them, like Cheetahs FANG, PAWS and HASL, and the aforementioned Cherokee, Lima Fox. I hated flying G-JULY and refused to take her solo. She was a perfectly normal Cheetah like all the others, but something about her gave me bad vibes. Later she would have several incidents including an engine fire (thankfully on the ground) and was eventually written off after another engine failure resulted in a crash.

'Why not try the Warriors instead?' suggested the aero club. So I flirted for a year with the bigger, more modern (mid-Seventies) and more expensive version of the Cherokee, the PA28-161. While they looked stylish with tapered wings and generally smoother aerodynamically, the bigger fuselage and extra four feet of wing span made them considerably heavier on the controls for an eight-stone wafer to handle. On a positive note, I only needed two cushions to see over the instrument panel! The lack of thrill was just the same, except I was now paying more for the privilege. Then for some unfathomable reason I was persuaded to start instrument training in the Warriors, spending time 'under the hood' unable to see out and flying purely by navigational aids, as guided by an instructor. What was the point of flying if you couldn't see the view? I don't know why I persisted with learning a skill that I would never use, but I was still drifting, unable to rekindle the spark in a once joyful activity that had now become mundane. In an effort to save money while sliding further down this senseless slope, I found myself at Booker airfield and fell in to the company of the remarkable Monique Agazarian, known by all as Aggie.

What a character she was! Sister of Jack and Noel, and sister-in-law of Francine, all recognised for their courageous wartime exploits, Aggie herself flew throughout the war with the Air Transport Auxiliary, ferrying all types of military aircraft around the country. When hostilities finally ceased, she got a commercial licence and ran her own air charter. She could fly anything and had done, but the Spitfire remained her one true love. Now she was running a ground school operation using a charming link simulator, the Gat-1 which she affectionately referred to as *Gatty*.

From the outside it looked like a truncated Cessna 150 cockpit, mounted on a mechanism encased in a rubber skirt. Inside the single-seat cockpit were all the fully functional controls of a light aircraft, which was started up and 'flown' in the exact same manner. Tricky to get the feel of at first thanks to the lack of feedback produced by control surfaces in actual flight, it felt like sitting in a tin can that was balanced on a marble, but it had real character and was truly evocative of the sixties era of flight. I would love to know what happened to it after Aggie's death, sadly just a few years later. Hopefully someone rescued it to be preserved for posterity. I see from my log book that I 'flew' fourteen hours in *Gatty*, shut in my own little world seeing nothing but the panel in front of me, trusting the instruments, altering course by the stop watch and Aggie's prompting in my headphones. On completing the lesson having landed and shut down just like the real thing, I climbed out and Aggie would decipher the tracing that recorded the accuracy (or not!) of her 'Little Mouse' as she dubbed me.

After a couple of initial wobbles, one day I scrambled out of *Gatty* to see Aggie beaming at me, holding up a trace of perfect racetrack patterns complete with teardrop approaches. She told me I had 'extraordinary ability' and really should have more faith in myself. I still have that trace which she autographed for me, proof that I once made the grade albeit more by luck than judgement, but I knew deep down that the confidence to fly in real instrument conditions, unable to navigate visually from map to ground would forever elude me. If I messed up my timings or strayed off course in *Gatty*, there were no serious consequences and no lives were at risk. That wouldn't be the case if I messed up for real in the air.

*

My low self-esteem was programmed in at birth and became generally fortified throughout the course of life. I'm my own worst enemy, sabotaged by my lack of confidence before I even start. If I listed all the skills and important responsibilities from past employment and set them down as if advertising a vacancy, I would immediately think there's no way I can do that – despite the fact that I already have. I drive myself mad! A natural reluctance to credit success probably stems from an inbuilt distrust of bravado. Self-praise has no value, any idiot can say how wonderful they are. Merely relating my modest achievements in these pages leaves me somewhat reticent, and no doubt these days it would immediately be slapped with some form of 'Mental Health' label, the fashionable pretext for being less than perfect.

Weirdly it's become something of an essential badge of honour among the younger generations, a free pass for failing to cope with some minor aspect of everyday life. Unwilling to venture beyond the babbling confines of social media and free themselves from the toxic negativity of Snapface, Twitbook and

Chattergram, they flock towards the latest trend, terrified of being the one who didn't conform. The façade of social media harbours the *Star Trek* reality of the Borg, and there's nothing social about it at all. It's life Jim, but not as we know it. Those of us not permanently welded to a smart phone embrace reality and adapt accordingly to the whims of life. So I am what I am – deal with it!

*

It was during my instrument training phase of 1989, that I discovered another facet of the aviation world: *homebuilt* aircraft. Currently playing with the Piper Warriors, it was all getting too serious and complicated for my liking and the thrill had long gone out of it. A visit to the Popham Microlight Fair was a revelation. I thought my Grumman Cheetahs were small and dainty after flying the heavy Warrior, but here were tiny quirky flying machines that made them look enormous. I discovered the Popular Flying Association (now re-branded as the Light Aircraft Association) whose members were committing aviation in all kinds of miniature aircraft that they had made themselves. I signed up at once and took a trial flight in a Chevvron motor glider, a real life-sized Airfix kit. The squat-looking machine was simple in structure and surprisingly light on the controls despite a wingspan *nine feet* longer than the Warrior. I was charmed by its no-frills appearance, the exposed cables and fittings normally concealed in standard cockpits. It was fun – it had heart – something sadly lacking in mass-produced aircraft, and so began a long-term investigation of this parallel universe with a view to somehow knitting a machine of my own.

*

Flying the Chevvron proved to be a pivotal moment. The Warriors had been a different challenge, but for me it was a road to nowhere. February of 1990 found me back in the faithful old Cherokee, plodding round the patch burning my wages once a month to fend off the added expense of a dual check. My mum was always a keen passenger, and it was nice to take people up who wouldn't normally have had the chance. There was generally a crowd of spotters gathered around the car park at White Waltham and one of these regulars was a slightly eccentric character known among the group as 'Old Willie', although I seem to remember him telling me that his real name was Henry. He was just a harmless old chap whose few pleasures in life were a drop of rum and watching aeroplanes. He lived with his elderly sisters and from what I could gather, was glad to escape the house and head to the airfield for a bit of like-minded company. The other spotters regarded him with tolerant humour but he was clearly the outsider, unshaven in his scruffy coat and battered old Austin Maestro, hanging around on the fringes hoping for a sign of acceptance. I felt a bit sorry for him and perhaps he recognised a fellow misfit as he latched on to me, but I dearly wished he wouldn't call me 'Sweetie-pie'!

There was an American pilot based there at the time, a familiar sight in his vintage Waco biplane: a beefy fixed-undercarriage tail dragger painted in cheerful orange and yellow, its fuselage adorned with a large sunflower on either side. The Waco was later joined by a pristine Beechcraft Staggerwing, which caused great excitement among the spotters. We watched this beast of a biplane taking off not long after its arrival at the airfield, tucking its wheels up neatly inside the lower wings, giving it a clean yet somewhat pugnacious demeanour. Willie turned to me as the big yellow machine growled away from the circuit, drew himself up and declared importantly 'That one's got a detachable undercarriage.' I sincerely hoped it hadn't.

He was there on his own one day when Mum and I arrived for our regular patch patrol, so I asked if he would like to come along. Well, after that we were best buds – I couldn't get away from him! White Waltham aerodrome is a very pleasant place to just to sit and watch the flying while soaking up the ambience. Poor old Willie, he only wanted some company, but it got so bad that I had to slow down by the entrance to see if his car was there and drive on by accordingly. It was like trying to dodge a guided missile, he would find me no matter what. He flew with me several times in the end, a glutton for punishment perhaps, but I think it gave him a sense of status among the spotters. He had a pal to take him flying – he wasn't just a spectator anymore. It was worth going round the patch for.

I KNOW WHAT I WANT, WHAT I REALLY *REALLY* WANT!

Bensen B8 with Volkswagen engine

My twenty-ninth birthday was approaching and I felt like doing something different to see out my third decade in appropriate style. It was another one of those moments. As a one-off, just-for-the-hell-of-it I took a trial flight in a Robinson R22 helicopter. If the Chevvron had revealed new possibilities, this was off the scale! Visibility from the fishbowl cockpit was far better than any aeroplane, but

I found it very difficult to filter through all the vibrations and make an actual connection with the machine. The weird T-bar cyclic quivered loosely in my hand muddling any feedback through the controls, but despite the manic clattering, I was thrilled. It could reverse, climb vertically, hover and fly sideways – so light and manoeuvrable – *so expensive!* It was brilliant. Helicopter training was completely out of the question with my limited budget already at full stretch, but the taste of rotary-winged flight had really got under my skin, sowing the seeds of what was to become an incurable addiction. It's kind of ironic therefore, that now older and a tad wiser having become familiar with the intricacies of autorotation, I'd be pretty reluctant to trust a small helicopter again.

Less than three months after discovering those unattainable delights of rotary-winged flight, it was pure coincidence that I saw the late, great Wing Commander Ken Wallis fly his James Bond display with the famous *Little Nellie*. My mum loved hot air balloons, so I had taken her to Bristol for the annual Balloon Fiesta, unaware that fortune had set me a new path. A forgotten spark of recollection from dim and distant childhood flickered into life as we perused the program of events. A television documentary about an amiable old gentleman and his tiny gnat-like flying machines had captivated me as a teenager, and well over a decade later, with no idea of who he might've been, somehow I knew that this was the same man. And of course, everyone knows *Little Nellie.* In sweeping contrast to the lazy elephantine bulk of the balloons, Ken and *Little Nellie* blew the crowd away with manoeuvres unimaginable in the light aircraft world. Fast and agile they flew confidently within the confines of arena at heights that rarely exceeded the surrounding treetops, stopping in mid-air, reversing and turning on a sixpence. It was electrifying! It was everything that a fixed-winged aircraft wasn't. My new found addiction took a massive hit and life had changed forever. Only a gyroplane would do.

The eccentric little rotorcraft had completely stolen my heart, but digging deeper into my new favourite subject revealed an unexpected snag in that no two-seat gyroplanes were yet available in Britain. Apart from a few scarce second-hand machines on the market, the only way to own one (and so learn to fly) was to build it, and the very limited number of approved plans to choose from were all single-seat. After four years of drifting and trying to recapture that initial thrill of flight, I had found the answer I craved, but with it came a lot of soul searching. I wanted to fly a gyroplane – but a single-seater? No passengers? To spend a vast chunk of my savings on something that I couldn't share? I toyed for a while with the idea of small twin-seat aeroplanes, but the appeal just wasn't there and all roads inevitably led back to the gyroplane. I hadn't even flown one and I was hooked!

Chatting casually with my work mates one day, we got on to the subject of flying and my current predicament in particular. Both were typical lads, a pair of comedians who had flown with me a couple of times, and they didn't see what the problem was at all. If that's what I really wanted to do, then *do it!* The banter stopped abruptly as Tony turned to me and said in all seriousness, 'Shirl, we'd be just as happy watching you fly, coz we know you're happy up there.' It was a most unexpected change of mood and I was touched by his sincerity. He made up for it later by peeling a banana and poking it in my ear – an act so randomly peculiar that I remember it to this day! But such is life. Cheers Tone, you gave me a moment. And I don't mean the banana...

*

Apart from some minor skills mainly gleaned from the pages of *Practical Classics* while renovating a Trojan bubble car in my early twenties, I possessed no particular skills suitable for the construction of a flying machine. I work reasonably well with pliable metals that can be hand-shaped to a certain extent, but accuracy of any kind is really not my forte. I can't cut a straight line to save my life, and the drilling of perfectly aligned holes in a length of aluminium box section would be too hit and miss to even contemplate. How on earth was I going to build a gyroplane? Consequently, I kept a close eye on the adverts in each eagerly awaited issue of *Popular Flying*. Second hand gyroplanes were very few and far between, so when an advert appeared listing an 'Immaculate red Cricket' for sale, it seemed too good to be true - and so it was, but I had to drive from Berkshire way up to the wilds of Cumbria to find out! Being a complete novice with no idea of what to look for in a second-hand gyroplane, it was a great relief to be accompanied by experienced gyronaut Hugh Bancroft-Wilson, who kindly offered to cast a practised eye over this allegedly immaculate machine. With my brother Graham along for moral support, we journeyed up to the quiet Lincolnshire town of Grantham to stop overnight before collecting Hugh from RAF Cranwell the following day.

He was already waiting outside the air station next morning so off we went on our way 'up North', and way up north it proved to be. Yorkshire has always signified *up North* in my tiny mind, so it was quite surprising to see just how much of England lies beyond - there's a hell of a lot of North! Many miles later we were escorted into a large dusty barn where disappointment awaited. It was immediately apparent even to a complete novice that this tired little gyroplane was nowhere near immaculate and to describe it as such had certainly stretched the bounds of credibility. It was as dusty as its surroundings, apparently not worth the effort of a quick wipe over with a rag, and worst of all, the rotor blade assembly was suspended high up in the rafters. This very important, nay - *critical* - part of the gyroplane had not been made available for scrutiny. How many hundreds of miles had we come for this? Hugh got to work and showed me all over the forlorn little rotorcraft, pointing out things to look for and discovering several anomalies that he really didn't like, much to the disgust of the owner who seemed thoroughly indifferent to Hugh's opinion. I felt sorry for the poor machine, but it wasn't worth a fraction of the asking price, especially without seeing the rotor blades. This excursion had already cost me enough in wasted time and fuel, which I wouldn't have minded had we been presented with an immaculate red Cricket, or even just a tidy one with rotor blades! So that was that.

Dropping Hugh back to RAF Cranwell very late at night, he took the time to show us over his own gyroplane, an open-frame Brock that looked like a tiny blue insect lost inside the vast echoing hangar that housed it. I learned a lot from Hugh

Bancroft-Wilson in those early years and was grateful for his encouragement. Sadly, he didn't have long to live as a recurring brain tumour took him far too soon. In comparison, I later discovered that the owner of the aforementioned 'immaculate red Cricket' hadn't taken me seriously at all, and rather arrogantly decreed that I would never fly a gyroplane. I rest my case.

PATIENCE IS A VIRTUE

Campbell Cricket with Rotax engine

Hugh was organising a gyroplane meeting at Barkston Heath, a satellite airfield of RAF Cranwell, and suggested that it would be beneficial for me to attend. I'd already concluded that being a gyronaut was a long-distance hobby (she says, currently stuck 700 miles away from her gyroplane!), a rare and unusual fellowship to be sought out far from the madding crowd. My mum was always keen for a road trip and new adventure, so once again I pointed my car to the North and we set out for the flatlands of Lincolnshire to see what we could see. A pleasant couple of days were spent at leisure around the city of Lincoln, waiting in keen anticipation of my first ever gyroplane event.

The day in question arrived with a disappointing grey overcast, but the weather was dry and predicted to improve. We parked as directed alongside a scattering of cars overlooking a taxiway in front of a large military hangar, where two gyroplanes waited by an intersection. It was clear that after decades of air shows and fixed-wing events, my perspective was in need of some adjustment – these things were really tiny out in the open! A white Cricket with a yellow nose was flying at a 100 feet or so, back and forth along the runway accompanied by the tinny moped whine of two-stroke resonance. Hugh's blue Brock came taxiing in to view and parked with the others at the intersection, and that was it: two Crickets, a Bensen and a Brock. Only the black Bensen B8 had a mechanical pre-rotator, the others all started their rotor blades by hand and used the wind to get them up to flying speed. Sadly it's a dying art these days.

Maybe a dozen people were in attendance: a few enthusiasts clustered round the machines chatting to the pilots, so we wandered over for a closer look. I really don't know what my mum thought as we hung around observing these mad little contraptions that looked about as substantial as a flying deck chair, but if she worried for my safety at all (and surely she must have done) she didn't let it show. In fact, never a word of discouragement came from either of my parents during the transition from 'proper' aeroplanes to eccentric flying egg whisks, so I guess after three decades they had come to accept that their daughter's blueprint wasn't stored in the Conventional file and had just given up. That said, it was around this same time that my brother had taken to clambering up sheer rock faces armed with nothing but a bag of chalk, so perhaps flying a gyroplane didn't seem so crazy after all!

There wasn't a great deal of action during the day with only three pilots and a student under the watchful eye of his instructor, but this was the best that I had seen so far. The miniature rotorcraft were just as exciting and manoeuvrable as *Little Nellie*, far more appealing than any aeroplane. Hugh joined me briefly to point out Tony Melody, a very experienced gyroplane instructor and inspector, someone I needed to get acquainted with if I was going to pursue this most desirable form of flight. Here was the chance I'd been waiting for: an actual instructor who could help me become a gyronaut – but did I go bounding over and introduce myself? Did I heck. I wanted this more than anything, but I could not go up to Tony (a very pleasant and approachable chap) and say hello. Something that simple, I was quite incapable of making a move and drawing attention to myself. We had travelled hundreds of miles hoping to find a way forward in my quest for autorotation and now it was within my grasp, only for me to fail miserably at the first hurdle. I hung around the periphery all day, hiding behind my camera and hating myself more and more as every opportunity to catch Tony in a quiet moment went to waste. I felt so stupid, knowing how badly I would regret it once back at home. The other enthusiasts took no notice and probably assumed that I was with one of the spotters. I was only a female after all and they didn't fly gyroplanes, so there was no reason to think I might be a genuinely interested party in my own right.

It was my mum who saved the day - and not for the first time! Stepping up for her idiot daughter struck dumb upon the grass, she went over to Tony and did the honours as the afternoon drew to a close. I was filming the white Cricket again, and captured off camera in the background is Tony's surprised reaction on hearing of a potential female gyroplane pilot. How do you know if a gyroplane is female? Already being fixed-wing qualified helped to bolster my limited credibility and Tony was very supportive, telling me that the best way to start was by learning to fly a gyro-glider, which would teach me all I needed to know about handling a free-spinning rotor blade. Back then it was the only method of sampling autorotational flight with an instructor on board.

Imagine going through all the effort and expense of building your own gyroplane, only to find yourself unable to master the delicate art of rotor handling, or perhaps to discover that you didn't like being aloft in such a minimal flying machine after all. It did happen, but I was absolutely convinced that it wouldn't be a problem for me. To seek out a gyro-glider was prophetic advice that altered the course of my life, and three years after we met at Barkston Heath, Tony did indeed complete my transformation into a gyroplane pilot - thanks to my mum's timely intervention.

*

Following the trip to Cumbria in abortive expectation of an immaculate red Cricket, the long slow pursuit of my future gyroplane continued. Again without the instant access of Internet search engines, all hopes were pinned on a handful of adverts placed in the occasional rotorcraft newsletter or bimonthly homebuilt aircraft magazine. The 'for sale' adverts in the particularly short rotorcraft section was the first page I turned to as soon as the latest edition of *Popular Flying* dropped through the letterbox. Every two months it brought a potential Christmas Eve. Would there be any gyroplanes for sale? Might there be a suitable machine and within my budget? Had someone else got the magazine before me and already snatched the prize from my grasp? It was a roller coaster of emotions, and all done and dusted in a matter of minutes with hopes inevitably dashed, only to reassemble during the next sixty days of publication anticipation when the cycle would start all over again.

The minimal autorotational knowledge I had acquired so far was helping to narrow the search, and my preference was leaning towards a Cricket, not that there's a lot of choice as the very few British approved homebuilt gyroplanes are all some variation of the Bensen B8. Crickets wear a small semi-enclosed cockpit known as a pod, which gives them a more streamlined and business-like appearance, not quite as eccentric as the naked flying deck chairs. However, a Cricket's beauty is only skin deep with the deck chair being merely cloaked by the pod. I didn't think that I'd mind flying on a bare-bones airframe, but a streamlined pod could only be beneficial in terms of economy and protection from the elements. The fibreglass shell offers little in the way of accident protection so any structural benefit beyond the superficial is merely an illusion, but Crickets looked nice with their tubby little cockpits and that was about the depth of priority that my experience allowed at the time.

Regarding engine power, the air-cooled Volkswagen varieties (I had learned) were heavy, required hand propping to start, and were on the excessively noisy side which made them unpopular at many airfields. As gyroplanes fly relatively slowly compared to aeroplanes, the noise tends to hang around and irritate the neighbours. I really didn't fancy having to hand-swing the propeller either as I'm quite attached to my fingers and harboured no desire to part with any, so Volkswagen engines were scratched off the wish list. That left me with a choice of the Rotax two-strokes, which were steadily replacing the older Volkswagens and now favoured by the majority of gyronauts. Lighter in weight, they wore proper silencers to reduce noise, and were fitted with a recoil starter similar to that of a lawnmower for ignition, happily eliminating any requirement to place fingers in the vicinity of the propeller arc. Therefore, my future flying machine was going to be a Cricket, powered by a Rotax engine.

But second-hand gyroplanes were few and far between, and as I had no realistic hopes of building one of my own, I would have to take what I could get. It was the summer of 1992 when an advert appeared for a partly built Cricket project for sale in Somerset. Nothing more suitable had been available up until then and I was beginning to think that maybe the only way forward would be an attempt to build after all. A case of little hope or no hope, although my brother is a good mechanic with useful skills. But even if we got that far, could I really trust a flying machine knowing that *I* had put it together? That was doubtful at best! The advertised project consisted of a completed airframe – keel, mast, axle, flight controls and rotor head – signed off by the build inspector, plus fuel tank, pod and a set of plastic rotor blades. The engine mount was for a Volkswagen but it could be adapted to fit a Rotax. There was still a lot of work to be done, work that was well beyond my ability, but as it was relatively cheap there would be funds left over to pay someone capable of doing the difficult bits for me. If only I could find someone...

It was definitely worth a look, so we disappeared on a day trip to Chard where we met George and his embryonic gyroplane. George and I would cross paths many times in the years to come, but his broad Somerset accent (as strong as mature Cheddar!) never gets any easier to understand. I managed to decipher that he had given up on the gyroplane because microlight aircraft were far more accessible and a lot less hassle. He had a point. Microlights were everywhere: you could train on a two-seat machine with your instructor onboard, before selecting an aircraft of your own. There was no need to purchase or build one before you could take instruction, nor risk that same precious machine by training from scratch, alone in the seat.

A bare aluminium airframe sat there waiting on its wheels, already looking like a basic gyroplane. There are many pairs of holes to be drilled in an airframe, demanding an accuracy that I couldn't hope to achieve – but here's one all complete – inspected and signed off ready to go. Did I ever learn the hard way! Green as I was, it seemed like the answer I had been waiting for, a step in the right direction to finally break the interminable cycle of sale ad disappointment. George seemed like a genuine chap, I was happy to trust him and so the deal was done.

There I was, the proud owner of an airframe, a pile of parts and a large set of plans that somehow had to be turned into a gyroplane, but how exactly that was supposed to happen I had not the faintest idea. The phrase winging it couldn't be more appropriate! The rotorcraft association's newsletter was compiled at the time by Peter Lovegrove, former employee of Campbell Aircraft back in the Seventies, and who was in fact the designer of the Campbell Cricket gyroplane. Who better to ask for advice? In reply to my letter, he kindly offered to come down and cast an expert eye over my new acquisition, which seemed like a good idea at the time. If perchance you have seen the television episode of *Salvage Squad* that featured a rebuild of the Campbell Super Cricket, you may have got the impression that Peter is just a teeny bit on the pedantic side.

My newly acquired airframe had been checked by an inspector and the build stage signed off in the project book, which (I stupidly believed) surely meant that it met the required standard. But no, that's not good enough – throw it away. *What?!* The rotor head and control stick didn't make the grade either: scrap them and never mind the signatures in the book. Eh? Did build inspections count for nothing? In Peter's opinion, apparently not. The plans George had followed were copies drawn up by a veteran gyroplane inspector who had managed to incorporate an error – an error relating to a

Volkswagen engine that I wouldn't be using anyway. But guess what... Oh and just for good measure, the rotor blades were not acceptable either, being amateur-made copies of a genuine article they were only suitable for ground training. Well, at least they'd have some use.

All that remained were rudder pedals, engine mount, wheels and stub axles, fuel tank and pod. George had made a nice tail fin and rudder out of plywood but while the assembly was judged to be far too heavy, for once the phrase 'scrap it' hadn't been applied. I had myself a Maybe pile. Having trashed all my hopes along with the basis of my future gyroplane, Peter then added insult to injury by stating that I'd be better off not getting involved with gyroplanes at all, and had I thought about having a microlight instead? Wow.

YOU DO KNOW TIZ A *GYRO*-GLIDER...?

The purest art of autorotation

It was around this time in 1992 that *Popular Flying* magazine ran an article featuring one of the very few established gyroplane groups in the country, based at St Merryn airfield in Cornwall. I was already aware of this particular autorotational enclave as it was listed as a Strut, a sub-division of the Popular Flying Association that caters for specific localities or aircraft types around the British Isles. Several letters to the group's co-ordinator garnered no response, setting a precedent that continues to this day. He never replies in *any* respect! The magazine article featured two veteran gyronauts, Chris Julian and Tony Philpotts, both of whom were to become very important to me in the following years. The reporter had taken some rotor handling instruction on the gyro-glider and was later treated to a demonstration of what powered gyroplanes are capable of, which made me even more determined to pursue my goal. I *had* to do this!

I was working an average sixty-hour week trying to keep up with British Airways' insatiable demand for uniform name badges, each of which was laboriously typeset and printed by hand. My mum was concerned that I needed a break, so on condition that any potential excursion would include a thorough investigation of St Merryn airfield, I agreed to take a week off and hopefully sample some real autorotational flight in to the bargain. The only form of contact back then was either by letter or telephone, which for someone verbally challenged meant mailing a letter via pigeon post. I'm hopeless at small talk and struggle with telephones, but the resulting conversation was surprisingly easy.

Answering the insistent ring of the dreadful implement one evening, a cheerful Cornish accent came back down the line and thus I met Chris Julian. We chatted about the aircraft I'd flown, then came a pause before he asked hesitantly 'You do know tiz a *gyro*-glider?' So improbable was the idea of a female gyronaut that Chris automatically assumed I was looking for fixed-wing gliding. Not a chance, I could do that anywhere should the fancy take me, but a gyro-glider was a very rare bird indeed, hence the planned expedition to the far South West. He seemed genuinely intrigued that I wanted to fly gyroplanes, but why was it such a big deal all the time? Accustomed as I am to being an oddity, I found it puzzling to be viewed as such a freak of nature – women had broken the sound barrier and flown in space, for heaven's sake! What was so difficult about a gyroplane that only men could tame them?

Now, in my fleeting association with the small British gyroplane community, Chris's reputation as something of a 'ladies' man' (to put it politely) had already preceded him. Further telephone conversations frequently went off on a tangent beginning with the phrase 'So, what are you wearing?' I don't know what kind of dolly bird he imagined was on the other end of the line, but a buck-toothed flat-chested tomboy who hadn't worn a skirt since the last day of school probably wasn't high on his list of expectations. This was well beyond the bounds of my very limited experience of that nature (frankly, zero), but I soon grew used to it as just Chris being Chris and began to play along. My descriptions of various outlandish combinations such as a pink chiffon tutu with green wellingtons and a bowler hat were much appreciated judging by the chuckles that came back down the phone line. I caught him beautifully one time, not missing a beat at the predictable enquiry, 'So what are you wearing?' I immediately replied 'Nothing.' The gale of laughter lasted nearly a minute before he had to ring off, helpless, unable to speak.

Humour became my trusted weapon in diffusing a situation, as I was no match for him physically. Chris was completely brazen and not the slightest bit fussy: anything remotely female with a pulse was fair game to him, so being remotely female with a pulse, I think he saw me as a challenge! Years of popularity on the speedway circuit with attendant groupies vying for his attention had helped condition his often-repellent attitude, although some women clearly found it flattering to be referred to as 'a nice bit of stuff'. It was a different world back then. Although we got on very well in the main, Chris could be a real pest when the mood took him, and quite frankly he had the morals of a tomcat. I'm well aware of how our friendship was viewed by those who knew him, but pals are all we ever were. It was an unfortunate flip side to the otherwise likeable happy-go-lucky character that he was. He seemed to enjoy his sleazy reputation and I think it was a case of living up to the legend, but as time went on, the crude advances became increasingly half-hearted and more in jest, merely going through the motions as if it were expected of him. The boundaries of mutual respect quickly became established between us quite naturally: Chris would keep his trousers to himself, and I wouldn't kick him in the shins.

*

Having arranged a convenient time for both Chris and his trusted towing partner, Tony Philpotts, the date was fixed for my first real taste of autorotation. Mum and I packed our bags and headed off to Cornwall and the start of a new adventure. St Merryn airfield is well hidden from the road and we wasted a whole morning going round and round the nearby village and its environs, exploring all the narrow country lanes to no avail. The only clue was a large sign fixed to a farm entrance proclaiming it home to the Cornwall Parachute Centre, so there must be an airfield here somewhere! Through the gate we went, bouncing along a dry rutted track that led to some deserted buildings and a distinctly agricultural looking area devoid of anything remotely aeronautical. But over on the far side across some fields peeped the top of what could possibly be a hangar. Trusting that we wouldn't be shot for trespassing, we jolted slowly back along the track following a wire fence that appeared to lead towards the distant hangar, but on rounding the corner our path was barred by a padlocked gate. We hadn't seen a soul in all this time, nor any evidence of flying activity and it was now well past midday. Several hours and many miles covered had achieved precisely nothing, so it was only fair to take Mum down to Padstow and find some lunch.

As luck would have it, just as we returned along the village road later that afternoon, a gyro-glider rose up out of the fields to our left and shortly disappeared down into the grass. *Aargh,* follow that glider! Another few minutes driving nervously round what looked like private property, we discovered an entrance by a shabby black hangar from which a rough perimeter track led towards a distant control tower where the gyro-glider was just pulling in. How did we ever manage before mobile phones and satnavs? A dumpy figure clad in open-necked shirt and corduroy trousers hailed us loudly in a familiar Cornish accent. So this was Chris Julian! He had been wondering where we were after telling everyone that there was 'a young gurl' coming down to fly the gyro-glider. He must've been so disappointed...

Chris introduced us to the rest of the crew, all veteran gyronauts of advancing years. Tony Philpotts, Chris's partner in crime: a trim white-haired Yorkshireman with a mischievous twinkle that belied his seven decades. In the few years that came to I know them both, Chris often exclaimed in apparent disbelief, 'Tony, he's sempty you know!' Dear old Tony, eternally seventy. Also present were Les Cload, Trevor Johnson and airfield owner Bob Partridge, all of whom owned and flew Crickets, which had been Britain's answer to the American Bensen B8 back in the seventies. While there was a certain amount of surprise at my serious intention to become a gyronaut, right from the start these veterans took me under their collective wing and showed me nothing but encouragement.

Three storeys of sun-bleached red brick cube, the remaining bare bones of the old control tower, stood watch over a long low building attached to its side. This was the gyros' nest. Rows of blocked-up windows left their imprint clearly visible in the tired walls, of which over half the length had been demolished to accommodate the wingspan of a Cessna 182 belonging to the parachute club on the other side of the runway. A pair of long rickety doors filled the breach, one of which sagged wearily on its hinges, propped open by a length of heavy drainpipe. Thin shafts of sunlight filtered through holes in the roof between broken ceiling panels, peeling drunkenly from exposed rafters. Hunkered down at the foot of the derelict tower, the old building had such character, standing defiant against time and tempest. I loved it. The parachute plane seemed enormous, squeezed into one half of the hangar with inches to spare. Odd bits of farm machinery lay scattered along with other clutter of uncertain origin, trip hazards aplenty as we picked our way carefully through the gloom behind Chris, stepping over axles and dodging propellers. Grubby blankets draped over rotor blades made a thicket of shrouds concealing a handful of sleeping gyroplanes – a couple of ancient Bensens, several Crickets, and the sleek Wombat Gyrocopter prototype. I had found my utopia.

Alongside the hangar stood a modest block hut, which served as an austere clubhouse. We were ushered inside the bare block walls and invited to choose from an assortment of chairs clustered round a battered wooden table. A row of rusting metal lockers stood along one side, cobwebbed shelves sparsely cluttered with dirty rags and empty oil bottles that looked as if they hadn't moved in years. A collection of tattered diagrams and fading photographs pinned to the wall hinted at an exciting lineage of autorotational action. This was the real deal. Tony kindly offered refreshments, delving into a cardboard box to produce several flasks of black tea, a tin of powdered milk, and a stack of peanut butter and marmalade sandwiches to be shared among us. This as I would later learn, was an established ritual of many years standing. Frequent tea breaks and Tony's sandwiches (exclusively peanut butter and marmalade) were an essential part of the fabric of the St Merryn Gyronauts.

Suitably refreshed it was time for the main event. Mum settled in the car alongside Tony, while Chris introduced me to the gyro-glider. It wasn't much to look at: a skeletal airframe of 2x2 inch aluminium box tube consisting of keel, axle and mast with a pair of rotor blades that rocked like a see-saw on a simple rotor head. It had no rudder or tail plane, just a vertical plywood fin fastened on the back of the keel. The only concession to comfort was a sagging weave of tired elastic webbing wrapped around the seat frame, a central three-pronged control stick sprouting like a trident from beneath. A foot bar bolted on the nose wheel assembly provided steering on the ground, the brake being applied in much the same manner via a block of wood that was pressed directly against the tyre. It was all wonderfully low-tech. Five feet of heavy rope attached us to the tow car, acting as a shock absorber to take the whip out of the hundred feet of steel cable locked in a release mechanism on the nose of the glider. Our only instrument was a tatty piece of string tied to the bracing wire to indicate wind direction, proper grass roots stuff. I could hardly wait to get started.

Unlike helicopters, which alter the individual pitch of their rotor blades, gyroplane rotors are fixed at the hub bar so control inputs alter the pitch of the rotor disc as a whole, an amalgamation of ailerons and elevators in a single control surface like a giant frisbee. Once airborne, gyroplanes are controlled in much the same manner as a fixed-wing, the crucial difference is getting *into* the air as wind-powered rotor blades will not fly until they're ready. Attempt to take off before they reach flying rpm and you'll get a short sharp lesson in just how much energy is generated by a free-spinning rotor disc. It only takes a few seconds. The rotors take control and everything goes to hell in a handcart as the gyroplane beats itself to death. It can really ruin your day. I'm reluctant to get into too much detail having twice related the process in *Short Hops* and *Spinning on the Wind,* and it's not easy to describe and still make some kind of sense, so apologies if the following sounds familiar. I'll just summarise the basics as these fantastic little rotorcraft have a unique method of operation that may not be apparent to all.

Facing the glider into wind, I held the control stick fully forward so that the rotor blades were flat to the breeze. It was quite a stretch for a short arse to push against the trailing edge of each blade while keeping the stick down, the dead weight of 23 feet of rotor span rested heavily on the controls. Slowly the blades began to gather momentum. Chris explained that trying to force airflow through the rotors by bringing the stick back too soon would result in flapping. In an exceedingly small nutshell, until they are turning fast enough, the rotor blades can flex violently if given too much airflow and will destroy a gyroplane if not corrected in time. It's a common cause of wreckage these days, but modern gyroplane wreckage is ridiculously more expensive than it was back then.

Judging that we had sufficient rotor speed, Chris told me to bring the stick back a bit and give them a little more air. Suddenly the rotor blades seemed to wake up to the breeze, taking on a life of their own and swishing round ever faster. How could a pair of inert metal planks become a living breathing wing? It's a fascinating transition. Centrifugal force was doing its thing and pulling the rotors out straight, so to complete the equation and get airborne, we now had to generate *centripetal* force by spinning them even faster. Tony took up the slack in the cable and began a steady acceleration as Chris talked me through my first take off. The rotors were a whistling blur and I could feel the energy building above our heads as the nose wheel lifted itself off the ground – the fail-safe indicator that autorotating blades are ready to fly. Putting the stick forward a little to balance the machine on its main wheels, the glider suddenly soared into the air with little assistance from me.

I loved the floating sensation at once. The lightness and response were an unexpected joy and I was barely aware of moving the stick at all. It seemed like only seconds before we reached the end and the car was gradually reducing speed, lowering us smoothly back down to float just above the ground.

The rotors shouldered the load with a loud whopping sound and the glider obediently settled itself on to the runway, the rotor disc acting like a huge air-brake stopped us in our tracks. It was every bit as thrilling as I'd imagined!

The aged seat webbing retained very little of its original elasticity which made for a bone rattling ride back along the ground, the metal frame digging into my thigh as I struggled to keep my foot hooked under the steering bar. Turning into wind back at the threshold, Chris showed me how to retain as much rotor speed as possible so that it was safe to move off almost at once. I could hear the rotors picking up speed as our forward motion increased airflow through the disc, a tangible resistance growing through the controls as their constantly changing *swish* provided me with a running commentary. I loved everything about it. So effective was this stripped-back-to-basics method of training that I was already developing valuable autorotational skills. Reading the rotor blades by senses alone quickly became second nature, but flying the glider was so much fun that it didn't seem like learning at all.

For such an apparently simple wind-powered flying machine, it's easy to underestimate just how much inertia is contained in a free-spinning rotor disc, but stopping them by hand dispels all illusion! Modern gyroplanes are too tall for the manual method to be practical so they apply a rotor brake from the cockpit instead, but there's no fun in that. Patting the leading edge of each blade as they come around is the perfect illustration of why these machines demand respect. Even my lightweight rotors can knock me off my feet should I attempt to slow them too soon, but I love patting them down and enjoy the physical contact, an emphatic reminder of the power that I'm dealing with.

After a couple of hour-long lessons, Chris asked if I felt ready to fly solo. I'd enjoyed every minute but natural caution dictated that I fly one more dual session, as he was a lot of ballast to lose in one go. So we went out to play some more, varying on a theme by describing shapes through the air as we flew. The James Bond run was my favourite. Tony snaked the car back and forth across the runway while I kept the glider in position behind it, swinging the machine from left to right and back again to keep the cable taut. Super fun! The hour flew by and it was time for the obligatory tea break once more. I was having the time of my life – and so apparently were Chris and Tony!

Refuelled once more with tea and sandwiches, I felt ready to face the gyro-glider alone. This time, Chris strapped me in to the middle of the seat, just as it would be in my Cricket. As he started the rotors, he explained that the machine would take off and fly at much slower speed with only me on board. For the first run I was to keep it straight and level and simple, and with that last instruction Chris put his fist to his teeth and pretended to chew his nails, grinning broadly as he scuttled back to the car. The rotors kept their momentum on the breeze and we moved off straight away, the glider felt feather light in my hand and the nose wheel popped up almost at once. I caught it with forward stick and had barely balanced on the main wheels before the machine lifted smoothly into the air of its own accord. It felt more natural flying from the middle of the seat, just floating like a soap bubble as we crept along the runway at jogging pace. Chris hung precariously out of the passenger door, laughing and shouting but watching my progress like a hawk. Allowing plenty of time to coax the glider back down as runway's end approached, it seemed to hang in the air reluctant to descend, and forward speed was almost zero when it finally fluttered onto the ground. Superb! Chris burst from the car crowing with delight, and Tony beamed across at me as he manoeuvred around to take up the cable. No problem remembering *that* first solo! We finished the day by going through all the exercises again, but this time I flew alone while Chris directed me from the car, hanging out of the open door waving his arms like a mad conductor.

Taking a break between lessons during that marvellous first week of discovery, I experienced something of an epiphany as the four of us (Chris, Tony, my mum and me) sat outside on the grass. Tony was sitting on a rickety wooden chair propped against the hut, sheltered by a thick patch of wild grass alongside that stood taller than his head. With a mug of tea in his hand and a beatific smile on his face, he was the picture of contentment, totally at one with his surroundings. In that very moment I knew that this was where I needed to be. It came out of the blue. I was happily settled in my job of ten years, but I knew in that instant that nothing would be the same again. My only intention had been to spend a week and see if I could actually fly a free-spinning rotor blade – no thought of radical shift in direction had even entered my head. I was content living at home with my brother and our parents, repeating the same routine week in, week out. It was comfortable, safe and secure, yet in a matter of days everything had changed. When Tony suggested that I bring my collection of parts down to Chris's workshop for assembly, my fate was sealed.

The week had flown by in more ways than one and it was an awful wrench to say goodbye and return to the reality of life 'up country'. Back in harness at my workbench, haunted by the marvellous sensation of flying the gyro-glider, the previously safe yet predictable weekly grind transformed into a millstone round my neck, but all those years of overtime stashed away in my bank account would now begin to pay off. However long it took, I was going to fly my own gyroplane. I'm ashamed to say that I didn't give a second thought to my parents: how they might feel or how they would manage without my income, although I was in my thirties, so perhaps they thought they'd never get rid of me! Only a few years earlier we had discussed buying our rented house together, so what a relief that I didn't get caught in that trap before I discovered gyroplanes. It would've been very difficult, if not impossible to extract myself and leave them to bear such a financial commitment alone. And what a boring ordinary life to continue with – albeit a boring ordinary life that I'd been perfectly content with for the past decade! But I wasn't me anymore. That version of me turned to dust in the moment the gyro-glider left the ground, and the touch of the rotors on the wind took my soul.

A Moth to the Flame

Grabbing as many long weekends away from work as I could muster, excitement grew with each hotly anticipated visit to the workshop. The bare aluminium airframe mounted on a pair of go-kart wheels looked more like a land yacht than a flying machine, a deceptive simplicity that masked the critical time-consuming accuracy involved in creating a gyroplane. Measure twice, cut once as the old engineering adage goes, or in my case, measure half a dozen times and still miss it completely. As an absolute beginner with a steep learning curve ahead, I was fascinated by this pre-metric world of micrometers and slide rules which I had little hope of comprehending. There were no computers, no digital programming, nothing but traditional manual skills using imperial measurements calculated with pad and pencil from scaled plans, drawn on huge sheets of paper pinned to the wall.

Enthusiasm far outweighed my ability (still does!) but I was keen to learn, helping as much as possible with any small idiot-proof tasks – suitable for a small idiot – that Chris would save to coincide with my visits. At the other end of the scale, critical precision components such as rotor heads were entrusted only to Ray, a retired machinist who assisted in the workshop on a casual basis. After three self-taught decades of building gyroplanes, Chris was perfectly capable with both lathe and milling machine. He could turn a billet of aluminium into a rotor head with no problem at all, but such was his respect for Ray's professional skills that anything requiring the most accurate of measurements was always put to one side for when Ray came in.

There was quite a production line going in what was little more than a large garage, but this anonymous workshop at the bottom south-west corner of the British Isles was an important focus of gyroplane expertise. People came from far and wide to seek Chris's help and advice, bringing their machines for servicing or repair, plus the neophytes like me, starting from scratch. Already there was another Cricket in the construction queue behind mine, and taking priority along with most of the floor space was Tony's almost completed Wombat Gyrocopter, a modern streamlined creation of Chris's own design, and sister ship to his prototype at St Merryn. Reminiscent of a Wallis autogyro, I would have loved to have flown one. Officially only two were built but in reality there were four. The Mk2 was Chris's crowning glory, specially modified to go through the British certification process, but time wasters and tragic events would put a stop to it all.

When the prized new Rotax 582 arrived at the workshop, I was startled to read on the first page of the instruction manual, 'This engine, by its design, is subject to sudden stoppage.' Well, that inspired confidence. The single most expensive component of my gyroplane – an engine that was designed to stop! Had there really been such little progress since the days of the notorious McCulloch and the dreaded *Mac attack?* Built to power military target drones during the 1960s, the compact and incredibly noisy McCulloch engines packed a punch of horsepower that made them a perfect fit for the newly emerging fraternity of tiny rotorcraft. But there was a snag. Reliability is the most desirable attribute of an aero engine, as the sudden expeditious landing and subsequent recovery of a defective flying machine is a disagreeable exercise at best. The McCulloch (a cheap and cheerful power plant bolted to the business end of a target drone) met no such expectations, and in its original state was dependable only in the respect of being thoroughly unreliable, the in-flight failures being so common that they became known as Mac attacks. Three decades later, staring in disbelief at my new Rotax engine, it appeared that things hadn't much improved. On the bright side, retrieving a poorly gyroplane from some inaccessible field is considerably less complicated than extracting a sick aeroplane.

Tony's new Wombat, pristine in red and gold, was duly completed and moved to her new home at St Merryn, leaving my Cricket to take centre stage. The square-tube airframe seemed draggy and outdated compared to the clean lines of the Wombat, and Chris was quick to expound the superior performance of his design, confidently asserting how much I was going to enjoy flying her. He was in no doubt that another Wombat would soon be in the pipeline for me, and had fate not intervened he would've been absolutely right! But first there was a small matter of actually *learning* to fly a gyroplane, for which my heavy and docile emerging Cricket would be the ideal mount. She was a stocky little moorland pony beside the elegant racehorse of a Wombat, but it was on her dependable broad back that I would earn my spurs before stepping up to the thoroughbred.

Official registration received from on high decreed that she be anointed G-BVDJ, and the letters adorning her tail now determined her name, *Delta-J*. She was beginning to look the business. The fuel tank was in position, caged inside the heavy steel cradle of the engine mount, upon which perched the Rotax 582 ready to be plumbed in. On the back of the keel tube, her freshly painted tail fin and rudder offset the equally glowing scarlet pod mounted on the front, completing the look from a purely visual standpoint. But there was so much more to be done, vital time-consuming tasks that revealed little progress to the casual observer. I helped as much as possible under the guidance of my mentors, becoming so familiar with my tiny rotorcraft that when the time came for preflight checks, I could tell at a glance if something was out of place.

By this time, I had made the move permanently to Cornwall, keen to continue my evolution from fixed-wing pilot to gyronaut. Since that first week on the gyro-glider, I'd gone back to White Waltham for a dual check ride just to keep my hand in, but that brief taste of autorotation had ruined me! It was as different as driving a bus is to riding a motorbike. The plodding droning flight of the steady old Cherokee had bored me before, but now I just plain hated it. Poor G-AXIO, it wasn't her fault. A light aircraft's inert wings cannot compete with the vivacious energy of a free-spinning rotor – a truly living breathing wing – and so 14 August 1993 was the very last time that I rented an aeroplane.

*

I sometimes regret wasting so much time and money on flying aeroplanes after getting my fixed-wing licence, but looking back, it was a natural progression that couldn't have happened any other way. The instrument training in particular was always going to be a dead end, as I lack both the intelligence and the confidence to do it for real. But if I hadn't tried, I would've missed the special encounter with Monique Agazarian and *Gatty*, the charming little simulator with considerably more heart than any modern digital counterpart. I really hope it's been preserved somewhere, it was so unique and very much a part of Aggie. It was an honour to have known them both.

Every stage of flight training has a defined objective for the student to aim for, obviously structured towards qualifying and receiving a Private Pilot's Licence at the end of it all, but having acquired that expensive bit of dreary brown card left me in something of a vacuum. It was a special privilege to take friends and family aloft for a bird's eye view, so I don't regret that side of it at all, especially as it wasn't possible to share my gyroplane in the same manner. So all in all, fixed-wing flying became an important piece of the puzzle, giving me a good grounding in aviation procedure that would otherwise have been lacking when it came to the gyroplane. It was a strong foundation to build upon, and a valuable part of my evolution into a gyronaut.

There's a clear division between logic and intuition, especially where flying is concerned. Logical types tend to reduce everything to black and white, a product of physics and maths that can always be explained by some equation or other, and neatly filed in the appropriate compartment. Intuitive types go with their gut feeling, trusting their senses and accepting the existence of grey areas. Personally, I'm the latter: I'm not technical at all. It's a struggle to correlate theory with reality and I'm equally hopeless at maths. One of my many afflictions is a weird sort of number blindness that randomly confuses threes and fives, sixes with nines and vice versa for no apparent reason.

A blown fuse, a fault in the circuitry or I'm just wired up wrong in general, but show me a page of graphs and equations and my brain throws its hands up in despair, disconnects and goes for a wander. Sometimes it doesn't come back.

Calculating the weight and balance of a particular aeroplane left my grey matter fizzing in a flat spin: I grasp the concept well enough but struggle to translate the data into anything remotely useful. Weight and balance by the way, basically ensures that the weight carried by an aircraft is correctly distributed between set parameters, meaning the aircraft will be properly *balanced* in the air and not overloaded or tail heavy - both of which are bad things. I couldn't afford to go touring so there was no baggage to worry about in the rear fuselage, but I knew that flying with full tanks and a full cabin had the potential to make things interesting. To err on the cautious side therefore, I only took two adult passengers at a time, meaning there was no requirement to wrestle with the dreaded weight and balance calculation.

Back in the mid-nineties there were no gyroplane schools as such, and snaring one of the small handful of mainly itinerant instructors in the country required a large butterfly net and a certain alignment of planets. To learn to fly a gyroplane we first had to own one - build it or find a used machine - there was no other way. Next, having procured the services of an elusive instructor, we dragged our rotary-winged chariots often hundreds of miles from home to congregate with other chosen neophytes at the particular airfield of operation. Classrooms were non-existent and any ground school was pretty much ad hoc and often taken on the hoof in the parking area. Factor in the great British weather, mechanical gremlins and instructor availability (training for most instructors was a part time vocation that fitted around other commitments) all of which made becoming a gyronaut an achievement that took endless patience and perseverance. You *really* had to want it!

Later in my autorotational years, a professional helicopter pilot was horrified because I couldn't plot a drag curve for him. I could explain it well enough, but I couldn't put the numbers on the lines, and that (he informed me with a look of disgust) makes me dangerous. Everything has to relate to facts and figures in order to know what's happening in the air, and yes, for a complicated multi-engine, passenger carrying helicopter he had a point. For a tiny single-seat gyroplane that does everything best at around 55 mph give or take a bit, things are considerably less critical and it's only my neck on the block if I get it wrong. But should I get into a situation for whatever reason, I won't be wasting time trying to remember the appropriate numbers for whichever bit of the graph I'm supposed to be on – I'll be too busy paying attention to what my machine is telling me.

So, while performance charts and suchlike leave me cold, put a control stick in my hand and some wind through the rotor blades and I'll tell you exactly what's going on. Feedback through the controls is everything, which probably explains why I'm hopeless at flying computer simulations and model aircraft! I was taught to autorotate by a veteran gyronaut who began back in the 1960s with a gyro-glider made of exhaust pipe tubing. He couldn't do maths either, he could barely read and write – but by god he could fly! So everyone can relax, safe in the knowledge that there's not the remotest possibility of me being left in control of a complicated multi-engine, passenger carrying helicopter. You're welcome.

THE WACKY WORLD OF *THE CHALET*

Happily for me, Chris collected waifs and strays. His bungalow with adjoining workshop was divided into several small flats, augmented by a couple of shabby caravans that he rented out cheaply to a handful of life's misfits. I slotted in very well. He and his partner Judy knew exactly how to work the system, and life at The Chalet was never dull, in fact it was quite an education for the innocent that I was.

*

A modest single room flat was built especially for me on the footprint of his television repair shed, which was shifted forward in the yard to mask the construction going on behind. Planning permission was for softies! The entire homestead was powered by electricity that Chris had somehow managed to split off from the three-phase supply to his workshop. We knew when he started the lathe as it drained every drop of current from the property, simultaneously dimming all our lights until the heavy machine had gathered sufficient speed.

A large storage heater had been appropriated from a dubious source, which Chris insisted on installing in my flat. It only had one setting and that was full afterburner, great during winter but when summer arrived there was no way to turn it off, which probably explained why it had been dumped in the first place! Being cunningly built so as not to exceed the height of the wooden shed concealing it from the road, the flat's low ceiling merely trapped the heat and turned the room into a sauna. Summer months were unbearable. My pleas to disconnect the thing were countered with a pledge to do it dreckly. Now *dreckly* is a Cornish idiom which refers to a fleeting and elusive moment that occurs as and when at no particular time that can be specified or adhered to, and is the same length as a piece of string.

So it was during the second summer of roasting in my block-work oven that Chris finally got round to tackling this malevolent furnace. After a morning of rattling around with various electrical accoutrements and voltage reading paraphernalia, he disappeared leaving the sweltering appliance to cool down at last. Relief was short lived. Washing my hands ready for lunch, I was startled to feel the stream of water pulsating with electricity, as did the taps and draining board! How the heck...? Out of interest, I switched on the shower (after finding a piece of wood to stand on) and that was electrifying as well. I don't know how Chris had managed it and neither did he, refusing to believe me until he came back to see for himself. Somehow every metal surface in my flat was conducting electricity! Another bullet dodged. The storage heater was duly stripped of all external wiring and there it remained, a solid bulk of uselessness.

*

Chris was by nature quite a stocky chap, but a combination of middle age and a surfeit of Cornish pasties had expanded his waistline to a modest paunch. 'Sixteen stone! Tiz terrible!' he would complain in disbelief, clutching his rotund stomach in the manner of an expectant mother. Various diets had been attempted before but healthy eating just wasn't his style. Fish and chips featured heavily on the menu several times a week, and Sunday evenings invariably found us gathered at the local chippy after a busy day at the airfield. So when Chris discovered the SlimFast weight loss program he was delighted. All he had to do, he explained enthusiastically was mix up one of these magic milkshakes to satisfy his hunger in place of a meal. As dietary plans go, I think it was a little more involved than that, but Chris was convinced that this marvellous concoction was the answer that he craved.

The new regime lasted perhaps a couple of weeks, but in fairness, to be sat in the kitchen with a milkshake for lunch, surrounded by the warm aroma of freshly cooked pasties as everyone else tucks in to a steaming plateful, what's a proud Cornishman to do? He did try to conform, adding an extra scoop of powder to the mix, or doubling the number of milkshakes per day in desperate hope of suppressing his appetite, finally resorting to a milkshake and half a pasty when all else failed. It was funny though. He had this air of perplexed innocence and couldn't understand how this miracle cure had failed so miserably to reduce his waistline. Truth was, Chris had got so confused experimenting with different combinations, that in the end he was eating his normal meals and having a milkshake in between! Not quite the diet plan that SlimFast had intended.

*

Our favourite television programme at The Chalet was *The X Files*, everything stopped when it came on and we all gathered in Chris's front room to watch. He was particularly impressed by their car phones, the chunky handsets that kept agents Mulder and Scully in touch with civilisation while out in the wilds chasing aliens, so he was thrilled when a newspaper advert appeared for one of these new-fangled mobile phones. Plagued with constant calls to the house phone, now he could stay in touch wherever he happened to be, just like the FBI. His theory was faultless, but reality along with technology had yet to catch up with the potential. Cornwall is the end of the line as far as the British mainland is concerned, we're out in the sticks down here and even today there are a few places where phone signals can't reach. The hotly anticipated parcel arrived several weeks later, containing a plastic walkie-talkie with a keypad on the front and a skinny aerial extending from the top. I don't know what the advert had promised its customers, or how the phones were supposed to connect as there were no signal masts or indeed any networks at all at the time, without which the hardware had little more than novelty value. In Chris's mind however, it represented freedom from the insistent ring of the landline.

The following month saw a variety of experiments to make the alleged mobile phone function as advertised. It's perfectly obvious in today's ultra-connected over-sharing world that nothing was going to happen without a signal – but how he tried! Tin foil and various lengths of wire were wrapped around the flimsy antenna in desperate hope of improved reception. We even climbed up on the roof and attached it to the television aerial! Many a time he had me hanging out of the car window, brandishing the phone aloft as we rocketed down country lanes in the hope of intercepting a signal that wasn't there. From the Atlantic cliffs to the top of china clay country and the open expanse of Bodmin moor, we tried it everywhere. Chris deserved a connection for perseverance alone, but it wasn't to be. I wonder what he would make of it all now – the irony being that he'd get no peace at all. The incessant calls that pestered him at home would follow him everywhere, and the greatly desired mobile phone would soon be abandoned in disgust. Such is progress.

*

Chris didn't believe in wasting money on cars. His aged vehicles were barely roadworthy and in no condition to pass the annual inspection, so what was the point of submitting them! The poor old bangers proclaimed their distress with a range of loud knocks, squeaks and rattles which did nothing to deter him from driving like the ex-speedway rider that he was. Near misses were a way of life: speed was everything and he was fearless. I often told him that one day he would meet someone coming the other way who drove like he did, to which he always retorted that they would have brakes. I could only hope they'd be in better condition than his.

Once when my mum was down for a visit, he decided to take us all to one of his favourite local watering holes and treat us to a *cup o' tea*. Chris never touched alcohol: his chosen haunts were greasy-spoon cafés and roadside snack bars, providing the nectar of 'a nice cup o' tea.' For reasons unknown, he wouldn't call Mum by her name and always referred to her as 'Mother' instead of Mollie, which amused her no end. So with Judy in the front seat, we settled into the back of his rickety Ford Granada as he did his usual out-of-the-gate speedway start, at which point the bench seat on which we were perched shipped its moorings, upending Mother and me on to our backs with knees in the air! Twisting round to look over his shoulder, Chris was mortified. We lay there unable to move, utterly helpless with laughter and his startled cry of 'Ooh 'ell, Mother!' only made it worse!

Poor Mum. Life at The Chalet was an unpredictable step beyond, but she took it all with good humour. With only three of us in the car, Chris would insist that she sit beside him in the front for a better view of the scenery as it went whizzing by. He meant it as a compliment, the best seat in the house, but the last thing Mum wanted was a better view – she had her eyes shut! Watching from the back, I could see her tensed in anticipation of impending carnage, gripping the seat, feet braced against the floor applying phantom brakes as we shot through narrow twisting lanes at full pelt. Chris wasn't the most observant of drivers, and he was also quite deaf after years of flying with a McCulloch engine roaring behind his head, so even when Mum sat in the back she still couldn't relax. To hold a conversation with someone in the back of the car, Chris would lever himself up and twist the top half of his body round to face them, one hand on the steering wheel as we blasted gaily towards oblivion. Mum was always very relieved when we reached a destination, not that she would say anything to her well-intentioned host, but it really freaked her out when he did that. Flying a gyroplane was considerably safer than driving around with Chris.

Thankfully it was a different story with gyroplanes. When in instructor mode, student safety was paramount and his concern was genuine. He taught me everything about rotor handling, and our only instrument was a piece of string. It never lies, the batteries can't fail, the screen doesn't go blank. Thirty years of flying with a bit of string and yet to ding a rotor blade, all thanks to Chris Julian, faithfully assisted by Tony Philpotts.

Autorotation,
Baby!

Chris and the wonderful Wombat

I remember we had stopped at Bodmin Aero Club for a cup of tea one time (Chris never went far without a cup of tea), when a group of young RAF cadets were in residence. Dressed in his usual tatty pullover, a shock of unruly white hair sticking up from his collar like a mad professor, Chris chatted loudly in his broad Cornish accent, chuckling away as he teased the kitchen staff through the serving hatch. The cadets in their khaki flight suits gathered in a corner, sneering among themselves at what they perceived to be a classic country bumpkin. It was a shame we were visiting by road that day as had we flown in, they would've seen just how wrong they were in their assumptions. Chris was a virtuoso of the free-spinning rotor blade, there was nothing that he couldn't do within parameters and even a few things beyond. The Wombat was his masterpiece and in the skies above St Merryn he made her sing. Poetry in motion, they were a joy to watch - from a suitably sheltered vantage point where you couldn't be dive-bombed! He was a terror for that, the old devil.

Tony was more of a gentleman, the quieter of the two autorotational veterans, but he had a dry sense of humour that often revealed itself with a mischievous twinkle. He seemed a little abashed at times by Chris's earthy turn of phrase, and I don't recall hearing any crude language from Tony. His was the patient calming influence of the partnership, the yin to the yang of boisterous energy that was Chris Julian. They made a great team and took such delight in my progress that it was a pleasure to learn from them. I know I was something of a novelty for them in a way, but in a nice way. They hitched up the gyro-glider in all but the worst of wind conditions, sending me out to test my new skills and expand my limitations, hanging on gusts that bowled in over the cliffs straight off the Atlantic ocean. Strangely, my inherent lack of confidence failed to assert itself during what would now be frowned upon as extreme wind conditions for a mere beginner. Somehow this purest form autorotation came to me as naturally as a duck to water, and I trusted my mentors' judgement without question. If they thought I could do it, then let's do it! Pitting myself against nature's blast was the best training that any gyronaut could have, fine tuning my abilities, surfing the wind on the end of a hundred feet of cable. Tremendous fun!

Thanks to my lack of bulk, another favourite experiment was to see how slowly they could tow me and still keep the glider in the air. Tony crawled along in second gear watching the speedometer, while Chris trotted beside me watching the main wheels waver inches above the ground. I seemed to perplex him somehow. Anyone who listened was informed that 'she fly like a bit of silk' but in the next breath he would invariably add 'I can't understand it.' I even have it on video, a bewildered voice in the background saying, 'She got a pretty feel for a gyro. I can't understand it.' I couldn't understand it either. The gyro-glider was so easy to fly that I wasn't aware of doing anything particularly special to warrant Chris's confusion. He was building quite the reputation for me, which was a little unnerving if I had to live up to these expectations with my Cricket.

*

In order for a gyroplane to fly correctly we have to perform a hang check: basically, the machine is suspended by the teeter bolt (which normally secures the rotor assembly to the rotor head) and hoisted clear of the ground. The intended pilot in full flying kit then clambers into the seat, and various measurements are taken to ensure that the *angle of dangle* is within specified parameters. For us old school gyronauts, the hang check was our first opportunity to get a sense of being aloft in our own gyroplane. It felt quite vulnerable to me, swaying gently suspended five feet above the concrete floor at St Merryn, but that was more to do with the structural integrity of the rope binding us to a decrepit wooden beam in the hangar roof. Grass roots aviation, I love it! With all the requisite angles and control movements suitably adjusted and confirmed, it was a major step forward towards that maiden flight.

In 1994, we towed my almost completed flying machine up to Old Sarum, to make her début at a gyroplane gathering. These historic grass airfields have a special ambience all of their own, an abiding sense of past that resists the trappings of the modern world as if those adventurous souls from the age of wind in the wires still thrive just beyond our peripheral vision. Gyroplane meetings were few and far between back in the day, so it was always fun to get together with fellow enthusiasts from 'up country' and see some different machines. Delta-J attracted a lot of interest being a new kid on the block, her E-type gearbox in particular with its built in electric starter motor was the first of its kind to be attached to a gyroplane in Britain. Back in the Nineties when Volkswagen engines were still being brought to life with a flick of the propeller blade, many gyro pilots had upgraded to the Rotax two-strokes which employed a sharp tug on the cord of a recoil starter to induce internal combustion.

Chris got me to practice with the Rotax 532 mounted on the Wombat, but not once did I manage to generate a spark. It looked so easy when everyone else did it! Even after he'd warmed the engine for me, the compression of twin cylinders was still more than my scrawny frame could overcome, producing nothing better than a stuttering turn of the crankshaft that was far too slow to tickle a spark plug. Chris found it very entertaining: 'You'm only a wafer!' he would chortle at the laboured *hiss, phut, thunk* that accompanied each pathetic twitch of the propeller as I applied my inadequate strength to the starter cord. What hope for my autorotational aspirations if I couldn't start the engine! So the recent appearance of the E-type gearbox on the market was a welcome slice of luck that allowed me to substitute physical limitations with battery power. My engine retains the recoil starter at the other end, and it's been used in anger a couple of times when unseen faults have thwarted the application of electricity – but it wasn't me who hauled on the starter cord.

Jon Erskine, an old pal of Chris's from his speedway days, arrived during the weekend having flown his flexwing microlight over from Wales. As I had yet to experience altitude in a minimal open cockpit, Chris thought it a great opportunity for me to see what flying a gyroplane was going to be like, to which Jon very kindly agreed. The passenger seat looked like an afterthought in a compact design that crammed it into what little space remained behind the pilot, its occupant forced to adopt a Quasimodo-style hunch by the forward sloping mast. It was a snug fit even for me, and when Jon climbed onboard he was practically in my lap. Clearly this wasn't built for comfort, and in this somewhat absurd position I left the ground for the first time in a minimal open cockpit flying machine, curled around my pilot like a monkey on his back. Jon took us on a short tour of the locality, circling the castle and outskirts of Salisbury but it was difficult to see much beyond the wing, quite claustrophobic in fact. The flight was slow and ponderous with none of the joyous energy of the gyro-glider, which also boasted unparalleled visibility through the rotor disc. To be brutally honest, I found it boring and was glad that I'd resisted being diverted to the microlight world. But thanks to Jon, I now knew that being suspended in a minuscule machine with nothing but an open plastic shell around it gave me no qualms at all.

Returning to the airfield, we found Chris in conversation with a young couple who had been admiring my gyroplane. They owned G-AAWO, a pristine 1930s Gipsy Moth, and generously invited us both to fly some circuits in her. What an honour, she was gorgeous! I couldn't believe my luck as I was assisted up the wing and into the front cockpit of another age: it felt like sitting in a large bucket, straining to peer out over the leather-trimmed edge. The engine cowling pointed at the sky as if sniffing the breeze, and the broad spread of wings above and below effectively cluttered the pilot's view, not that it mattered as I was lost in the depths of the cockpit seeing little of the outside. With an expert swing of the propeller, the engine roared and the venerable old lady lifted her tail and took to the air as stately as a galleon. I followed through on the controls as prompted, watching the gauge in the wires to try and judge our angle of bank, but other than that I was flying blind. Sat deep in a cockpit of polished wood and leather with prop wash ruffling my hair, the sound of wind through the wires as we whistled in on final approach really enhanced the sense of a gentler age of aviation. Chris fared slightly better, being that bit taller he could just see out of the cockpit. But what an unexpected pleasure, and all because of Delta-J.

You'd Never Get Me Up in One of Those…

Homebuilt gyroplanes have suffered a bad reputation since appearing on these shores in the 1960s. Very little knowledge was available on this new form of aviation, so the early enthusiasts had no option but to teach themselves to fly their tiny home-made rotorcraft – starting from scratch – all alone with nothing but a set of written instructions to guide them. A literal case of trial and error, with no guarantee of a happy ending. Those early gyronauts really went out on a limb, putting their lives on the line to explore unknown boundaries just as the pioneers of the fixed-wing world had done since the dawn of the twentieth century, and that alone deserves respect. But unlike those fragile fledgling aeroplanes of yesteryear, the birth of the gyroplane occurred in a relatively modern age and the inevitable growing pains of accidents and incidents were there for all to see. Pioneer gyroplane pilots of the sixties and seventies were generally scorned as reckless nutters, and there's no denying that a few of them were, but in their own small way they all contributed to greater understanding of the autorotating blade. However, a spate of fatalities during the 1980s with a flawed American design did nothing to improve the gyroplane's image.

Light aircraft on the other hand, are a well-established cornerstone of the aviation world. Aeroplanes are perfectly normal – regulated, acceptable – the very antithesis of the much-maligned gyroplane. These fabulous little rotorcraft are the black sheep of the aviation world: a minority bunch of unruly renegades that fall out of the sky and litter the countryside with wreckage, so what on earth did my parents think as I veered from the acceptable to the allegedly downright deadly? Mum loved to fly and was always a willing passenger, but Dad was more reluctant. He wasn't really the adventurous type (and to be honest, neither am I), but he flew with me once just to say that he'd done it, and clearly once was enough as it didn't happen again! But right from the start of my autorotational journey and despite all the horror stories and negativity surrounding my new obsession, they both supported me every step of the way, and often came along to watch us training.

I'm not an adrenaline junkie by any stretch of the imagination, that's my brother's department. He's the confident daring one and I wouldn't do half the things that he has. Our parents merely accepted the unconventional antics of their offspring with stoic composure. Mum in particular had a very strict upbringing, so perhaps it was through us that she could enjoy the freedom that she had been denied. Most parents are content to see their kids grow up and find a partner, settle in to domesticity and breed, so I guess ours just got lucky! While that was never on the cards for me, my brother settled late into family life having found a like-minded partner to share his active lifestyle, albeit geared down considerably with the kids in tow. Our parents viewed the unorthodox in us as just us being us, and kept their concerns to themselves. When one day their son and daughter clambered out of an upstairs window and abseiled down the side of the house, neither of them batted an eyelid.

However, had they been present during the weekend of my first ever powered gyroplane flight, their calm exterior may have experienced a slight wobble – mine certainly did! The RAF 2000 was a kit-built gyroplane originating from Canada, and it was Chris Julian who went over to the factory in Saskatchewan and built the first one destined for British shores. This enclosed side-by-side twin-seat horrible excuse for a gyroplane remained at St Merryn while its many teething troubles were attended to. Heavy and noisy, with a bulbous canopy and small inadequate tail fin stuck on the back like an afterthought, its dangerously high thrust line has been a bone of contention to this day. The whole gang was there at St Merryn during one of several engine changes to this first machine, before it was upgraded to the more powerful Subaru Legacy. Tony Melody had come down to help Mike get the thing running properly, but this third or fourth replacement engine was splattering oil everywhere and didn't sound very well at all. Chris kept up a running commentary along the lines of 'I dunt like that. T'idden right. They shudden be flying that. I wudden fly it' every time the noisy great beast was hauled off around the circuit to return once more dripping in oil. This went on all weekend, as did Chris, loudly reiterating his dislike of the leaking under-powered engine. But as the Sunday afternoon wore on, he suddenly got it into his head that *I* should fly in the brute – after fervently expressing his misgivings about it for the past two days! Cheers, mate. What did I do to deserve that?

Thanks to Chris's insistence, Mike did take me up in it, which I wasn't at all thrilled about. We flew a couple of circuits, still spitting oil and it was every bit as awful as it looked. Heavy on the controls and lazy in response, it was like stirring porridge trying to get the feel of the thing. Its unstable nodding motion was quite disconcerting, and there was none of the delightful energy that I loved about the gyro-glider. In the video clip that Chris recorded of my first powered gyroplane flight, as the noisy bulbous machine taxis back like a fat bumblebee and shuts down on the tarmac, he remarks earnestly in the background 'I ope it avven put er off.'

*

Even now, almost three decades since I qualified as a gyronaut, there are still only a few dozen women in the world who fly them. It's baffling to me, yet no other flying machine so undeservedly endures the same stigma and prejudice as my miniature rotorcraft. Mention 'gyroplane' and the ignorant throw their hands up in horror – *dangerous* they cry! But hang on a minute, I can fly as slowly as I like, stop in mid-air and even fly backwards if the wind is favourable. This marvellous agility makes engine failure far less of an event than with an unwieldy fixed-wing, and using the rotor disc as a drag chute brings us to an instant halt on touch down. Thanks to my veteran mentors,

I can safely fly in wind speeds that effectively grounds all the allegedly 'safer' aircraft.

So permit me to add just a little bit of background in order to redress the balance. Fixed-wing aircraft will stall because wings require a certain amount of airflow in order to generate sufficient lift. Fail to maintain adequate airspeed and an aeroplane will express its displeasure by surrendering to gravity. While this isn't an immediate concern providing there's a decent amount of height in which to recover, inducing a stall at lower levels is unlikely to reach favourable conclusion. During the 1920s, Juan de la Cierva devised the original *Autogiro* concept as a flying machine that cannot stall. When in 1955, Igor Bensen took Cierva's legacy and created the homebuilt gyroplane, the aviation world was graced with the most delightfully agile, responsive and downright *fun* little flying machines that anyone could wish for. Unfortunately, the opinion held by the vast majority of the aviation world is precisely the opposite.

The diligence of Juan de la Cierva's work led to the later success of the helicopter, which ironically eclipsed its forebear and forever sealed its fate as the poor relation of the rotary-winged world. The paradox being that when a helicopter loses power to the main rotor blades it briefly becomes a gyroplane of sorts, autorotating down to land instead of dropping like the ton of proverbial bricks. But helicopters are very complex and expensive mechanisms compared to the lowly gyroplane, and they too have their Achilles heel. Screwing themselves into the air with engine power creates a huge amount of torque, which naturally tries to spin the fuselage in the opposite direction to the rotors. To counteract the torque and so enable the helicopter to proceed in an orderly fashion, a small and rather vulnerable tail rotor is stuck vertically on the rear end of the fuselage to push it back in to line. Anyone who walks away from a tail rotor failure is very lucky indeed.

Gyroplanes are far more civilised: our wind-powered rotors don't generate torque or create any sandblasting downwash. Our particular nemesis is negative G, so gyroplane pilots learn to stay away from negative G, just as aeroplane pilots learn to stay above stalling speed. The bottom line for any pilot is that *every* single kind of flying machine is potentially lethal, because gravity never loses. So it's all relative, but I never had this much fun with an aeroplane!

TEETHING TROUBLES

Mark in his Montgomerie Bensen

British homebuilt gyroplanes have a very limited choice where rotor blades are concerned, in fact the word *choice* suggests far more than is actually available! Our very few approved rotor blades are American made imports, but the original manufacturers were going through something of a transition in the early nineties, which is how Delta-J came to be wearing one of the first sets of Dragon Wings to be brought over. Smaller in dimension and lighter in weight compared to our original blades, they have a clean profile with a minimum of protruding rivets to spoil the airflow, but that efficient shape was proving extremely difficult to start turning by hand.

The first hint of trouble came when we fitted them to the glider so that I could get acquainted with their behaviour. The wind was far gustier than when Chris had test flown them on the Wombat, and we had an almighty fight trying to get them started. I couldn't push them anywhere near fast enough to settle them down, and even Chris was struggling. They seemed far more flexible than our old rotors, the advancing blade whipping up viciously on ill-timed gusts which our heavier sets would've ridden through with a stretch and a yawn. We managed a few flights in the end, but every time we towed back downwind the rotor blades were threatening to flap with almost rubber-like contortions. They were really tricky. Any autorotating rotor blades will object if they're forced to fly before they're ready, but where more placid types will accept a carefully judged nudge of encouragement, a similar encouraging nudge to a sensitive pair of Dragon Wings could well end in disaster.

My first time in command of my new Cricket was 28 May 1994, when I put the engine through its running in procedure, followed by a bit of taxiing to get the feel of the controls. Everything went well and Chris decided that the time had come to see what she could do. I was ridiculously excited as we drove out to the airfield next day. Naturally, Chris had told everyone, so there was quite a crowd to witness the first flight of a new gyroplane – *my new gyroplane!* Our friend Mark Hayward had flown in especially for the occasion, and he now stepped up to spin the rotor blades as Chris settled in the seat. These days, it's a well-known fact that Dragon Wings are absolute pigs to get started by hand, but we had to find out the hard way. Poor Mark would certainly earn his peanut butter and marmalade sandwich!

With about 12-15 knots of wind on the nose, it was fascinating to see the flexing blades visibly slowing where our old ones would have been gaining momentum. After about ten minutes with Mark shoving them round as hard as he could, Chris eventually got them to catch the breeze, and taxied straight out to the runway. We all chased after him and gathered at the intersection to watch as Delta-J took to the air on her maiden flight. I was thrilled. How small she looked in scarlet silhouette, so pretty against the sky, the sound of the rotors on the wind was music to my ears. But Chris was having trouble: she wouldn't stay level and he was struggling to keep her nose up. He brought her back down as light as a feather, calling for Mark to increase the tension on the trim springs, but a couple more circuits and Chris had had enough. The stick pressure was too much even for him – I would have no chance.

Several months of consultation and calculation followed with various ideas and proposed remedies floated around the gyroplane community. The root of the problem lay in that super-clean airfoil section. As they generated less drag than our old sets, the slippery Dragon Wings ran flatter through the air, which effectively pushed the nose down. Chris wanted to fit stronger trim springs but that would only mask the problem and I didn't like it at all. I wouldn't be able to hold her if a spring broke, and an abrupt pitch down is the last thing you want in a gyroplane. Further lengthy deliberations finally agreed on a modified torque tube to reduce the stick pressure. Hallelujah.

What couldn't be solved at the time was the spin-up problem. I needed the remains of my dwindling savings to cover training costs, so fitting a mechanical pre-rotator would have to wait. Mark was interested to see how the Dragon Wings would behave on his gyroplane – which had a pre-rotator. Only one way to find out. Mark landed at St Merryn one fine Sunday and we swapped rotor blades. He had a docile set of Rotor Hawks similar to those used on the gyro-glider, and I knew I could work them by hand. With my Dragon Wings installed on his gyroplane and maximum tension on the trim springs, Mark took off to return sometime later with a huge grin on his face, most impressed by the improved performance. A fair exchange was agreed and another problem duly solved.

*

Chris had completed the test flight schedule and we made all the necessary tweaks and adjustments so that my shiny new gyroplane was ready to go. I gathered the mound of paperwork, dotted the T's and crossed the I's, checked and double-checked that nothing had been missed before submitting everything in accordance with the requisite aviation formula, *when the weight of the paperwork equals that of the aircraft...* Weeks dragged by in anticipation of receiving Delta-J's Permit to Fly, after which I could properly begin to log training time towards my licence. But there was an unforeseen snag, a particularly tiresome snag that would waste another ten precious months before being resolved. A certain helpful person made the authorities aware that I weigh considerably less than any previous British gyronaut. This made them nervous. The test flying had been done by a pilot who was twice my size: how would this new Cricket behave with only a wafer on board? The eventual outcome was that the test flying all had to be done again by a pilot nearer to my own proportions. This was just peachy. No eight-stone gyronauts were yet available, so good old Mark was chosen to do the honours, weighing in at a svelte ten-stone-something. Providing all was satisfactory, I would then be allowed to partake of my new gyroplane, bogged down with an additional two-stone-something of ballast.

Delta-J's performance naturally improved with a much reduced load in the seat, and Mark duly reported on her excellent handling qualities. It went against the grain to add unnecessary weight to a flying machine, and Chris's views on having to weigh her down with ballast were unrepeatable. But what else could I do if I was to be allowed to use my gyroplane – and I desperately wanted to use my gyroplane! It was the only way we were going to get that coveted Permit to Fly, so somehow, we had to conjure up a suitably heavy attachment that could be safely stowed and secured inside the minimal fibreglass pod of a Cricket. It had to be carried as centrally as possible so as not to upset the balance in flight, but the only space available is a tiny compartment in the nose, definitely not the place to add such a substantial load. Sandbags were too bulky and difficult to attach without fouling the controls, and we were really struggling until Chris happened to find some strips of lead among the detritus at the back of our hangar.

They definitely had potential, being pliable and sufficiently weighty without the bulk of the sandbags. I selected a couple of lengths and trimmed them down to our target weight. Now, where to put them? The easiest way without boring holes through the pod was to stuff the hefty lead strips inside the seat cushions, nicely within the centre of gravity, and they couldn't get loose with my arse plonked on top of them. All I had to do now was get *that* arrangement approved! Suffice to say after what seemed like an age, G-BVDJ's Permit to Fly finally dropped through the letterbox, and at long last I had myself a legal flying machine. My veterans promptly got the lead out, and just as Chris had predicted, it didn't make the slightest bit of difference.

Finally ready to begin official training after two years of building, testing and fighting over paperwork, I promptly lost the services of my first instructor when he unfortunately failed his medical. Bear in mind that this was *single-seat* gyroplane training where the instructor remains firmly on the ground, and at no time does he attempt to squeeze on board with the student. Some considerable time later having at last nailed down a starting date with a second instructor, I was less than impressed to learn that he was off on holiday to America only days before we were due to begin training. Maybe he didn't fancy my chances but that was quite some distance to put between us, so I guess the prospect was just too terrifying. Third time lucky, then.

It's so easy these days! All the information world-wide is available at our fingertips in the comfort of our own homes. There are flight schools where you can train with an instructor in a two-seat gyroplane, then buy a machine of your own off the peg, the only drawback now is the price. People have no clue of how difficult it used to be, and not so long ago either. From that day in 1990 when my addiction to these miniature flying egg whisks began with the aerial poetry of Ken Wallis and *Little Nellie*, it took five years to attain my licence. Five years in which to track down and make contact with the few elusive gyronauts scattered around the British Isles. No such thing as search engines and email back then. Five years in which to give up everything I'd ever known and move 200 miles to the autorotational heart of St Merryn. Five years to help build my gyroplane, get her airworthy, get her legal, then to drag her 300 miles back up country for training at the third attempt. Five years to become a qualified gyroplane pilot – that's how badly I wanted it. And hell yeah, it was worth it!

GETTING TO KNOW YOU

Regardless of the lengthy quest for legality, Chris had already got me working with Delta-J as soon as he was satisfied with the initial test flights. Wise to the ways of authorities and the snail's pace of the paperwork trail, he saw no reason to waste any more time knowing full well that she was airworthy and as safe as could be expected - it was me that was the unknown quantity! In any case, the early stages of single-seat training are all done on the ground. It didn't count towards my licence as Chris wasn't an officially qualified instructor, but his knowledge and experience were far more valuable than any qualification. Thanks to the gyro-glider I could handle the rotor blades without thinking, leaving my lonely brain cell to focus on the consequence of adding a noisy 65 hp to the equation. 'Is that all?' you may ask. When you're basically sitting in your life savings with expensive equipment spinning furiously above and behind your head, and all it will take is a split second's inattention to reduce the whole lot to a tangled mess, believe me, sixty-five horses are plenty!

Waiting for suitable weather conditions was crucial. The wind had to be steady and straight down the runway: I would have enough on my plate without dealing with crosswind complications. Apprehension tempered my excitement, knowing that a smug minority expected me to come to grief just because *girls don't fly gyroplanes,* which only strengthened my resolve not to give them the satisfaction. Yet by the same token and despite the reassurance of my veterans, I too doubted my ability. I was about to learn from scratch on a flying machine that represented the major portion of my life savings - a *single-*

seat flying machine. I had just one shot and if I messed up it was game over, I couldn't afford to start again. Fear focussed purely on my own ineptitude and its potential to reduce my one and only gyroplane to a thrashing pile of scrap metal. The very real possibility of sustaining serious injury or at least a few broken bones in to the bargain, never entered the equation.

*

Before I go any further and to clarify a potential source of confusion, when I write about my adventures with Delta-J, I automatically use the plural as in 'we' and 'us' because she's as much a part of the story as I am. Without Delta-J, I wouldn't be me and none of this would have happened.

*

At last the day came when I pushed my rotor blades into life as pilot in command for the very first time, and I was happy to find that I could still hear them whispering over the noise of the engine. Chris instructed me to do a few steady runs at 15 mph to practice combining throttle with rotor handling, and if I felt out of control at any time, all I had to do was switch off the engine and stop. I repeated the exercise several times until Chris told me to take the speed up another 5 mph and do the same thing again. At 20 mph the rotors were whipping round and seemed almost ready to fly, but judging the attitude of my Cricket was considerably more difficult than the naked airframe of the gyro-glider. Half a dozen times we travelled up and down the runway, bobbing about with a rocking horse gait and feeling very disheartened, until summoned back in. I thought we were bouncing all over the place, but my instructor cheerfully informed me that we'd tracked perfectly down the centre line – it sure hadn't felt like it! Now I had to do it again at 25 mph. Feeding extra airspeed into the rotor disc would create more lift and help us to stabilise, or that was the theory. I was scared of leaving the ground before I could cope, but Chris assured me that it was still too slow to sustain flight, although a gust of wind might briefly pick us up, generating a small hop.

Off we went again, steadily feeding wind into the rotors and accelerating accordingly until 25 mph registered on the airspeed indicator. A palpable energy whipped round above my head like a caged tornado, pulsing its vitality through the controls. Suddenly the nose reared up and Delta-J sat back on her tail wheel. The angle felt quite alarming and I had an irrational fear of the rotors striking the ground behind, hastily cutting power and pushing the stick forward to set us back down. It's an early stage hurdle in single-seat training that always gets the adrenaline going! But we were over it now and after a few more runs to settle down and tune in, I was ready. As the nose came up I caught it with forward stick and kept the power on, and sure enough everything stabilised. I was 'flying' the nose wheel, holding Delta-J properly balanced on her mains. Chris capered at the side of the runway as we trundled past, laughing and shouting his approval.

Juggling engine thrust against rotor drag took a lot of concentration in the beginning. With practice came the beginnings of a wary confidence, but I was still uneasy about leaving the ground and resisted Chris's demands to go faster. I knew that holding the two-wheel-balance attitude and nudging up the airspeed would lift us off and (providing I didn't increase power) settle back down on the main gear after a short hop. I knew all of that. I just couldn't bring myself to do it. Not yet...

What Goes Up, Must Come Down

May 1995 found us 300 miles away at Enstone airfield, in Oxfordshire, where I was to reunite with Tony Melody and continue my training in an official capacity. The first week began quietly with only two students, but others would arrive during the course of the summer and a great camaraderie developed as we watched and learned from each other's mistakes. At times there could be up to four or five of us scattered along various parts of the runway, the more advanced students occasionally dropping into our midst to keep things interesting. Tony would trot alongside brandishing the first aid box, making us laugh and easing taut nerves. We helped and encouraged each other as best we could, united in the common goal of mastering our single-seat gyroplanes, a happy experience that remains one of the highlights of my life.

Chris had travelled up to keep an eye on me for a few days, and he advised me not to go out in the crosswind that persisted for the early part of the week. Simon had taken some two-seat gyroplane instruction in America but had only recently acquired his single-seat Brock, the machine built and formerly owned by Hugh Bancroft-Wilson. Despite this and undaunted by the crosswind, he chose to begin training and quickly progressed on to his first few hops. Watching from the sidelines I could see exactly what I needed to do, but when my turn came, I just couldn't seem to improve. All we needed was a little more airspeed, but my hand froze on the throttle and Delta-J skittered between her main wheels like an excited puppy. Seeing Simon fly the length of the runway after only a few hours with his new machine was most discouraging and I began to wonder if I really could master my gyroplane, unaware that we too had already begun to hop. Admittedly it was only a matter of millimetres but even so, our wheels had left the ground.

In the end, it really was no big deal. When the time is right it'll happen - and it did. Trundling along carefully balanced on the mains one day, a little more power was all it took and a few inches of daylight showed beneath the wheels. After several more runs it was easy and I wondered what had taken me so long, but caution is the best policy in a single-seat machine when you only have one shot. Balancing on the main wheels like this is basically a slow motion take off, so now the fun begins! Squeezing on just enough power to lift off resulted in several gentle hops down the runway, a modest foot or so above the ground and a couple of rotor spans in length, an exercise we repeated over and over again. The increase in engine power was directly proportional to the increase in confidence levels, as short hops gradually evolved into extended hops until we were flying the runway in one luxurious bound. It was brilliant! This was only the beginning, but I already knew that this crazy little flying egg whisk would be everything I had dreamed of.

Now I could get her in the air, I had to learn how to keep her up there, and to do that we needed to level off. The first bit was straightforward enough: take off as before and climb to the dizzy heights of 30 feet - and that's where the problem started. Try as I might, I could not get the nose down and Delta-J was dragging her tail: we were coming in too slow, relying on the engine to cushion the touch down and prevent an axle bending arrival. It was another hot summer's day and a large thermal had parked itself over the intersection, right where us fledglings were beginning our descents. Engrossed in coaxing our tiny rotorcraft back to earth, we were each caught in turn and tossed back into the air like a set of juggler's clubs.

I had already flown a frustrating couple of hours trying to correct our approach speed. Buzzing along at 30 feet getting progressively more annoyed with myself, I put the stick firmly forward as we hit the thermal and bounced aloft, reducing power to set up an approach. That was all fine and dandy had the buoyant cushion of air not spat us out seconds later and all the lift vanished in an instant. The rotors lost their grip, scrabbling furiously above my head like a cartoon character charging over a cliff and running on thin air, just before they fall. We were falling too. I added power and we shot back into the air as the nose reared up again, now we were too high and the runway was getting shorter. This was somewhat disconcerting. I had over-corrected and Delta-J started to porpoise. *Pilot induced oscillation!* No problem, just slow things down and let the airframe catch up with the rotors. However, there was a minor inconvenience in being only about 20 feet off the ground and just to make it interesting, hurtling towards the hedge at the end of the runway. Slowing down would drop us rapidly with very little room to recover before becoming intimately acquainted with the hedge.

A warning from a fellow student popped into my head. Some months earlier when caught in a similar situation (too high and running out of runway), he reacted by closing the throttle and consequently lost all his airspeed. The machine dropped rapidly, landed hard and tipped over, trashing itself in the process and dislocating his shoulder. I could hear him telling me 'If you run out of room and can't get in, for Christ's sake DON'T take the power off!' It was excellent advice and gratefully received. I knew there wasn't time to stop the roller coaster and sort myself out in the short space of tarmac remaining, an experienced pilot could do it but not this rookie. I remember very clearly rationalising the options in barely a matter of seconds as we swooped and climbed with ever-increasing severity towards runway's end. The choice was simple, we *had* to fly.

Going up into the circuit didn't faze me at all, Delta-J's survival depended on it. Throttling up to 6,000 rpm was considerably more power than I had used so far, and I was unprepared for the startling kick in the pants as she stabilised immediately and rocketed over the hedge. *Wow,* I wasn't expecting that! Chris was in my head, telling me to keep the airspeed on as we turned downwind. Already at 250 feet (eight times higher than we'd ever been before), crossing the main road beyond the hedge was a step too far. I made a tight 180 and steamed downwind beside the runway at an enthusiastic 70 mph. This was awesome! She handled like a dream, and I was sorely tempted to play, but a glance down to my right revealed a group of anxious faces staring up at us from the bottom half of the runway. *Behave. You're not ready yet...*

Thankfully there were no aeroplanes in the circuit to complicate matters, and centre stage was all ours. Delta-J turned on the proverbial sixpence and I was thrilled with my tiny flying machine as I lined her up over the gyroplane half of the runway, throttled back and put the nose down as best I could. Passing 40 feet, I nudged on a few more revs and slid back in to the 'straight and level above the runway' position where we were supposed to have been all along, yet again landing too slowly and cushioned with power. Aaargh! After all that, I *still* couldn't get it right.

Collective relief was much evident as I taxied sheepishly back to the fold, and we couldn't help laughing as Tony feigned heart failure. I was delighted with the brief taste of my Cricket's performance, yet disgusted with myself for having triggered oscillations, and could imagine the earful I was going to get from Chris when he heard. But Delta-J was still in one piece and that was all that really mattered. Later, as I sat with Tony recounting our little escapade, he recognised the problem straight away – and I wasn't entirely at fault. Before leaving for home, Chris had flown my machine and adjusted the stick pressure to what he thought would be suitable for me. Not knowing any different I'd accepted it without question, believing it was my own incompetence preventing me from flying on an even keel. Going over to Delta-J, Tony released all the tension from the trim springs and it was as simple as that. I wasn't such a failure after all – merely a wimp.

*

One of the best day's training was when the local flying club closed early for the day, giving us free rein over the full length of the runway. Along with Kieran who had reached the same stage with his thunderous Volkswagen powered Bensen, we now climbed to 100 feet above the runway to practice power-off landings. Levelling out over the centre line, we reduced as much power as we felt comfortable with, building our courage and working towards landing with an idling engine. It was a little scary at first! Only when we were pointing at the ground at about 45 degrees did the airspeed begin to rise. It felt uncomfortably steep, like standing on the rudder pedals looking down over the nose, but after dropping back to 50 feet we were in familiar territory – we had done this bit before.

Later in the day as a variation on a theme, we began combining landing lessons with S turns. Apart from my unscheduled circuit, everything up to now had been done in a straight line (some straighter than others) and we were ready and eager to try some new directions. Again, bit by bit, we gently explored the flight envelope of our miniature rotorcraft, tipping them over into increasingly tighter turns and loving the raw energy of the rotor disc. It was such tremendous fun that it didn't feel like learning at all. With a deserted airfield to play with, Kieran and I made absolute pigs of ourselves as we chased each other back and forth across the runway, snaking from side to side and revelling in the superb manoeuvrability of our gyroplanes. Dropping down for landing practice at the end of each run, we turned around and fast taxied back up the side of the runway to keep our rotors spinning, and leapt into the air again. I couldn't remember fixed-wing training being so utterly joyful.

Following another session of reduced power and *almost-but-not-quite* spot landings in a crosswind, our next treat on the agenda was to discover the delights of slow flight and hovering. Circling above the grass to reach the dizzy heights of 700 feet, we turned into wind and steadily raised the nose, throttling back and keeping a close eye on the altimeter. Delta-J began to wallow, the controls growing mushy and sluggish as the airspeed bled away. With 40 mph on the clock, I nudged on some power to hold her there and trickled across the grass at 500 feet, just feeling it out. This was really cool. Regaining airspeed at the end of each pass and climbing back to 700 feet, we flew slower and slower until finally we were hanging stationary in the air. The engine roared its heart out with nothing more to give, but the drag of the rotor disc was too great to overcome and we slipped into a vertical descent. Again the attitude was steep. The nose pointed high at the heavens blocking everything from view, and I lay there looking up at my feet on the rudder pedals. This was prime negative G territory, a potentially lethal situation for a gyroplane: push the nose down too quickly and the rotors will slow in a heartbeat, flap down and cut off the tail. I wasn't scared, though. I knew what to do. 400 feet now, still sliding down on our tail, and that was low enough for a first time recovery. Reducing power while gently lowering the nose returned us safely to an even keel, before powering back up for another go. You can't do that with an aeroplane! Flying as slowly as possible before pulling into a vertical descent was a great confidence builder, and it's still one of my favourite things.

The wind increased during the day and became strong enough to support us in a hover. Slowing to zero airspeed we balanced on the wind, finding that point of equilibrium which kept us hanging in the air (another manoeuvre I never tire of), drifting backwards above the grass like thistledown on the breeze. I grew less reliant on airspeed and altimeter, sensing the touch of the rotors on the wind and the sound of their song in my ears. Delta-J had become part of me, and a movement with rudder and rotors was as natural as moving my finger and toes.

Brief Encounter

This unique and memorable moment took place during a training exercise in 1995. The flight itself wasn't remarkable at all and the magic that happened required no skill on my part, it was merely a spectacular coincidence. Having completely missed my Spitfire escort at Blackbushe eight years earlier, I couldn't have dreamed that one day I would collect the whole set.

*

Along with Simon, I was nearing the end of the gyroplane conversion course, so we paired up to explore the local area and complete our cross-country flights. The day of the British Grand Prix dawned overcast with showers, but a reasonable cloud base and good visibility between the wet patches was all the encouragement we needed. Simon suggested buzzing over to nearby Silverstone to take a look at the Formula One festivities. As fixed-wing pilots we were both well familiar with the intricacies of map reading and course plotting, the essential difference now was to ensure that our charts (and everything else!) were securely nailed down to avoid littering the countryside with propeller shredded confetti. A phone call to the ops desk advised us of pertinent airspace restrictions and granted permission to proceed, *providing* we kept well clear of the circuit itself.

It was about a 40-mile round trip with a decent bit of wind to play with, and the occasional deluge to avoid beneath a ceiling of around 1,400 feet. I didn't like to fly in such conditions with an aeroplane: they were too unwieldy for my in-built safety margins and I was always nervous of being forced down by a lowering cloud base. On a day like today, other than a spot of circuit bashing, I would have left the aeroplane firmly on the ground. There were no such qualms with our agile little gyroplanes, the heavy overcast didn't bother me at all. The air smelt fresh and earthy as we floated through the ashen void like a pair of tadpoles in a fish tank. The thick porridge of the cloud base spread like a canopy above our heads, a damp grey blanket supported here and there by feathery columns of rain. Heavy downpours were clearly visible as dark smudges brushing the earth, easily avoided. A few hidden showers lay in ambush to be quickly side-stepped as the first drops splashed across our visors, and we just nipped through the lighter drizzly bits.

Flying at 120 knots snug inside an aeroplane is as mundane as driving a car. Shielded from the elements, there's little sense of motion or velocity without scenery flashing past the windows. (Advisory note: with the exception of take off or landing, scenery flashing past the windows of an aeroplane generally isn't a good sign). 70 mph in an open cockpit gyroplane is something else! The wind roared in my ears, a riotous concussion that snatched at my flight suit and blustered tirelessly around the pod like a gang of boisterous puppies in search of mischief. Anything not tied down would be ripped away without mercy. Simon must be getting pummelled out there on his open-frame machine, he had no protection at all. Sailing an invisible tide through the pale silvery light, we skipped between the showers bobbing like surfers on a swell, our rotors busily harvesting lift from the eccentric flurries of wind. Delta-J was alive in my hands: I could feel everything, every movement as she reacted to the airflow swirling around us. This was *really* flying!

The cloud was beginning to break a little as Silverstone gradually crept into view, shafts of watery sunlight glinting on a carpet of toy cars tightly packed in distant parking zones. Far beyond, the dark urban sprawl of Milton Keynes skulked on the horizon beneath an ashen sky, streaked and smudged like a bad watercolour. A thick wooded area formed a natural boundary between us and the race track, so we stayed above the fields to watch from a respectable distance and indulge in a spot of hovering. Several light aircraft were also in the vicinity, clearly visible as distinct black crosses pinned against the cloud base. It proved delightfully simple to keep an eye on them, pivoting on the spot in tight 360s to check our very few blind spots, accompanied by a delicious *whop* from the hard working rotor blades.

It was beginning to look quite dark back towards Enstone, so we turned our noses for home and challenged the wind almost head on, sprinkles of fine rain misting our visors. I didn't worry about the weather. It wasn't threatening to that extent (not for a super-nimble gyroplane), and there were plenty of good fields along our track for a precautionary landing if things took a turn for the worse. I'd been a bit concerned about wet plugs as we got splattered on the periphery of several heavier downpours, but the engine seemed unperturbed and maintained its healthy roar as we battled against the wind.

Then it happened. As well as the British Grand Prix that day there was also a big air display being held at Duxford, due east of Silverstone. I couldn't believe my eyes as just ahead of us, the only airworthy Lancaster bomber in the world emerged from the cloud base, closely flanked by a Spitfire and Hurricane. The Battle of Britain Memorial Flight in full splendour – what a magnificent sight! It was completely unexpected, not a mention of them in our pre-flight briefing. I brought Delta-J to a halt and hung her on the wind beneath a nebulous vault of pearly-grey, watching in stunned amazement as the iconic old warbirds crossed our track. To meet them in their own element for one priceless moment was beyond words and my heart was in my mouth. Veils of mist caressed their wings and they slipped back into the heavens and vanished as suddenly as they had appeared. Wow. Just *wow*.

Even now it gives me chills. To share the sky with them for one brief moment – the enormity of all they epitomised – what an incredible privilege that was.

THE END IS NIGH

30 July 1995 found us back at the charming aerodrome of Old Sarum, where along with Simon, I was about to take my final flight test for gyroplane qualification. I hadn't flown Delta-J from grass before, but the runway looked well rolled so I wasn't unduly worried about that, my main concern was being able to take off at all. It was a scorcher of a day: not a breath of wind to ripple the sultry air and the lifeless windsock hung dejectedly from its pole like a wilted flower. Simon had no worries with a pre-rotator to drive his rotors through the danger zone, but hand starting mine would be test enough in itself, never mind trying to coax them into the air!

The setting was idyllic. People filled the picnic tables sitting in the sunshine, or lounged in scattered groups across the grass. Air traffic was sporadic in the summer heat, and the thought of climbing into a baking Spam can and sealing the lid didn't appeal to me either. On the other hand, an open cockpit gyroplane would be delightful on such a day - if only I can get her off the ground... After confirming arrangements with the tower, it was time to saddle up. Being small and slow and difficult to spot, we were given exclusive use of the microlight circuit, flying our exercises over the secondary strip running parallel to the main runway. Tony gave us a last briefing and explained what we needed to do, as in demonstrate as much of the latter part of the syllabus as was practical in these conditions. Accustomed to our exclusive little world at the bottom of Enstone's runway where we made our mistakes in private, I was more nervous about performing in front of this large crowd of spectators than doing the test itself. And I just knew my rotors weren't going to co-operate...

Finally strapped in and baking nicely inside my electric hat, I parked Delta-J behind Simon's machine ready to catch his prop wash through my rotor blades. Tony shoved them round as hard as he could to give them a good start and we moved off towards the holding point at the other end of the airfield, but despite taxiing closely in Simon's wake, the rotors felt sluggish and weren't gaining any momentum at all. Simon engaged his pre-rotator and turned straight on to the runway but before I could follow, a Cessna called 'final' over the radio and we were left stranded at the hold. With no hope of saving the rapidly decaying rotor rpm, I turned away and parked up ready for a fight with my rotor blades.

It was far too hot for such exertions. Stretching to throw my weight behind every turn of the rotor blades quickly sapped what little strength I had, leaving me gasping in despair. This was a battle I knew I couldn't win. The moment I stopped pushing and flopped back into the seat, by the time I'd buckled up, plugged in and fired up, all that remained of my efforts was a lazily mocking *swish* that was not even close to being recoverable. Luckily, Tony guessed what had happened after seeing Simon take off alone, and heroically trotted over half the length of the runway to come and save the day. Pausing a moment for traffic to clear the circuit, Tony got the rotors turning as fast as he could and waved us away. Delta-J fired at once and we taxied straight to the runway with a brief 'lined up and rolling' call to the tower, ambling forth along the centre line with full focus on my reluctant rotors.

The grass strip wasn't as good as it looked. Four-inch wheels and no suspension made for a very rough ride indeed, but it was impossible to get airborne any sooner without any wind to shorten our take off run. Accelerating gently to nurse the rotor blades, it seemed like an age before they began to wake up and I could finally feel some energy building above my head. I gave them an extra nudge of power as encouragement that *now* would be a good time, and Delta-J grudgingly sat up on her main wheels. That'll do. I opened the throttle but the response was markedly subdued and with the last third of the runway remaining, my little Cricket reluctantly hauled herself off the deck and sauntered into the air with her hands in her pockets. I kept her nose down to gain airspeed then traded it for height, pulling up in a lovely long swoop as we reached the airfield boundary. Performance was definitely lacking today.

Once aloft I was much happier, the hard part was over! It was wonderful to be in the air and I even forgot about our audience as we circuited the airfield to fly a different exercise on each pass along the runway. Slow flight wasn't particularly slow in such unresponsive air (just in case the elastic snapped), neither could we demonstrate our hovering and crosswind capabilities, but Tony had seen us do it all before. After twenty-five minutes of entertaining the locals, we slotted in behind a fixed-wing on final and managed to make a passable landing opposite our parking area, where Simon was already down. Rolling to a halt, the heat hit me like opening an oven door. I couldn't get out of my electric hat fast enough, and Simon agreed that the best place to be was in the air. But first a debrief: how had we fared on our flight tests and would I have to do it again? Thanks to Tony's endless patience over the past few months and despite the challenging conditions, we had both managed to pass. Sitting down to complete the formalities over welcome refreshments, we discovered that the rest of the day was ours to do as we pleased, so naturally there was only one way to celebrate our graduation – go flying!

With the aid of some local instructors and a large map on the briefing room wall, we planned to visit an ancient chalk carving known as the Westbury white horse, routing via Stonehenge. This would take us through several danger areas over the army firing ranges on Salisbury Plain, including some disturbingly marked *High Impact Areas,* although we were assured that they weren't active at present. Wouldn't that just be typical, to get shot down on the day I qualified for my licence! Our intended track also took us close to the busy parachuting centre at Netheravon, and for that we needed permission. A subsequent phone call granted us a narrow corridor to fly down, hugging the west side of the main road that passes between their zone and a danger area. Maximum altitude would be 800 feet, with strict instructions to call for clearance before skirting the zone boundary. A high impact area to the left and parachutes to the right, quite the incentive for accurate navigation.

We chased Simon out onto the runway, harvesting his prop wash through the rotors and took off in a much tidier manner. Stonehenge was in view as we climbed out of the circuit side by side, and in the distance, the smooth runways of Boscombe Down looked like rolls of grey carpet laid out on the grass. We sailed through the warm summer sky, savouring the moment, elated by a sense of almost overwhelming disbelief that here I was, a newly qualified gyronaut piloting my very own gyroplane. Against the odds, I had done this thing! Looking down at a crowd of people dwarfed by the giant standing stones of the ancient monument, I felt extremely lucky indeed, and glancing across at Simon, felt sure that he too would have a big soppy grin on his face.

With a farewell pass around the enigmatic stones, we headed over to the road that we were to track along, and turned north. I could see dust trails on the distant ranges raised by invisible tanks, and sincerely hoped that our information was correct! The parachute centre was about five miles to our right, where a twin engine aircraft was climbing above the circuit, and the controller held us at the zone boundary until the drop was complete. We circled tightly as a dozen parachutes blossomed in the sky, watching the canopies drift down to collapse on the ground until we were cleared to go on. A thick mauve haze hung like a dirty curtain above the parched landscape and there was a definite lack of vitality in the air, my rotors felt slippery as if unable to get to a grip on it. Suddenly we crested a spine of hills, the ground abruptly falling away beneath our wheels as we flew straight into a wall of cool air, the gift of instant energy. The rotors grabbed it at once, greedily harvesting precious lift and we bounced skywards feasting on the updraught. Flying a wide circle over the flat plain that had opened up below, we turned back on ourselves to see the white horse standing crisp against a backdrop of green hillside, overlooking the downs. Miniature people walking along a footpath at the top of the hill, stopped to watch as two gyroplanes swept in from across the plain and roared triumphantly over their heads.

We returned safely to Old Sarum after flying a final circuit of Stonehenge to celebrate, and landed together for the last time. I felt mixed emotions as we packed away and loaded our machines onto their trailers. We were both fully fledged now: it was time to leave the nest and our fellow students under Tony's wing and go our separate ways. I was grateful to have qualified without doing any damage, yet there was a tinge of regret that a unique chapter of my life had come to an end. For this proud member of the Enstone 95 gang, the training was over - the learning about to begin.

I was lucky to be going home to a group of veteran gyronauts who would keep me on the straight and narrow. I knew that I'd be under close scrutiny until I had proved myself, especially from Chris. He was waiting in the road when we arrived, scooping me up in a massive bear hug, impatient to hear all about it. As soon as Delta-J was tucked away in the yard, he hustled me inside demanding to see the video evidence of my training. Sprawled on the sofa with copious mugs of tea, we watched it through again and again and yet once more, Chris picking faults and cheerfully voicing loud criticism as I cringed at the memory of some of those landings. It was good to be home!

Come Sunday, the weather was perfect and I knew I would be on trial as we towed Delta-J back to the airfield. Everyone was there to welcome us; Bob, Les and Derek, and dear old Tony down from Bude. There was no chance of a quiet maiden flight, they all wanted to see me perform, even the visitors who had come down for gyro-gliding after Chris had finished broadcasting to all and sundry. Les offered to escort me round the local landmarks and before I knew it, we were parked at the threshold of Wendy's runway as Chris started the rotors. Everyone gathered to watch. I tried to ignore the stage fright by concentrating on Les as he prepared to take off in his loud two-litre Volkswagen Cricket. It wasn't a good runway for our debut, the aged tarmac cracked and choked by a thick carpet of weeds bulging like blisters from the once immaculate surface.

I would try a short take off as we had some wind to help us on our way. The rotors accelerated nicely as Chris lifted the nose of the pod, letting more air through until they would spin no faster. Setting us back on three wheels, he beamed at me and put his fist to his mouth, pretending to chew his nails as he skipped out of the way – and I knew we were going to be all right. Les was circling overhead waiting for us to catch up. I added some power and already Delta-J felt light and eager to fly. I held her on the main wheels for a moment just to show that I could do it, then opened the throttle to bump briefly over ragged tufts of vegetation before sailing into the air. This was what I'd been waiting for. Looking down at the familiar pattern of runways where it all began with the gyro-glider, the circle was complete and at last I really was a St Merryn Gyronaut.

Joining up with Les, we chased him around the local area for thirty-five minutes, a beautiful blur of coastline and countryside, but I was more intent on keeping up with him than noting my surroundings. I was used to flying with Simon who liked to go low and slow, and Chris had warned me that Les flew with unerring purpose – he wasn't kidding! The airspeed indicator quivered beyond 80 mph as we raced to keep up with our veteran guide, who had a worrying habit of shooting out to sea. That was a line I wouldn't cross, so we loitered above the cliff tops playing with the updraughts until he came back in. When flying a tiny rotorcraft with the glide ratio of a house brick, it's best to stay over something you can land on should the need arise! We took the shortest route across the Camel estuary, but I climbed an extra couple of hundred feet as we flew over the muddy looking waters, just in case. The twin coasts of Cornwall's narrow peninsula with its numerous clusters of wind farms make navigation a simple matter, so even on our first time out, St Merryn was surprisingly easy to find.

I could see the glider in action on the runway as we headed home, and knowing that Chris and Tony would be having fun with their students reminded me of my first visit, a know-nothing-wannabe with a collection of parts and an improbable dream. Now I was about to land on that hallowed ground for the first time in my very own gyroplane. I circled while Les made his approach, waiting our turn as he touched down then followed him in to make a half-decent landing. Taxiing to the back to the hangar and stopping the rotor blades, I felt quietly euphoric. The improbable dream had come true.

Spinning on the Wind

It was a cracking autumnal day of October 1995: an ice-white sun glared out from a pale sky, with a howling south-westerly that snatched the breath from our lungs. Perfect kiting weather! In such a wind as this, the gyro-glider can be tethered and flown from a stationary point instead of being towed. No one would dream of flying in such conditions in the fixed-wing world, and as a newly qualified convert in the art of autorotation, I have to admit that I would've been reluctant to indulge had our veterans not been with us.

There were four of us eager to play, so we dusted off Tony's old glider for a rare outing to blow away the cobwebs. Chris Shilling settled into the seat as we hitched it to the car and Tony pulled them out to the start of the Gyro runway, directly into wind. With Old Faithful tied on to my car and Derek installed at the wheel, I grabbed my video camera and hopped onboard with Chris as Derek began to drag us out in to the teeth of the gale. Away from the shelter of the hangar it was a struggle to move against the wind and even harder to stop going downwind – I was almost blown off my feet! Chris-S was already in position with his glider at the threshold, the car parked a tow rope's length away with Tony wisely sheltering inside. The seething tide of air plucked the speech from our mouths, scattering words like paper in the wind and we had to shout to be heard.

Starting the rotor blades was going to be a challenge in a wind this strong. Derek went to help Chris-S with Tony's glider, while I hung on to the stick as Chris began to push our rotors into life. He and Derek shoved like crazy while Chris-S and I grimly nursed the bucking control sticks, trying to stabilise the rotors long enough to form a disc. A slight error of judgement in the relentless 40 mph wind could send them flapping out of control and wreck the gliders in a instant. Perseverance eventually paid off, Chris-S being the first to get airborne with his lighter load. Chris had joined me on the seat to help hold us down until the rotors had settled, and now I gingerly slid off to fight my way over to the centreline and do some filming, waddling with difficulty inside two padded flying suits comically inflated by the wind. Chris opened the furiously spinning rotor disc to the wind, and soared into the air. Synchronised kiting – you don't see that every day!

The wind was shoving me in the back, threatening to bowl me over like a tumble-weed as I struggled to steady the camera and keep a pair of delighted gyronauts in view as they bobbed gleefully on the roaring torrent of air. A brief lull settled the machines gently back to earth, and Derek took the opportunity to scramble on board with Chris-S. Their glider struggled up to about 5 feet but the extra weight proved too much, as Chris on Old Faithful waved mockingly from above. He yelled at me to come back and fly, planting the wheels firmly on the deck for me to climb on. Although our combined weight wasn't much different from that of Derek and Chris-S, our longer blades gave us an extra bit of rotor disc that made all the difference, and we rose easily.

Once into clean air the glider went up like a lift as the wind blew even stronger – this is awesome! Chris let it climb to the full extent of the tow rope and handed it over to me. The stick bucked in my hand and the airframe pulsed as the rotors fought against the constraint of the tow rope, fastened to my little car some 50 feet below. Chris made a game of testing me, seeing how accurately I could position the glider where he wanted it. I was careful not to jerk the rope, so powerful was the pull of the rotor disc that it wasn't hard to imagine us lifting the car up as well. But what terrific fun! Chris-S was happily floating alongside, so I picked up my camera to do some air to air shots as Derek and Tony added to the entertainment by towing us down the runway at a snail's pace.

Chris-S crossed our path with some enthusiastic wide turns

and steep banks as I tried to keep him in camera range from my own soaring perch, which throbbed to the beat of the rotors. They were a rough fibreglass set of doubtful integrity that bounced energetically at the best of times, and now they were spinning like crazy. The cars crept down the runway straining against the tremendous drag of the rotors. Normally the gyroglider lands as the tow car reaches the end of the runway, and the whole caboodle is turned around and hauled back downwind to do it again. Not this time: Derek and Tony switched off their engines and surrendered to the forces of nature. It was brilliant – imagine an umbrella catching the wind – an umbrella 25 feet in diameter! We opened the rotor discs and used the wind to push us back through the air, pulling our cars along below. The gliders rarely touched down, riding the gale to kite stationary, then crawling down the runway to reverse back up and do it again, a joyful game that we played for hours. It was the longest time that we'd ever gone without a tea break. After a while I swapped over to fly with Chris-S and take some film of Chris from Tony's machine, another bronco ride beneath a rough set of plastic blades which unfortunately didn't improve the recording of a memorable day, but it captures the spirit if little else. The autumn chill began to make its presence known after several hours of riotous autorotation, seeping inside collars and cuffs, numbing feet and hands until we reluctantly called a halt and returned to the hangar, tired and stiff and absolutely elated.

As we shared peanut butter and marmalade sandwiches, huddling round Tony's Thermos flask for warmth, the drone of an approaching Rotax heralded the arrival of our mate Mark popping in from Liskeard. As usual it took a few minutes to pick out the buzzing micro-dot high in the sky, which steadily evolved into a familiar yellow gyroplane that dropped down to perform a neat spot landing in front of the hangar. I hadn't planned to fly my machine as the wind strength was well beyond the limits of my new skills, so when Mark suggested that I accompany him to Bodmin, I was about to decline. Chris thought otherwise, telling me that despite the excess velocity it would be good experience because both wind speed and direction remained constant – and anyway I'd been flying in it all day! A squadron of nervous butterflies took wing inside my stomach as I extracted Delta-J from her nest. Chris and Mark wouldn't expect me to fly if they didn't think I could handle the conditions, the trouble was that *I* didn't think I could handle the conditions. It was a bright day with fairly good viz but despite being wrapped up like a Telly Tubby, I was chilled to the bone. Shivering inside my pair of flight suits, I decided to compromise and escort Mark as far as the wind farm, just under halfway to Bodmin.

Chris started my rotors, having to really push them hard to avoid trouble. Even with the stick fully forward I could feel they were right on the edge of a flap, a bad situation to be in when you can't close them down any further, but Chris was on hand to shove them out of it. Finally the rotors caught and I was able to nurse them up to speed, being very careful not to let the wind catch the disc and bowl us over as we taxied to the runway. We two-wheel-balanced on the spot as Mark lined up and took off immediately, gunning the throttle. Not knowing any different, I did our normal take off (albeit with zero ground roll) steadily increasing power intending to climb out at 50 mph, but oh no we didn't! Delta-J leapt into the air and stayed there, we were going up sure enough but not forwards. This was novel. I put her nose down and increased to maximum power, trying to push through the headwind. Mark was well ahead of us by now and seemed to be making normal progress, so what was I doing wrong?

Airspeed was already in the 80s, the pointer quivering uncomfortably close to the red line at 90 mph. How was I supposed to raise ground speed without increasing airspeed? After what seemed like an age, we had fought our way to the edge of the airfield still climbing, with no chance of catching Mark. We were like a bug suspended in amber and could've been stuck in mid-air until the fuel ran out, which was one way of getting down. I managed to contain our height to 800 feet but as we were clearly not progressing in the direction of away, I had to pluck up courage to turn back. That may not sound like a big deal, but I was alone in the strongest headwind yet encountered and the usual procedures didn't seem to be working. Adding power got us climbing again, but reducing it saw us being pushed backwards: the rotors felt as if they were turning faster than they'd ever gone before and the disc felt like a solid lump resisting the wind, which roared all around. Imagine trying to paddle a tin bath upstream against rapids – the elements very much had the upper hand.

I was scared of turning crosswind, feeling like we could be blown over as soon as we presented a broadside. What I *should* have done was let the wind push us back and reverse up the runway, but my fixed-wing mentality wasn't yet fully suppressed and being distracted by events, it didn't occur to me to do what we'd been doing all day with the gliders! I remember very gingerly feeding in left stick with a touch of rudder, but as soon as Delta-J's nose moved away from the airflow, the wind grabbed us and pushed gleefully against the pod, whipping us through 180 degrees and we shot downwind pursued by furies. *Whoa!* The transition from barely perceptible ground speed to a ground speed of what seemed like Formula One proportions happened in a matter of seconds. I could feel the rotors losing their grip as the wind swept them along from behind, like running downhill and losing control of your legs as gravity forces them to go faster.

Not wanting to be blown too far downwind, I raised the nose and reduced power before turning tightly on to approach. Instantly we hit a solid wall of raging air. I retained enough presence of mind to get the nose down and whack the power on as we turned, hoping to gain momentum to battle upwind, and sure enough the threshold was creeping closer. Delta-J bobbed like a cork on the tide as we clawed our way home, but we seemed much too high at 600 feet (fixed-wing conditioning again) and I had no clear idea of what to do other than making it up as we went. Eventually by standing her on her nose and juggling the throttle, I managed to coax her down and we settled onto the runway about two thirds along, after what was possibly the longest short final of all time!

We were back on the ground but it wasn't over yet. There was a very real danger of the wind flipping us over, and it took perhaps a couple of minutes to bring the rotors down to a manageable speed before I dared to turn around and taxi in. Parking in the shelter of the hangar to kill off the wind, I couldn't drop my guard until the rotor blades were stopped and safely tied down, only then could I breathe a sigh of relief. Chris was waiting to give me an earful: instead of doing a normal take off, I should have gunned the throttle like Mark to punch our way through the headwind. *Now* he tells me! I was just grateful not to have hurt my gyroplane, but of course Chris was right as usual – it *was* an experience.

HAPPY DAYS

Lawrence of Bodmin

By the summer of 1996, I had scraped enough money together to fit Delta-J with a pre-rotator. The docile old Rotor Hawks had served me well and looking back now, it's plain to see that some of our earlier escapades may not have ended so favourably had we been able to use that original set of sensitive Dragon Wings. Chris had trusted me with a trial flight of his Rotordynes while the Wombat was in dock following a crankshaft failure, and even my limited experience could tell how much better they were. Unfortunately, as Rotordynes were no longer available, the only upgrade option was another set of Dragon Wings. The forced impetus of a mechanical pre-rotator masks that wonderful transition from inert mass to living wing, and I was reluctant to lose the hand-start capability, but Dragon Wings were gaining a reputation for improved performance and that's what I was looking for. When our second set arrived in August, I began learning another new way to get airborne. Delta-J's performance was much improved by her slippery new rotors, but by boy they're a handful.

*

One late December afternoon in the midst of some general lurking at the airfield, Chris suddenly decided we were going to fly over to visit our neighbours at Woodlands Barton, a perfectly kept microlight strip some fifteen minutes hop away on the other side of the wind farm. The air was crisp and clean with a frosty chill that nipped at fingers and toes. It was almost four o'clock when we eventually got airborne after dressing for battle with the cold, which in Chris's case meant doing up his top button and donning a scarf.

Forming up together and heading towards the glinting wind farm, we made lazy progress through a crystal blue void. The sun took on a pale peach hue as it slipped lower in the west, and a dusky haze began to shroud the horizon. A light breeze toyed with us as we flew a rotor span apart from the sleek Wombat Gyrocopter riding the air so easily alongside. Chris was clowning, waving both hands and pulling faces at me, laughing when I returned the compliment, steadying the stick with my knees. Two gyroplanes sailed alone through the fresh winter sky. The steady buzz of the engine faded into my subconscious and all was peaceful – but by 'eck, it was cold! I wriggled in the seat, trying to get some feeling back in numb extremities. My feet had parted company some time ago and two blocks of ice rested against the rudder pedals.

The velvet green runways of Woodlands Barton came steadily into view, the windsock fluttering half-heartedly towards the short one. I held back to follow the Wombat as Chris peeled away and slid down an invisible ramp to touch daintily upon the grass. I closed the throttle and we whistled in steeply to settle in behind - not too bad at all. Several weeks of frost had made the ground as hard as iron, and the grass already felt slippery beneath the cloudless evening sky. Thankfully someone was still at home. Peter the Kitfox pilot came out to meet us as we extracted ourselves with some difficulty from the machines and followed him inside to defrost over the gas stove. Steaming mugs of hot chocolate were gratefully received to assist the thawing out process, and my boots were tingling nicely by the time that Chris was ready to leave. We'd been on the ground about thirty minutes and dusk was upon us. The light breeze had long given up and gone home, leaving the windsock undisturbed. Oh well, we can use the longest runway.

Chris hand started his Rotordynes and was away easily, but my Dragon Wings just didn't want to know. Fast taxiing on frozen grass was a new experience and it didn't feel safe at all as we bumped and slipped across the runways. After several laps of the airfield in all directions, the nose wheel was just considering picking itself up as we hared towards a low wire fence at the boundary. A flat open field lay beyond, but the rotors still weren't biting as the gap closed all too rapidly. With visions of *doing a Philpotts* (Tony's famed impression of a carrier landing, demonstrated by catching the tail wheel on a wire fence), I chickened out, cut power and popped the airbrake, which brought us to a reassuringly abrupt halt some 40 feet from the fence. We might have made it, who knows, but better safe than sorry. Despite nipping back down the icy runway as fast as I dared in vain attempt to generate some airflow, the rotors rapidly lost momentum and clearly weren't going to oblige.

Watching from above, Chris could see that I was getting nowhere and came back down to help, bringing a lovely 60 inch fan with him. Just what we need. Parking behind him at the threshold, I engaged the pre-rotator and edged forward into his prop wash to boost my lazy rotor blades, and at last they began to wake up. Quickly scooting in front of the Wombat to return the favour and give him a blast, we accelerated together in a formation take off, flying a farewell pass to a bemused Peter who was finding it most entertaining. We put our noses down and raced through the freezing twilight to find St Merryn before it vanished in the dusk, landing in Braille, chilled to the bone and glad to be home. Chris was eager to put me right: I should have driven the pre-rotator harder and taxied faster. Thirty-plus years of experience meant that he was right as usual, and this third year rookie learned another lesson on that trip.

*

One of the lovely characters to come into our world at St Merryn immediately became known as *Brian the vicar,* and yes, he actually was. Like many before him, he had succumbed to the charms of the gyro-glider, and bought himself a partly built Cricket, which Chris was completing for him in the workshop. Brian loved flying the glider and became a popular member of the crew, always making the effort to pop over between Sunday services. To give Chris his due, he did try hard to curtail his language out of respect for a man of the cloth, but Brian was totally unfazed which was just as well as Chris had more than a few lapses in his good behaviour. Poor Brian, he needed a sense of humour with us lot. His Cricket was registered G-BWHT which I couldn't resist naming God Be With Holy Terrors. It was all Tony's fault, a habit that he instilled after working out that my Delta-J stood for Better Visibility for Damsel Jockeys. 'Damsel' was stretching the imagination a bit, but given Tony's eyesight...

Chris took me to act as gofer when Brian started the early stages of groundwork at St Merryn. In those days we tuned our radios to 123.45 to talk between ourselves, being in the back of beyond it didn't seem to bother anyone. Our Holy Terror beamed from ear to ear as he sat in his smart new gyroplane with everything turning and burning for the very first time. Chris began to instruct him over the radio, accompanied by gestures and arm waving which grew ever more animated as Brian remained grinning happily from the cockpit, obviously not hearing a word. Eventually Chris ducked under the spinning rotors and yelled in his ear, which had the had the desired effect, scuttling clear as Brian slowly headed off down the runway. Chris got back on the radio but there was still no response over the airwaves.

After a while the rattle of an idling Rotax grew louder, and in due time Brian cheerfully trundled past, completely oblivious to Chris's increasingly earthy transmissions, and just as well really – you shouldn't say things like that to a vicar! Getting more and more agitated, Chris finally managed to flag him down, only to find that Brian's radio was indeed switched on and functioning correctly on 123.45, whereas his own set had one digit astray. Instead of 123.45, Chris had tuned to 123.40, which happened to be the tower frequency of nearby RAF St Mawgan! Luckily, they hadn't picked up his broad Cornish expletives, the volume of which could well have been heard across the fields without the aid of radio, but Chris was totally unabashed as always. *Ooh 'ell!* he chuckled. Brian got on well, after that.

*

Chris was reluctant to fly so much in those later years, which I couldn't understand at the time – it's a beautiful day – let's get up there! Now over two decades later I'm also content just to fly when I feel like it, savouring the moment rather than gobbling it up and reaching for more. But looking back now, a bizarre incident had clearly affected him more than we realised at the time, which perhaps combined with the imminent arrival of his sixtieth birthday was a wake up call that no one – not even Chris Julian – is truly invincible.

I was in my flat one evening when Judy knocked on the door to ask if I had any plasters, as Chris had been bitten by a dog. Her calm matter of fact demeanour gave no cause to imagine anything more than a couple of puncture wounds, so I was horrified to find Chris dabbing a tissue at a bloody crater in the end of his nose. It looked just like a bite taken out of an apple. I couldn't believe it – they wanted a plaster for *that!* Having been asked to look at a faulty television set at someone's house, Chris had bent down to stroke their dog ('a big black bugger') which promptly leapt up and ripped a chunk out of his nose. Not realising the extent of the damage, he refused all offers of help and casually drove home clutching a fist full of toilet paper, with blood dripping down the front of his shirt.

It took a lot of persuasion to convince him that the gaping wound needed proper medical attention, but he refused to let me take him to hospital and insisted on driving himself. Concerned that he might pass out on the thirty-minute journey, all I could do was grab a coat and go with him. It was very late by the time we got to the emergency department where the wound was temporarily dressed, but the missing flesh needed attention from a specialist unit at nearby Duchy Hospital, so Chris was kept in for the night. That left me in charge of his big old wreck of a car (the remains of an Austin Princess), nervously creeping home in the small hours accompanied by a worrying variety of knocks and rattles, willing it to keep going and hoping the brakes would work as required. Chris was duly patched up and sewn back together later that day, and I went to collect him (in my car!), bringing home a somewhat subdued and more circumspect character to go with his sculpted new nose. After countless accidents and serious injuries suffered during his speedway days, this last incident far removed from the perils of the race track was the one that really got to him, and Chris lost some of his spark that night.

*

Our last flight together was on a perfect Easter Monday of 1997, a quiet day at St Merryn for a change with just the two of us out to play. We spent a leisurely couple of hours cleaning and checking our machines, happy just to be there, doing what we loved. Later we flew across to Bodmin to enjoy a pleasant lunch, sat outside on that lovely grass airfield, chatting about everything and nothing as we watched the world go by. It was a lazy sort of day, colours bold in the spring sunshine against a backdrop of blue and green.

Chris wanted to treat me to an ice cream, but I was too full to eat anything else, so he bumbled off to order one for himself, which is when he realised he had sunburn on top of his head. I gave him a duster from the pocket of my gyroplane, which he fastened over his head with a couple of small bungees and behold, Lawrence of Bodmin was born. When his 'bockernockerlorry' arrived (Chris couldn't pronounce knickerbocker glory) the image was complete and I had to take a photo, never dreaming how poignant it would become. As we drove home later that evening at an unusually sedate pace, he looked across at me and said reflectively 'You some dear little gyrocopter pilot really, Shirley' and reached over to squeeze my hand - after wiping his nose in his palm. I really wished he wouldn't do that!

But less than seven weeks later, Chris along with our new friend Bob Bond, were both dead, killed by another's incompetence while flying someone else's gyro-glider. Chris had lost his glasses a few days before they went on that fateful trip up country. Losing his glasses and keys happened so often that I threatened to buy him a handbag, but he would only lose that as well! We searched everywhere, even going back to St Merryn to see if he'd dropped them out there. We never did find them and I sometimes wonder if things might have been different if we had - would he have seen that those critical bolts were missing from the rotor head? But none of the other gyronauts on and around that machine spotted the deadly omission either. Russian roulette with a defective gyro-glider decided Chris and Bob's unhappy fate to be the ones on board when it came apart in the air.

It was ten weeks after Chris's sixtieth birthday. The impending milestone perplexed him hugely as he approached the end of his sixth decade, and he just couldn't get used to the idea. 'Tiz terrible when you'm sixty' he often remarked in bewilderment as old speedway injuries made their presence increasing felt. His brother Terry gave him a £50 note to mark the occasion (none of us had ever seen one before) but unlike his shrewd sibling, Chris couldn't hold on to cash. Once when he won twenty pounds on the Saturday night lottery, he was off down the road to claim his prize as soon as the local shop opened next morning. With twenty quid burning a hole in his pocket, Chris insisted on taking us all to McDonalds for a Sunday breakfast treat. True to form, we were duly rounded up and driven down to the Port and Starboard to indulge in fish, chips and mushy peas with the obligatory 'big mug o' tea' courtesy of Chris's £50 note. Poor old devil, sixty was the end of the line for him, but I doubt that he would have coped well with advancing years.

A Matter of Perspective

The other side of the fence was home to the Cornwall Parachute Centre, and we shared our hangar with their Cessna jump plane, *Charlie X-ray*. She was a big ol' bird and it took some careful manipulation to wiggle her in and out of the hangar door, which exceeded her vital statistics by the merest of inches. A car full of jump-suited students would arrive from the other side of the fence, eager to get Charlie into the air and hurl themselves out. Being neighbourly types, we always stopped to assist with the delicate extraction process and pass the time of day with the two Johns, pilot and instructor respectively. Their victims would hang around in various states of fear and bravado while Charlie was being checked over, eyeing us gyronauts with barely disguised suspicion as they observed our pint-sized machines, the go-kart wheels, the 'lawnmower' engines. You could almost read their thoughts. *Look at those things – it's just a deck chair with a rotor on top – they've got to be mad! You'd never get me up in that!*

We in turn, eyed them back in a friendly yet sympathetic manner, these poor demented souls tightly fastened to small backpacks by a spaghetti of buckles and straps. Our thoughts? *Spend fifteen minutes crammed in the back of Charlie just to come down in a couple of minutes hanging off a bed sheet? What a waste of effort. You wouldn't catch me doing that!*

*

You can have some gentle fun with unsuspecting folk when you fly an unusual bird. I was with Mark at Dunkeswell one time, having been invited along for the ride when he towed his gyroplane up for its annual inspection. An RAF 2000 was parked by the fence and as is usual with a gyroplane, a few people had gathered to take a look. We sidled up to the group, and this is how it went...

'That's a strange looking thing.' says Mark innocently. 'A helicopter with a tail fin.'

'It's an autogyro.' replies one of the onlookers, authoritatively.

'Oh really?' says Mark, 'An autogyro. How does that work then?' To which the fount of all knowledge gives a brief, but not altogether accurate description of a gyroplane to an apparently enthralled Mark, who simply cannot believe that such a heavy looking machine can fly purely by spinning the rotor blades with the wind. 'How ridiculous! Whatever will they think of next!' He strings them along like this for a few more minutes before turning to me, perfectly straight faced: 'Well that doesn't sound safe to me at all. You'd never get me up in one of those!'

*

Mark struck again during the annual Popular Flying rally in Bedfordshire. Having gone to procure a weather update before embarking on a local flight, we returned to find our birds surrounded by spectators - which seems to bring out the monkey in him.

'Oh look at these funny things!' he cried, gleefully advancing on the unwary. 'Microlights with rotors on!'

There's always one who can't resist the bait, and soon Mark was having a guided tour of his own gyroplane from a well-intentioned bystander. Several more people stopped to listen in - then came the conversation stopper.

'Well that sounds easy enough.' says my mischievous pal, 'Do you think it would be all right if we had a go?'

Nervous chuckles from our tour guide: of course he can't be serious... 'It's okay' says Mark brightly, 'I've got a microlight licence and my friend has a PPL-A. We'll be very careful, I'm sure they won't mind!' And so saying, he goes over to Delta-J and pulls out my flight suit. 'This looks a bit small for me, Shirley. I think you'd better have this one. You heard what the nice man said didn't you? It all works the same as a microlight but we have to spin the rotors round first. We can manage that, can't we!'

By now the *nice man* is getting increasingly nervous as realisation dawns that Mark has every intention of 'borrowing' two gyroplanes, armed only with the information that he's just helpfully supplied. So we continued the pantomime, trying on each other's crash helmets for size, and 'what does this lever do, and what's this button for?' Mark keeps asking the poor guy who was now desperately looking to escape, much to the growing intrigue of our audience.

'Don't worry, it's all fine.' Mark assured them helpfully 'It's got the same engine as my microlight!' Then with a parting shot to his hapless victim as we fumbled to start the machines - pointing to the rotor tie down, he called out 'Do you think we should take these bits of string off the rotor blades first?'

IF *YOU* CAN DO IT...

It was 1934 when Miss Joan Mayne and the Right Honourable Mrs Victor Bruce became the first women in Britain to fly gyroplanes, piloting the huge Cierva Autogiros that couldn't have been more different to my diminutive Cricket. Regretfully the evolution of the helicopter soon outpaced that of the original gyroplanes and consigned them to the annals of rotorcraft history, so these courageous ladies were the first and last of their kind. It wasn't until the 1950s that homebuilt gyroplanes began to appear, inspired by two wartime gyro-gliders, the *Bachsteltze,* and the Hafner *Rotachute*. In 1960s America, Marion Springer became the first woman gyronaut of the homebuilt era, and France gained a couple of lady gyroplane pilots in the 1980s, but another decade would pass before Britain got one of its own.

*

Being a lone female in the predominantly masculine world of autorotation wasn't an issue for me. First and foremost I'm a gyronaut and the rest is immaterial. Inevitably there were a few sceptics when I first started training, but when they all had their accidents and I somehow got through unscathed, opinions began to change. Our rotorcraft association wanted to use me for publicity, but I felt very uncomfortable when there were far better pilots more deserving of the attention. It's only coincidence that I became the first female gyronaut – I would still want to do it even if there were hundreds of women flying gyroplanes! A far more credible motive came from our chairman at the time, Hugh Bancroft-Wilson, who informed me with a grin that 'If *you* can do it, anyone can!' Fair point, well put.

So for the greater good I reluctantly subjected myself to some minor publicity, hating the spotlight and intrusive lenses, yet without fail they all printed a load of absolute nonsense. One inventive piece stated that I became infected with autorotation while watching a James Bond film at the cinema, which was total rubbish. Another related the lunatic fantasy of me going flying so as to land in a field and go for a walk – as if I'd leave my precious gyroplane alone in some random field! Idiots. Why waste time doing interviews only to publish fictitious twaddle?

Best of all was the *Daily Mail*. About a year after Chris was killed, I got a job as a gilder in a small craft workshop, forty miles away. While I loved the skill and creativity of the work, unfortunately the wages were dirt poor and barely covered the fuel costs. My savings had dwindled to nothing and I didn't have a spare penny to my name. Then out of the blue, along comes the *Daily Mail*. 'Can we do some air to air photography with you?' I hate being arranged in awkward poses like a specimen laid bare beneath the prying eye of a microscope, but airborne and captured from a distance safely hidden beneath my electric hat – no worries! Mark kindly agreed to do the honours and chauffeur photographer Colin Davey in his pea-green Shadow microlight. It's really not easy getting in and out of the back of a Shadow. It helps to be a bit of a contortionist in order to thread yourself between wing and struts and collapse gracefully into the narrow depths of the cabin. We all met at St Merryn one afternoon, and spent an enjoyable hour flying round the coast in loose formation, while Colin struggled to aim a beast of camera at my tiny gyroplane from the rear confines of the Shadow.

He did a super job. Digital cameras were new technology and it was amazing to see the results within minutes rather than having to wait days for the film to be developed. Back in the hangar we were most impressed as his shots appeared on the laptop screen. My little red bird showed up beautifully above the cliff tops, dramatic waves breaking over the rocks below. Her pod and tail made a bright splash of colour against a patchwork of countryside, the rotors captured in a perfect blur. It looked stunning: is that *really* me?

Disbelief continued when a cheque for £150 arrived in the post, and I was happy to learn that Mark had also been rewarded. Two weeks' wages for an hour's flying, that was the best job ever! But no word of a lie, the very next day my old Volkswagen Polo blew its head gasket. I don't subscribe to any religion and am uncomfortable with the term 'angel' due to its biblical connotations, but that's just one example of many that something somewhere keeps an eye out for me. Without that cheque I would've been completely screwed, unable to get to work or pay for repairs, but it was an awful shame that the photographs were lost in the post and I never saw those amazing shots again. They *paid me* to have a professional aerial photo shoot! Sometimes I just can't believe my luck.

MAGNI'S DAY, 1997

The Magni family wonder if this is a good idea...

I had the grand total of 84 autorotational hours in my log book when the opportunity arose to fly my first new type of single-seat gyroplane. We were in the north of Italy at a private grass airstrip near Milan, visiting a rotary-winged gathering organised by veteran gyroplane manufacturer Vittorio Magni and family. Three days earlier, our group of ten from all corners of the British mainland, converged on a remote Welsh village and piled themselves and a mountain of camping equipment into what was basically a school minibus. We left the same evening and headed for the Channel Tunnel, where we spent a sleepless night in the terminal waiting for the early morning shuttle. I remember very little about the second day except for feeling absolutely exhausted, having been on the road from Cornwall to Wales to Kent and crossed to France in under twenty-four hours. Our route from Calais took us down through the Champagne region to arrive that evening somewhere around Épernay, where we pitched our tents at a pleasant lakeside spot with the wonderful name of Camp Bouzy.

It was bliss being able to stretch out in my tent for a proper night's sleep after two days propped up semi-comatose in the minibus, and I greeted the new dawn fully revitalised and eager for the journey ahead. We faced a day of travel down through Switzerland and the Alps to the top of Italy, so there was a moment of disquiet when we discovered that our minibus boasted a mere 1.8 litre engine and not the anticipated 2.5. There had been some suspicion of its sluggish performance when driving out of Wales – now we were facing the Alps! With tents and baggage packed away and hurled up on the roof rack, we scrambled aboard for a brief detour to a nearby supermarket for supplies before continuing our marathon trek down south.

It was another long and tiring day. Our heavily loaded minibus struggled gallantly over increasingly vertical terrain while we stared out at spectacular – almost manicured – Alpine scenery that exuded an air of prosperous serenity. The rugged foothills had been draped in a lush green velvet that was perfectly tailored to their flowing contours and neatly trimmed off at the edge. Dark forests clinging to the upper slopes bore scars of raw earth slashed by the violence of avalanche, and beyond the tree line, stark rock grasped at the heavens with jagged claws. Snow dusted the higher peaks like icing sugar and the air grew cooler as we staggered ever upwards, passing through some impressively long tunnels burrowed deep in to the mountains. Everywhere was spotlessly clean.

Half-timbered dwellings of pale cream and white capped with angular slate roofs gradually softened into more typical Swiss-style wooden chalets as we descended from Alpine heights towards the frontier. A growing Mediterranean influence replaced earthy tones of wood and slate with shades of ochre and terracotta, the increasing warmth of the colours nicely complementing the increasing warmth of the climate. Late in the afternoon we cheered our brave chariot as it carried us across the border into a sunny Italy, sweltering in 30°C and impeccably timed to hit the outskirts of Milan during the frantic Italian rush hour. It was best not to look.

And so Friday evening, dateline Milan. At a quiet airstrip nestling on the fringe of the global centre of style and elegance, an asthmatic minibus wheezed to a halt and disgorged a steaming heap of humanity, modelling a uniquely dishevelled look after three days folded inside. The British have landed! We tottered into the relative cool of the main hangar where Lisa and Micky Magni dispensed welcoming coffee, most gratefully received. The airstrip of Speziana is housed on a large private estate set amidst the flat plain of the river Po, with the skyscrapers of Milan in the distance. A row of Magni gyroplanes stood in front of the hangar, bathed in the warmth of the evening haze. Sleek tandem M16s and the wedge-shaped single-seat M18s, arranged against a backdrop of tall rustic buildings, the intricate red brickwork decorated with multicoloured flags and streamers. Revived by the infusion of caffeine and perked at the prospect of three nights ahead without having to pack up and move on, a merry band of nomads gathered round to unload our gallant little bus, which by now had sunk to its knees. A pleasant spot had been reserved for us at the foot of a sturdy three-storey building, sheltered by a thick crop of maize growing alongside. A soft percussion of mallets thudded into the sandy soil as a small hamlet of tents mushroomed in the dusk. Little did we know...

Accommodation sorted, it was time for a celebratory barbecue but some uninvited guests had other ideas and it was *us* who were on the menu, poor Keith being flavour of choice for a squadron of particularly voracious mosquitoes. Micky came over with gifts from our hosts, a bottle of wine and cans of insect repellent, and as the evening wore on I think they drank both. Sausage and kebabs liberated in the morning raid on the French supermarket went down well, topped with a sprinkling of baked mosquitoes. Tired and content, we relaxed around the glowing coals until fatigue had quietened even the most raucous of tongues, slipping in to a companionable silence beneath the stars. Bus lag – it's a thing.

Saturday dawned deceptively bright and calm, yet it was decidedly overcast in at least a couple of tents! Clearing the remains of the barbecue, we were alarmed to discover a spill of red wine had actually eaten into the plastic tabletop overnight. No wonder some heads were sore. Despite the early hour it was already humid and uncomfortably warm, even with a freshening breeze. Lisa and Micky spared a few minutes from their busy schedule to come and visit, Lisa being my Italian counterpart, the first lady in Italy to fly gyroplanes. Married to Vittorio's eldest son Pietro, she had her hands full with a young family but still loved to fly whenever the chance arose, and Micky now translated Lisa's generous offer of the previous year to lend me her single-seat M18. Twelve months earlier with only 50 hours of gyroplane flight time in my log book, I'd played safe by opting to fly with Pietro in the M16 instead. Despite a nagging reluctance to trust myself with someone else's machine, I had a little more experience and didn't want to appear rude by refusing again, so we parted company, with Micky promising to fetch me when the time came.

Leaving the hangovers to recover in their tents, the rest of us wandered off to explore the airfield, greeted everywhere by vivacious Italians. Tucked away in a corner of the hangar, we found the intriguing sight of an M16 tandem gyroplane wearing what appeared to be a small jet engine, looking strangely incomplete without a propeller. Vittorio and sons, Pietro and Luca were busy adjusting the rotor blades on another M16, which would later be giving pleasure flights. The workshop was immaculate with neatly laid out tool chests, rows of blade racks mounted on the walls, and a nifty little winch hanging from the ceiling for changing rotor assemblies. Outside, a brace of M18s departed to later return accompanied by an M14, a sort of one-and-a-half-seat gyroplane, with the passenger perched awkwardly astride behind the pilot. A couple of American open-frame designs stood out among the uniform ranks of Magni machines: a pair of Air Commands along with a spindly-legged Dominator, all rare birds to British eyes, as were the M18s. It takes fathomless pockets and the patience of several saints to get a new type of gyroplane approved for use in our heavily regulated skies, so it was marvellous to actually see some different flavours that we'd only been able to read about.

The clouds had thickened rapidly during the morning and the wind blew stronger as a dark ceiling descended ominously across the plain. The flight briefing for the competitions coincided with the first drops of rain, and two M16s had barely begun passenger flying when the heavens opened with a vengeance. I was pleased to see Glauco Dalbo's open-frame Dominator arrive just in time, squeezing in beneath the turbulent cloud base and taxiing rapidly to bail out at the flight line, his partner Gina huddled in the back seat. We first met at Enstone, when he was passing by on a business trip and had witnessed my rodeo ride over the hedge. We kept in touch and he and Gina had since come to visit us at Chris's workshop, so it was nice to see them on their home turf. Activity for the rest of the day was confined to the hangar, swapping stories and sharing photos with our jovial Italian hosts while outside the weather grew even wilder. Distant thunder rumbled on the horizon, and the remaining machines were hurriedly pulled from the flight line and stowed under cover.

Seated at long trestle tables, the evening meal was set against a backdrop of Wagnerian proportions as lightning whiplashed across the sky, punctuated by thunderous reverberations and torrential rain. The hangar doors were slid in to place, closing out the worst of the elements while several hundred happy gyronauts enjoyed a convivial evening inside. A leggy white mongrel patrolled beneath the tables, weaving through a forest of feet in search of discarded morsels. The minibus crew gathered at one end, wondering if we would find anything left of our camp when the night was over - it was brutal out there!

I was sitting next to Keith who was struggling with a dietary dilemma. For reasons I can't remember, he couldn't eat the risotto and didn't want to offend our hosts by leaving it all. The rest of us had enough on our plates already and were unable to assist, but then the dog emerged from under a nearby table. Spotting his chance, Keith managed to attract the hopeful canine and began slowly transferring his food to the waiting jaws below. It was funny. Keith nonchalantly chatted away, his hand moving furtively from the plate to slip beneath the tablecloth and back again. This went on for a couple of minutes, yet Gill and Jim sitting opposite were completely unaware of what he was doing. As Keith's meal quietly diminished, I peeped under the table to see a growing mound of risotto scattered at our feet and no sign of the dog! Intercepting the next handful, I lifted the cloth to point under the table and we both cracked up with laughter, much to the amusement of the others who had no idea what was going on.

After coffee and dessert came the prize giving. The Magni family in their matching orange flight suits took centre stage to present an array of trophies and gifts, the lively audience greeting each award with boisterous cheers and applause that completely drowned out the heavy rain hammering on the roof. Of course we didn't understand a word of it, but their expressive enthusiasm made a welcome change from the restrained ambience of our British gatherings! Maybe we need more wine... Live music and dancing rounded off the festivities, which were still in full swing when the tent dwellers finally gathered our collective courage and headed out into the storm.

Outside was pitch black and howling, ankle deep in water that oozed over our shoes. We picked our way by torchlight and dramatic slashes of lightning, illuminating a dense curtain of rain driving deep into the saturated ground. The tents were hunched black shapes thrown into stark relief by the brilliance of every flash, accompanied almost instantly by a deafening crack of thunder - this was flipping dangerous! Bent and battered by the deluge, our tents clung grimly to the earth, swamped in three inches of water. It was beyond salvage. I grabbed my rucksack from the black lagoon inside and fled through the tempest behind Ian and Olga to hurl ourselves into the sanctuary of the minibus. Thankfully it wasn't too cold as we struggled out of the worst of wet clothing and arranged ourselves across the seats, resigned to an uncomfortable night. Lightning split the darkness revealing a flurry of movement outside as Ray came pounding through the spray to join us. Incredibly his tent remained watertight, but consequently attracted every insect on the plain, delighted to find a dry spot – they'd thrown him out.

Subsequent events took on an even more surreal quality as we settled down to whatever sleep we could get in a minibus parked in the very forge of Hades. Suddenly the door flew open and the rest of the crew piled in on top of us, accompanied by a torrent of wind and rain. *Shut that door!* The engine fired and we lurched over sodden ground befuddled and disorientated like cattle in a truck. Leaving the airfield, we embarked on a mad midnight dash through storm lashed villages, pursuing a guide who lead us disbelieving into the car park of a four star hotel. I can't afford *this!* A bedraggled band of refugees trooped in through an elegant lobby and huddled nervously on the carpet, expecting the imminent arrival of some burly Mafioso types to come and sling us out. Instead a pack of chambermaids appeared, chattering rapidly in Italian. A flapping of arms corralled us towards a long corridor, where couples and singletons were somehow identified and deftly split from the flock with a jingle of keys. What just happened? I'd been soaked to the skin and curled up on a bus seat in the midst of a raging storm – now I stood gaping in disbelief at three large beds in a magnificent chamber that was bigger than my own flat. It was all wonderfully insane.

I have to admit that Sunday morning felt a whole lot better than it would've done after a night in the bus! I tiptoed carefully around the room trying not to contaminate anything, a budget-conscious camper overwhelmed by the magnitude of this four star accommodation. Peeping through heavy drapes at the window revealed a pale silver dawn, silent and still as if the forces of nature had battled themselves to exhaustion. I wondered where we were. Caution was thrown to the wind when an ornate adjoining door opened on a large well-equipped bathroom. A long hot shower did wonders, but my choice of apparel plucked from a wet rucksack was either crumpled, damp, or both, and I felt ashamed to be seen in such a fine establishment. Then Keith arrived at the door, also squeaky-clean having partaken of the excellent facilities and totally unfazed by our posh new surroundings. With no time to rescue his bag before we were abducted, he'd turned up the heating to full blast and dried his wet clothes overnight. Why didn't I think of that – I was afraid to touch anything! It was still quite early and all was quiet, so we wandered off along the corridor to see what we could see.

We came across a plush dining room, which I vaguely recalled tramping through somewhere after midnight. The tables were all neatly set and a group of staff were already on duty awaiting guests to feed. We smiled back with self-consciously muttered *bon giornos,* whereupon two homely ladies ushered us towards a table and pulled back the chairs, gesturing for us to sit. They didn't seem to care who we were or where we had appeared from! A pair of polished wooden trolleys arrived, laden with a variety of platters: everything from bread and honey, fruit and cold meats, to yoghurt, pastries, eggs and cheese, and apparently all for us as our two ministering angels began piling the table with delicacies. We had no common language but their plump hands and faces spoke volumes, as if nothing could give them greater pleasure than the simple act of serving our breakfast. They were quite enchanting. A large jug of coffee was placed meaningfully in the last available space on the table and seeing that we were now quite surrounded by food, the lovely ladies retreated to the sidelines where they stood ready to attend, beaming at us encouragingly like a pair of indulgent aunts.

It would've been rude not to. Keith was particularly peckish after the comedy with the risotto, so we tucked in appreciatively while he told me his version of our midnight adventure. While Gill and Jim had bailed out to an adjacent barn, and the four of us fled to the minibus, Rowland surveyed the waterlogged camp in dismay and returned to the hangar, where our hosts were most concerned to hear of our sodden plight. Despite the late hour, several phone calls were made on our behalf to procure alternative accommodation, and a kind local offered to lead the way to the hotel. Quickly gathering the remaining troops, Rowland hurried them into the bus to follow our guide through the raging night. And here we were. Speaking of the others... Sudden activity from our ladies of plenty, as the rest of our merry band began to trickle into the dining room. We sat back to watch in amusement as the dear ladies revolved tirelessly among the tables, lavishing attention on our companions who seemed just as overwhelmed. Personally we were stuffed. When at last everyone had eaten their fill, we bade farewell to our new friends who seemed genuinely sorry to see us go, making me feel guilty about the mound of washing up left in our wake. How sweet were they.

We returned to our faithful minibus abandoned in the car park, scrambling into our seats wondering what carnage awaited us at Speziana, and how far across the fields we'd have to go to retrieve our tents. Dark clouds were low and threatening, but the rain held off and the wreckage of the camp didn't seem so bad in daylight. Most of the water had drained away though the sandy soil, and remarkably all the tents were still in place - a little battered and misshapen - but given the violence of the storm, we'd been expecting a hell of a lot worse! The day was warm despite the strong wind blustering across the plain, and it didn't take long to get everything shaken out and dried off again. Mosquitoes returned to the attack and it was my turn to be targeted, presumably there was no room left on Keith. The insect repellent had run out so we hurled the empty cans at the little blighters, who promptly hurled them back. Gill and Jim had found a good place to roost in of one of the barns, housing some dusty weight-shift microlights, so Keith, Mike and me thought it prudent to join them in case of further flood. Our tents were all self-supporting so we just picked them up between us and carried them fully assembled to the barn, a comical procession of tents on legs. The rest of the crew opted for a night in a local hotel with considerably fewer stars than the last one.

The planned fly out to a neighbouring airfield had to be cancelled as it was still waterlogged, but at Speziana the clouds were lifting and prospects were looking more favourable, thanks to a combination of strong wind and sandy ground. Later Pietro and Luca made some tentative flights to check runway conditions and it wasn't long before the air was buzzing again. The M16s resumed their passenger flying, and a pair of dainty Angel helicopters arrived to display their agility before settling lightly on the grass. Then Sergio appeared with a huge grin on his face. Micky was looking for me: time to fly. Suddenly I was very nervous. Flying a new single-seat machine without first getting the feel of it was normally unthinkable, but hops and groundwork were out of the question with a busy public display in progress. This could be a stretch for my travel insurance...

I followed Sergio to the flight line where Lisa and Vittorio were waiting to fasten me into her gyroplane, as Micky translated their instructions. It felt strange. Higher off the ground and more upright, like sitting in a chair, it was a nicer seating position than the sort of go-kart style, elongated squat imposed by the Cricket, which always gives me a dead leg after about forty minutes. The control stick was base-mounted instead of a welded fork, and although a familiar Rotax 582 perched behind me, its familiar rpm gauge was replaced by a digital readout. It also lacked a piece of string to indicate wind direction, the most important 'instrument' of all. I can live without an rpm gauge but I *do* need a bit of string! Word had got around and an embarrassingly large audience gathered to watch as Vittorio accompanied us out to the runway. I taxied slowly, trying to get the feel of the M18: it seemed very solid and rode the bumpy ground well, but I didn't like the digital readout.

Over the weekend I'd noticed the different technique employed by the Italian gyronauts to get airborne. Using the pre-rotator, they drive the rotors much harder and go straight in with the throttle rather than a steady acceleration until the nose wheel lifts. It was a hard habit to break. The wind was strong yet constant, and right on the nose as we lined up on the runway. Vittorio applied the pre-rotator and wound up the rotors, waving us away as he ducked to the side, but ramming the power on went against everything I'd been taught. My Cricket-trained hand eased on the throttle and we wallowed forth, feeling it out. A touch more power and the wedge-shaped nose reared up in response – that's what I want – now I've got you! Drop the nose a bit, give it some throttle and suddenly we're suspended 10 feet in the air, flying slowly but rock steady along the runway. Without a red line on the digital rpm gauge, it was a case of power up until it felt right, trusting to luck and the seat of my pants as we climbed away, anxious to get clear of the busy circuit. The skyscrapers of Milan made a great reference point as I headed across the plain to where I remembered flying with Pietro, making sure to stay in visual contact with the airfield. Rowland told me later that Vittorio thought I was making for Switzerland!

The rotors were set up beautifully, very smooth on the controls which was a pleasing new experience. The unfamiliar slant of the M18's pod and missing piece of string gave me a little difficulty in judging balanced flight, but the machine felt very sturdy in the turbulent air, remaining steadfastly on course when I let go of the stick. It wasn't quite as responsive as Delta-J due to the heavy rotor blades and large tail feathers, but that was no bad thing, and having thrown it into a few tight turns and figure-eights, I was startled to find that fifteen minutes had elapsed. Not wishing to be greedy (and more importantly, I didn't know how much fuel was on board!) I finished with a brief but splendid hover and pointed the nose back towards the airfield, ready for the acid test. The air was still very disturbed in the aftermath of the storm, and the wind was pushing us hard as we flew back over the open fields and distinctive red-roofed Italian farmsteads, gradually slipping lower. I set up a long final approach to give myself time to sort things out, which unfortunately brought us straight in over the maize field. The digital rpm gauge was no help at all: the numbers bore no relation to my own Rotax engine so it was seat of the pants time again, nudging back the throttle as the M18 hung contentedly on the wind. Maintaining 55 knots on the clock, I brought us in with airspeed and altimeter until the machine began a more determined descent, then increased power to carry us to the threshold.

Vittorio was watching from the runway's edge: which of us was more anxious? Glancing at the left main wheel, I checked back on the stick to put the gyroplane in what I judged to be a more or less two-wheel-balance attitude and closed the throttle, using the big tail feathers to counteract the feisty wind. And just like the take off, touch down happened by itself. Poised on the mains and tail wheel, it took a second or two for me to realise that we were back on the ground before quickly planting the nose wheel firmly on the deck. Vittorio came over to stop and lock the rotors and escort us back to the flight line, beaming all over his face – which of us was more relieved! My first new type and I hadn't disgraced myself. It just goes to show how forgiving the Magni gyroplanes are. Lisa and Micky were waiting to greet us, leading the applause as I switched off the engine, smiling faces crowding round. Delighted to return her fully intact gyroplane, I thanked Lisa sincerely for trusting me with it and promised to do the same for her should she ever venture onto British shores. Sergio came bounding over, and in his inimitable style summed everything up in one marvellously accented sentence: 'Ay, my little flier! I worry about you, but then you take off – *and you bugger off!*' Yep, that's exactly what happened.

I followed Sergio into the crowd to find the rest of the gang grouped at the end of the flight line. Apparently I'd been causing some anxiety on the ground, and Jim's Panama hat would never be the same again. Angela had it tucked under her arm while Jim went for a flight in an M16, but she grew so nervous watching my exploits that she'd unwittingly squashed it flat. Her partner Frank had been airborne in an M16 at the same time, but she wasn't at all concerned about him! Glauco told me that going from a Cricket to an M18 was easy, but to do it the other way around wouldn't be so forgiving, and I had to agree. Lisa's machine took off and landed by itself with little interference from me. I wondered what she would think of Delta-J.

The air pulsated with the delicious beat of rotor blades until one by one, the gyroplanes began returning to the flight line. Finally, around 19:00, the chatter of the last engine was silenced, its dying echoes fading away as dusk began creeping over the plain once more, and it hadn't rained all day. Rowland had arranged for us all to eat at the local hotel where some of the crew would be spending the night, and it was with some reluctance that Keith and I boarded the minibus for the short trip down the road. We wanted to stay with the Italians who were having a barbecue in the hangar, and after a long drawn out meal of dubious origins at the hotel, I think the others might have agreed. The tent dwellers made our escape at well past 23:00 to find our way back to the airfield, where coloured disco lights flared in the darkness and a lively karaoke session echoed from the hangar. Too tired to appreciate the fun by then, we headed for the barn where our newly washed and dried tents awaited. Happily they hadn't shrunk.

Inevitably Monday morning arrived and we sat among the tents in the musty straw, chatting quietly and sharing stoves to make breakfast, loath to start packing away. Eventually the others returned from the hotel and came to round us up. Time to make a move. We took a last look around the airfield together, marshalling our thoughts and fond memories of a joyful weekend. Lisa appeared in her dressing gown, having hurried down from her room to say goodbye, a heartfelt hug and a few stumbled words of each other's language had to suffice, but we knew what we meant. Crammed on board the bus waving madly, we drove out of Speziana and began the mammoth trip home to our island in the north.

Returning through stunning alpine vistas, we paused in a small Swiss town to enjoy an alfresco lunch on the shores of Lake Lucerne. It was pure chocolate box. Elegant paddle steamers with rakish funnels slid through the crystal waters, furrowing the reflections of the mountains with their wake. The crisp mountain air felt wonderful after the Mediterranean heat, and I could have stayed there all day absorbing the marvellous scenery. It was almost too good to be true. That evening found us back at Camp Bouzy, where tents were extracted and inflated for the last time. The warm golden twilight was too good to waste so while the others went to the restaurant, I opted for a walk in the woods along with Keith and Mike. Later, back at the tents, we pooled supplies and cooked our own meal, lazing around the bubbling pot reliving events of the past few days as a pine scented dusk descended around us. You can't put a price on moments like that.

We had a relative day of leisure to follow before taking a late train through the Channel Tunnel, so with morning dew left to dry on our tents, Gill, Keith and I set off on a wander round the lake. It was bigger than it looked! The day grew rather hot as we strolled jauntily over springy turf and carpets of pine needles among the trees, spilling sand from our shoes as we tramped across pale beaches at the water's edge, a lovely morning to savour. But the universe keeps turning, indifferent to mere mortal pleasures and our time had trickled away. Hot and dusty we returned to break camp, hurling our gear back up on the roof rack ready for the last leg of the journey, which saw us pop out of the Chunnel and stagger back into Wales on Wednesday morning. We had to shoot the bus.

What an excellent adventure that was. A new flavour of gyroplane in the log book, fantastic scenery shared with a fine bunch of companions, and of course a whole lot of flying. Even the storm was awesome! I treasure the memories of Glauco and Gina, and particularly of Keith, who was a great mate and so full of fun. Sometimes we pay a heavy price for doing what we love best.

St Merryn Moments

Sitting alone on this historic airfield, I feel a deep connection with those who have gone before. Their echoes never fade and are particularly close on such a peaceful day as this. A few widely scattered clouds decorate a sky of vivid blue that softens to paler shades out on the horizon. A solitary breath whispers in from across the cliffs but the windsock sleeps undisturbed, hanging dead to the world like a deflated balloon. A drifting cloud briefly covers the sun, and a fierce white orb glares at me through feathery depths. Insects hum quietly as they go about their business, and rabbits creep warily into view, cropping the sun-browned grass ever shorter. Skylarks are busy in the fields, popping up vertically from grass and stubble, tiny wings a blur. Their cheerful warbles fill the air with a constant burbling chatter as they power skyward, incredible lung power. Pocket rockets - I love these little guys!

Delta-J stands beside me, a dab of bright scarlet against the natural tones of a late summer's day. She's all checked out and ready to go, but now is not the time. A turn of the key will shatter the silence and the moment will be lost. I'm happy where I am. Thick vegetation covers the protective arm of the old air raid shelter hunched companionably by our side, its weathered grey blocks peek out through a mass of brambles heavy with ripening blackberries. The derelict control tower stands guard over our hangar, empty sightless windows gazing out across the countryside. Nature has all but reclaimed the naval signal square hidden at its feet, a microcosm of time that triumphs over puny mortals. I like to seek it out, it restores my balance and I treasure it. A tangled carpet of ivy obstructs the path, choked with briar, gorse and nettles, a hurried rustling in the undergrowth as rabbits take fright at my footsteps and bolt for the safety of their burrows. Rusted iron rings that once secured bracing wires from the signal mast are still embedded in the concrete – if you know where to look. Decades of exposure weaken them, slowly crumbling amongst the weeds and soon they will leave no trace. Human existence is a mere blink of the eye in the great scheme of things. Nature will prevail, time is on her side.

It's hot today. The wind turbines up on the hill turn half-heartedly like unwound clocks, all pointing in different directions as if they can't be bothered to conform. St Uvelus church squats on the horizon to the right, marking the boundary with St Merryn's wartime twin, RAF St Eval, still partly operational as a communications hub. The scent of warm coconut fills the air as I stroll around the tower, a gift from yellow gorse buds adorning their vicious thorns, a spiteful contrast to the gentle fragrance. Blackberries complement the cheerful yellow with shades of crimson and purple, and thistles add a jaunty pink with their spiky punk-rock blooms. Buzzards circle high above the valley, wings stretched wide in silhouette soaring effortlessly on a thermal, their shrill calls float for miles. The surrounding fields are a patchwork of greens and browns, a melange of every shade from dark to light, dotted with bales like giant Swiss rolls spread beneath a flawless sky.

Behind the tower lies a scarred expanse of concrete, the footprints of vast hangars from the time of our island's most desperate need, gone forever after decades of the peace they helped to secure. A few derelict ancillary buildings endure beside the ghosts of the flattened leviathans they once served, weathered walls choked with ivy. Two smaller hangars survive, housing silage and discarded agricultural clutter in a forbidding gloom, fragments of glass clinging to the rusted frames of their shattered windows, such a sad and inglorious end. Abandoned Nissen huts hunch silently amid the undergrowth, corrugated walls curving over the classic half moon shape, thick with weeds inside.

The firing butts survive behind a tangled barrier of nettles and thorns, a distinctive shape of red brick walls rising above the decay that surrounds it. I love this structure and pick my way through the vicious foliage to reach its maw. Thick steel plates dulled and corroded by decades of Atlantic storms bear the evidence of a different battle for survival. Military aircraft were positioned here for armament calibration, leaving their mark for generations on the surface of the heavy plate still bolted to the walls. I run my fingers around the jagged edges of bullet wounds driven deep into the steel, an echo of unimaginable brutality and violence that's hard to reconcile with the tranquillity of this summer's day. I press my palm against the pitted surface and touch the past with respect. (Sadly, the firing butts were demolished not long after I wrote this.)

The sea sparkles on the horizon, shimmering in the heat as I wander along the taxiway going nowhere in particular. The old airfield sprawls peacefully around me, as content as a cat stretched out in the sun. Up on the hill, the wind turbines struggle to align themselves towards the west. The light breeze is no match for their giant blades and a couple remain pointing inland, unable to join the ranks. I look back at the hangar where Delta-J waits – how lucky I am! The sky is mine for the taking, but there's a powerful sense of calm today that's difficult to define. Everything is perfect, every atom, every molecule placed exactly where it needs to be. I can't shake this feeling. It flows deep beyond rational thought like a collective serenity surrounding my soul. *Respect the silence.* It defies explanation so I embrace it and am happy to concur.

Following the weed-encrusted path of the Short runway out to the intersection, I arrive at a small grass island sandwiched between the lanes of ageing tarmac. Here, somewhere around the foot of the windsock, lies a hidden gun emplacement. There's no longer any sign of the hatch that covers the narrow access shaft, and the circular concrete slab of the turret's roof is completely overgrown, but it's many years since I helped Chris and Tony to free it from vegetation. The gun itself was removed when the airfield was decommissioned back in the Fifties, and it must be over a decade since we last raised the turret. I have precious film of Chris larking about on the roof as it sinks slowly back into the earth. I'm not strong enough and no doubt the mechanism is too corroded by now, yet once a well-placed heave from below would activate a counterbalance and the turret would rise like a conning tower from the depths. Another forgotten treasure that no one cares about.

The airfield and its runways are a fraction of their former size, yet it's all still here, divided up and boundaries blurred beneath the insatiable spread of construction. Fifty years ago, these historic runways trembled to the sound of Seafires and Hurricanes, Corsairs, Hellcats, and the venerable Swordfish, Tiger Moths and Gladiators. Now all that's left are their echoes and a few homebuilt gyroplanes. Me and Delta-J fledged on these very same runways. Later, I would teach people to fly in the exact same manner, sharing knowledge handed down from the pioneers and given to me by dear departed friends. Sitting back by the hangar with Delta-J silent alongside, I know I'm not alone. The past is always here, close and ever present.

The light softens as the sun begins its descent towards the sea. I love the colour of a peaceful ocean at dusk, fading to a pale ice blue as the Earth slowly turns its face away, setting the western sky ablaze with orange, purple and gold. There's no artist like Nature. Twilight descends and with it come the bats, flickering black shapes darting around the abandoned buildings, so fast and nimble they fascinate me. Sometimes if I'm lucky, barn owls appear on an evening hunt, moving silently through the air in soft ethereal flight. Such peerless beauty weaves the rich tapestry of St Merryn airfield.

Darkness cloaks us, and the first twinkle of distant stars pierce the infinite void. I scramble up on a bale and lie back to watch a pin cushion of diamonds emerging above, stars and planets entwined in ceaseless celestial dance. Could some indiscernible life form be out there right now, looking back at the tiny speck of light that is planet Earth – looking back at me? The moon rises into the night above the shoulders of Bodmin Moor, an enigmatic face casting pale luminescence across the nocturnal landscape. The airfield becomes become stark and shadowy in repose, devoid of colour yet sharply defined like a black and white photograph, a different shade of splendour. I love this place. We didn't fly today but it doesn't matter. It was perfect all the same.

*

As we fly along the Cornish coast, I like to trace all the nooks and crannies with our wheels, another jolly game invented by Tony Philpotts. He taught me to line up a main wheel with the cliff edge and follow its course, snaking in and out of coves and inlets as we bounce in the turbulence rolling up from the rocks below. It's slow progress but super fun! One summer there was a young buzzard that used to come up and fly in formation as we played on the updraughts between Trevose Head and the river Camel. He would just appear out of nowhere, sliding through the air to come and have a look at us. Together we slowed to a hover and flew alongside for several minutes at a time, the buzzard casually hanging in the air with barely a twitch of feather along his impressive wingspan. He was merely curious and not in the least bit intimidated by this big noisy red thing. It was delightful to fly with him, but while he meant us no harm, I watched him as intently as he was watching me. This was his domain, changing position with such speed and grace that he could knock us out of the air in a heartbeat. I had to keep edging away as the youngster persisted in soaring too close to the rotor disc, which wouldn't have done either of us any good! What a beautiful bird, and such a honour that he came to share his piece of sky.

*

Cornwall is quite literally the end of the line. Forming the lower leg of the British mainland, it stretches out to the south-west dipping its toe into the Atlantic ocean, and the next dry land is American. The maritime environment of our narrow peninsula gives rise to some unusual weather conditions, and two notable flights spring to mind as unique encounters with a rare collusion of the elements.

Normally I don't venture up with sea mist around: it's too unpredictable, and losing visual reference is not recommended (or legal!) in a diminutive gyroplane with a minimal instrument panel. This memorable flight began with good visibility in a slight haze, the air was calm and just a little chilly as we climbed out of St Merryn and turned towards Padstow, where something unusual was afoot. Levelling off at 800 feet in bright sunshine, I could see a strange gloom hanging low over the mouth of the estuary just a few miles away. The sky was clear above and all around with no suggestion of anything untoward, so I stayed on track, eyes widening in disbelief as we approached the river.

Some unknown force had drained the Atlantic and filled it with snow. An unbroken blanket of glistening white cloud spread out beyond the cliffs for as far as the eye could see, covering the ocean entirely and neatly tucked in at the edges. This was incredible! We crossed the river, still climbing. Normally we potter around between 800-1,200 feet, but I was so utterly transfixed that we just kept on going. It looked unreal, supernatural even. So unbelievably perfect was the level of cloud against the cliff tops, slotting in to every cove and inlet like the pieces of a giant jigsaw puzzle, while the land remained bathed in sunlight. How is this possible? Reaching Tintagel and the limit of our fuel range, we levelled off at an unusually lofty 3,100 feet and turned to the west, lightly balanced on the breeze and gazing in wonder at the dazzling vista spread before us.

Further down the coast, the spell was beginning to break as ominous shadows billowed up around Port Isaac, creeping inland. Better make a move before we get shut out. I put Delta-J in to a slow descent and slid her out along the cliffs to watch our shadow flitting across a snowy plain. It looked so deceitfully solid that we could almost go down and land - *almost*. Dark feathery wisps reached up over the cliff tops in places, like spectral fingers exploring the ground ahead. Port Isaac was engulfed now, the cloud oozed into the village and sat there like a fat wet sponge. Headlights shone through the mist as cars broke out into daylight barely a mile inland. We gave it a respectfully wide berth and arrived back at the river mouth where the snowy blanket remained neatly tucked in, but a dense gloom engulfed the shoreline beyond Porthcothan. That's too close for comfort, time to go! Happily the sun still shone on the airfield and we raced for home, elated. Not a sign of the ocean - how amazing was that?

*

One of the best flights ever was again an unexpected surprise. There was nothing unusual about the sky that day: some thick fair weather cumulus around 1,000 feet with scattered patches of blue in between, and I had no notion of the extraordinary delights waiting above. Just for a change, I made a left hand turn out from St Merryn and flew up the valley towards the wind farm on the hill. The air was cool and we had bags of lift to play with, bouncing in the turbulence under the cloud base which wasn't as solid as it appeared from below. We circled around the graceful cluster of turbines and hung on the wind alongside, loving the vitality, a tangible synergy between the racing blur of my little rotors and the leisurely sweep of the huge blades working below. Patches of blue were expanding along the coast, so having feasted on the updraughts I decided to wander over to Wadebridge, then scoot back down the river to the sea. A touch of stick and rudder rolled us out of a splendid hover and we set off towards the town, brushed by clammy tendrils from the cloud base. After an orbit of the neighbourhood we zipped gaily back along the river to see what we could see, and arrived over Padstow to find an extraordinary arrangement of clouds.

Orderly rows of chubby cumulus awaited, all neatly sized and spaced like buns on a baking tray, and again the regularity was quite uncanny. No artist would paint a sky of such uniform consistency – it would look absurd – yet here it was in front of me! An aerial slalom designed for the pleasure of a passing gyronaut. Tony Philpotts introduced me to cloud-hopping, but opportunities to do it safely are few and far between, so this was too good to miss. I promised to do it justice. We swung around and headed down between the fluffy blobs, finding wide corridors with clear visibility all around, hardly believing my luck as I took Delta-J on a superb cloud-hopping ride. Some we went under, rotors slicing through the chill mist to flash back into the sunlight. Some we went over, skimming the tops with our wheels and chasing our shadow across the snowy flanks. We sat above the smaller wispy ones just as Tony had taught me, matching the drift before fluttering down through the middle in a vertical descent and climbing away to do it again. Fun with a capital F!

But change was afoot. Burly nimbus clouds swelled out to sea and the wind grew cold and blustery, shoving our chubby cumulus into disarray as they merged like flocks of frightened sheep. Game over. We dropped down beneath a thickening grey ceiling and shot for home, jostled by the turbulence. What an amazing flight! It's not often we get a suitably sized cloud with separation good enough to hop through, you really have to pick them carefully. To find rows of them perfectly lined up like that was quite exceptional. Thanks Tony – that one was for you.

KEITH'S BIT

It was inconceivable to me that Chris Julian's autorotational wisdom should be lost and forgotten after the Kemble tragedy. Somehow it had to be preserved, and so I began compiling as best I could, the how and why of everything that Chris had taught me, starting from scratch with the gyroglider. It was no easy task going back over all of my training stage by stage, breaking it down to analyse every step and remember how it felt to be a novice alone in the pilot's seat. All of that and much more besides had to be transcribed on to the page in unequivocal terms with nothing lost in translation. My head was in complete turmoil at the time and years would pass before I realised this self-imposed mission had served as a form of therapy.

I must pay tribute here to Robin Morton, a very clever man who had many an aviation string to his bow, including those of gyroplane inspector and enthusiast. Two months after the double fatality, stunned British gyronauts gathered from around the country at the 1997 PFA rally, still reeling in shock. We were all in denial. No one could believe it: not *Chris* - not in a *gyroglider*. The latest issue of *Rotor Gazette International* had been dedicated to him, and featured my unpolished outpouring. I don't remember much about that weekend, but I've never forgotten how an emotional Robin approached me and clasped my hands in his. 'You must *write,* my dear.' he implored, eyes bright with tears. Holding me close in mutual sorrow, he repeated softly 'You *must* write.' Thanks to you Robin, I did.

Budding gyroplane student Keith Balch was a keen supporter and willing guinea pig whose unfailing optimism encouraged me to keep going whenever my conviction faltered. As a newcomer to the gyroplane world, he was a great help in offering suggestions and verifying the clarity of my transcripts to a beginner. It was of utmost importance to get it right, but it wasn't just the flying side that I was struggling with. This was 1997 and the technology we now take for granted was a whole new ball game. Having started the project squinting at the monochrome screen of my word processor (accommodating five lines at a time, it was like typing through a letterbox!), I took Keith's advice and invested in a second-hand Windows computer. A lot of trial and many errors taught me how to write and insert diagrams and photos with Word 95, so it wasn't until eighteen months later that the resulting stack of typed notes and drawings came together to form the booklet known as *Short Hops.* But news had got around. Such was the dearth of gyroplane related subject matter at the time, that people from far afield began requesting copies of this crude handmade composition that was still a work in progress, and originally only intended for those at St Merryn.

So in 1998, in recognition of my attempt to preserve Chris's invaluable knowledge, I was shocked to be voted recipient of the Hugh Bancroft-Wilson memorial trophy. Keith was staying locally at the time, having brought his Bensen gyroplane down to do some early stage groundwork with me. He always had his finger on the pulse and typically knew all about the honour, assuming that I too was aware when he asked if I was going to the Cranfield rally for the presentation. *What presentation?* No one tells me anything! Eventually, having convinced me via the rotorcraft association that they hadn't made a mistake and it really wasn't a joke, Keith began insisting that I go and collect the trophy.

In reality, there was no hope of making the trip. Barely fourteen months had passed since losing my autorotational mentor, and the cottage industry of Wombat Gyrocopters had ceased to exist. All that was left were a couple of hours' work to bring in a few pounds, and my savings were depleting as I struggled to adjust and find a way forward. Driving to Bedfordshire was out of the question, but Keith (ever the cheerful optimist) had other ideas, and immediately declared that he would finance it for me. That's a real friend right there, but I couldn't accept his generous offer without knowing when I'd be able to repay him. Naturally he rebuffed any notion of debt and insisted that he was only too happy to see me receive the honour. We needed a compromise.

Delta-J provided the answer. As Keith admired the graffiti adorning her pod and tail, he decided he wanted to personalise his own gyroplane, so we agreed that I would repay his kindness by doing some nose art for him. There wasn't a great deal of room with it being an open-frame machine, but the angular nose cone enclosing the instrument panel was the obvious place to start. Keith was a computer boffin, mad about all kinds of gadgetry and technology which he invariably referred to as 'gizmos'. We shared the same sense of humour and love of the ridiculous. He rarely stayed still, being constantly upbeat and on the move, so I designed a blue-arsed fly to paint on one side of the nose cone, with the name *Gizmo* to go on the other. He loved it. I still have the drawings.

So we made the trip to Cranfield, and at the Sunday prize giving with Keith spurring me on, I stepped up to receive the Hugh Bancroft-Wilson trophy from Lord Trefgarne, and I still have it to this day, thanks to my good mate, Keith Balch. In *Short Hops*, I'd written about flying over the estuary and chasing the speedboats, which really appealed to Keith. He loved the idea and was keen to try it for himself, so I promised to take him when he had his licence, the intention being to complete his training at Henstridge, then return to St Merryn where I would apply his artwork, and together we would chase speedboats. Sadly, my debt remains unpaid.

At the end of May 2001, a gyroplane meeting was held at Henstridge airfield, in Somerset. Serious financial cramp meant that I couldn't afford to take Delta-J with me, and it felt like I was missing a limb as I wandered among the handful of Crickets and Bensens on the flight line. Then the raucous growl of a Volkswagen engine resonated through the circuit, announcing the arrival of a newly qualified Keith. I hadn't seen him actually fly his machine before, and was thrilled to watch him make a text book approach and landing. Later we went over to the gyroplane hangar housed in the former firing butts on the other side of the runway, where several students were preparing their machines for training. Despite his low hours, Keith seemed to have assumed the role of test pilot, confidently jumping into a different gyroplane and steaming off around the circuit, clearly loving every minute. This continued over the weekend and I was concerned to see him porpoising quite badly several times, although he was steady and competent in his own machine.

It troubled me that Keith was trying to do too much too soon, but as his instructor was present, along with several other gyronauts vastly more experienced than me, I kept my concerns to myself. He was having such a good time and no one else seemed worried, so who was I to spoil his fun? Hindsight is always twenty-twenty. I should have taken him aside for a quiet word – as should the other pilots who saw him trying to do far more than his experience allowed. Just five days later, Keith was killed flying a different gyroplane. He loved it too much and I lost a great friend, but we all let him down. I miss ya mate.

*

One year, when Mark came to do Delta-J's annual inspection, I was startled when he suddenly declared with a big grin, 'Shirley, you haven't had your accident yet!' Well if that didn't put the kybosh on it! Somewhat at a loss, I apologised for being so remiss, to which he replied, laughing sheepishly, that I was the only gyronaut he knew who hadn't broken anything! As backhanded compliments go, that's a cracker. I can only attribute my survival to excellent training and a more than a fair share of luck. But should gravity get me one day, it'll be because of something that I did or didn't do, and not because I happen to fly a gyroplane.

Everyone did their utmost to help and protect me during and after training – and who knows – perhaps if Chris Julian and Bob Bond hadn't been lost in that stupid accident, I might not have felt so strongly about helping others. Left to my own devices I doubt that I would've had the courage to teach people, but suddenly Chris was gone and the remainder of our devastated little group were looking to me to show them the way. *Me,* with a handful of hours and the ink hardly dry on my licence. How could I possibly fill the void left by Chris Julian? So I wrote *Short Hops*, took Chris's place on the gyro-glider and somehow we muddled through. Instructing seemed to come easily and I loved sharing the wonder of autorotation. Teaching *proper* rotor handling using nothing but the wind gave me some of the best moments of my life, and but for greedy Grenfell, I'd still be doing it now.

Chris's death changed everything. It pains me to think of others going through such an aftermath of tragedy, especially if something should have been said or done that could've prevented an accident - exactly like Keith. We should have stopped him before it was too late.

Don't Try This at Home

Making an exhibition of ourselves

In the summer of 1999, it was with great trepidation that me and my little bird found ourselves volunteered to do a turn at a local vintage fair, courtesy of an insistent neighbour. I really don't like doing that kind of thing, but having been put on the spot, they were so keen to have such a unique attraction that I reluctantly agreed to take Delta-J to the fair, and make an exhibition of ourselves.

In the weeks before the event, I drove down to check out available fields and get the lie of the land. The scenic Lizard peninsula is mainly scrubby open moorland with a few scattered villages, except that it's home to the Military Air Traffic Zone of RNAS Culdrose, the largest helicopter base in Europe, plus its secondary airfield at Predannack. There was also a small matter of avoiding the High Intensity Radio Transmission Area of Goonhilly Down, the largest satellite earth station in the world at the time. My 'landing strip' turned out to be earmarked for the visitors' car park, but I was assured that they would all be kept to the far side, leaving us plenty of room to drop in. As the prevailing wind is south-west, I checked out the field in that direction (rough), noted the proximity of the power lines (hmm...), and figured it was just about do-able. The organisers agreed to have marshals on hand to keep people clear and I would fly several circuits to give them prior warning, my condition being that we would only land if it was safe to do so. Plenty of fields surround the site, perfectly acceptable should the need arise for an unscheduled landing, so I planned a wide circuit to keep it legal, and our emergency options open. The only real doubt was our ability to take off again should the wind not co-operate on the day.

So with Delta-J spruced up and gleaming ready for her public (couldn't do a lot with the pilot) we awaited the coming weekend with mounting apprehension. Culdrose wasn't active apart from a couple of routine maintenance flights by the Search and Rescue squadron, and Air Traffic Control were happy to take our details over the phone. I planned to bimble straight down the coast through RAF St Mawgan's MATZ, land at Perranporth to top up the fuel, then head south across to the Lizard (preferably without being microwaved by Goonhilly) and follow the road to the show. The theory was good.

Zipping skywards from St Merryn on a bright and blustery Sunday, I pointed Delta-J's nose to the south-west and climbed up towards the MATZ boundary. I hate using the radio, but it had to be done, so an initial call went out to RAF St Mawgan. Silence. Give it a minute, try again. Silence. Orbit: try again. *Station calling St Mawgan, transmission unreadable – say again call sign.* So someone was at home. I said again call sign, and they said again that they couldn't read me. This was a good start. Trimming for a steady climb, I unplugged the aircraft antenna and carefully swapped it for the portable one. 'St Mawgan, Golf

Bravo Victor Delta Juliet....' Not a sausage. Fifteen minutes on the clock already and no one was talking to me. The stiff headwind was going to make the fuel situation interesting before long, so I made an executive decision and set course to skirt around the MATZ boundary, a considerably longer route than I'd bargained for. It was all going great so far!

We levelled off at 1,800 feet to fly around the moonscape of china clay works that loom above St Austell bay. Visibility was good and I could see for miles down the south coast towards our target area, the sea flecked with white horses whipped up by the wind. Small granite villages perched on the steep shoulders of clay country crept beneath our wheels, as I stared down into the mysterious blue pools that form in the craters of spoil heaps, like a strange volcanic region of some alien planet. Taking a wide track around the town of St Austell, we hopped between playing fields and patches of open ground before clearing suburbia and turning back towards the north coast to complete our circuit of the MATZ.

The wind now on our back whisked us along towards the wind farm at Carland Cross, which marked the edge of the zone boundary. I made a blind transmission, giving our position to anyone who was interested and informing them that we were changing frequency. Clearly no one was interested, so it was with little expectation that I switched over to Perranporth Radio and called in – to be greeted with a *Strength 5,* and *pass your message.* At last, someone was talking to me! I'd phoned the previous day so they were expecting us, but it was good to get proper joining instructions as we flew across the beach and over the cliffs for a downwind join. (The actual circuit pattern continues out to sea: not recommended for a tiny rotorcraft with the gliding ability of a teapot.)

Formerly an historic wartime base for Spitfires and Typhoons, it's a super airfield boasting six tarmac runways looking out over the Atlantic, and we practically had the place to ourselves thanks to the blustery wind grounding the normally active gliding club. Cutting the corner to avoid the wet bit, we scooted along the cliff tops greeted by the scent of warm coconut wafting up from the cheerful yellow gorse, nicely complemented by a spread of purple heather. We turned on to short final with a brief but spirited bronco ride bouncing through the turbulence off the cliffs, and air-taxied low along the runway to drop in at the intersection. Some of my early ground training was done at Perranporth under Chris's watchful eye, so it was nice to arrive properly and show what a gyroplane can really do. After confirming with the tower that there was no unexpected naval activity in the area, I retrieved my fuel cans and topped up the tank, complete with onlookers and *no, it isn't a microlight*, etc.

The wind was expected to moderate as we continued our journey south, which is practically a straight line from Perranporth to the Lizard peninsula. Climb up over Cornwall's rugged spine, giving wide berth to the radio mast at Four Lanes with its snaring web of bracing wires, then zoom downhill following the coast to Britain's most southerly point. What a view! A vast carpet of meadow and moorland spilled down towards the sea, the Earth Station looking like a set of china tea cups carelessly strewn on the lawn. To our right, a broad sweep of rocky coast and pale sands embraced the shimmering curve of Mount's Bay. RNAS Culdrose crept into view with its pattern of concrete aprons and immaculate runways, all mercifully quiet today. Ahead of us now, a cluster of wind turbines glinted in the sunshine beside a tableau plucked straight from science fiction. Massive girders supported the giant dishes of the Earth station, inscrutable blank faces staring intently beyond the heavens. We kept a respectful distance, careful to avoid their piercing gaze.

Not far to go now. Rounding the headland we flew over Cadgwith, a tiny fishing village squeezed into a steep wooded valley and funnelled down to the water's edge, where colourful boats bobbed in the narrow cove. Once clear of the valley it was safe to lose height, tracking along the road towards the fair where an unwelcome surprise awaited. Our 'landing strip' was three-quarters full of cars! This was novel. The wind had lost its earlier bluster but still retained enough strength to give us a reasonable hover, so I stopped to assess what was left of the field and weigh up our options. This attracted a lot of attention and I was relieved to see the promised marshals appear and begin herding people away. I decided to stick with the wind direction and come in steeply over the cars, leaving an escape route to go around over a flat area to the right of the power lines. It wasn't ideal and if I couldn't do it safely in three attempts, we would fly round, give 'em a wave and buzz off.

There's an awful lot of people down there – why am I doing this? Accelerating in to a circuit of the show ground, I tried to ignore the sea of upturned faces and concentrate on getting us down (preferably in one piece). I lined her up above the road and dropped down over the hedge in a steep approach, but it didn't feel quite right. Powering up again, I aimed for my chosen gap and successfully avoided the power lines, which is always a good thing! Safely back over the adjoining field, I let the momentum swing us up to our circuit height for another lap, the flags and bunting giving me a good indication of wind conditions. Another clearing turn to set up an approach and this time I brought my aiming point back towards the road, sinking vertically for a few seconds longer before levelling off in a short flare, and we were down. The field was rough and I quickly switched off before my vulnerable propeller blades could meet something hard and unyielding hidden in the scrubby grass, but we were here and still intact. Happy with that.

I hopped out to stop and secure the rotors as a growing number of children were gathering, and they do tend to leave a nasty dent in the rotor blades. Soon we were surrounded: I pulled the plug caps as an added precaution and turned my little bird around to meet her fans. A queue of delighted youngsters (and even a few parents) tried Delta-J on for size, asked all the usual questions and posed for photos while I explained that *no,* she isn't a helicopter, and *yes,* she is like the one in James Bond. *No,* it wasn't scary (unless landing in an unkempt field full of cars), and *no,* that's not a machine gun in the nose, nor does that button fire rockets. And so on, until the marshals came to our rescue and helped to push my tiny rotorcraft across the road to take her place at the fair.

She looked rather incongruous parked beside the ring among an array of muscular vintage tractors, classic cars and lorries, wreathed in a haze of exhaust fumes. The village hadn't seen anything like this before, she was the star attraction, a dainty red rose surrounded by heavy metal brawn. I was kept busy answering questions and keeping a watchful eye out for inquisitive fingers, but in fairness most children were well behaved as they sat in the cockpit pretending to be pilots (which in all honesty is exactly what I do!). Only one little brat needed growling at as he persisted in swinging heavily on the control stick. I'm a very passive person, but there are exceptions where Delta-J is concerned and that kid is lucky to be alive.

The sunny afternoon passed quickly in a blur of friendly faces, and we were well placed to watch the comedy. Heavy horses plodded round with quiet dignity, accompanied by the jingle of polished brasses and creaking leather harness, shortly followed into the ring by the manic chaos of a dog show. A random assortment of canines scattered to the four winds barking joyfully, in what was loosely termed the 'obedience' class. Gleaming vintage vehicles paraded slowly around the roped-off arena, the dimensions of which were now proving somewhat inadequate. Matters soon dissolved into farce when the procession of cars tried to extract themselves, only to meet a congestion of tractors struggling to get in. Discordant music drifted across the field from a local silver band competing manfully with the strident tones of a large fairground organ, thoughtfully placed nearby. The air was a heady mix of carbon monoxide and frying burgers, with a hint of cut grass and candy-floss.

One thing everyone wanted to know: when were we going to fly again? Good question. The wind had moderated as forecast, toying lazily with the flags and bunting as if it really couldn't be bothered anymore on a Sunday afternoon. The rough car park was unsuitable for anything other than a *very* short take off (out of the question without a gale blowing) and the adjoining fields didn't look much better, although they would do very nicely thank you if the elastic snapped on the way out. The show ground sloped downhill facing into what was left of the wind, and the surface was pretty good having been rolled for several days before the event. The best of the wind remained in the top left corner, well away from the sheltering influence of the hedge at the bottom of the field. Appraising it carefully, I thought we could make it by going diagonally, *providing* I could get the wheels off before the halfway mark as we would lose the wind further down. It would probably violate a chunk of the Air Navigation Order, but having considered that a worst case scenario posed minimal risk to all concerned, it was the best that I could do. Again I set myself three attempts, after which I'd be begging a lift to fetch the trailer. One way or another, I would not be leaving without Delta-J.

Proceedings began to wind down with the prize raffle draw, during which I inspected her closely to make sure no one had borrowed anything vital as a souvenir. But few people were leaving like I'd hoped – they wanted an air show and we were it. Stalls, tables and chairs began disappearing into the backs of cars and vans as I helped to dismantle the roped-off areas, watching the flags with increasing concern. We had to get going as soon as possible, the wind was fading rapidly and we needed every breath. The organisers were keen to help with what now appeared to be their grand finale, although I was praying that it wouldn't be *too* spectacular! I explained what was going to happen, adding that they shouldn't be alarmed by our strange manoeuvres as a gyroplane take off is quite different from the more familiar behaviour of aeroplanes and helicopters. All that remained was to walk the field from corner to corner, gathering discarded rubbish and scrutinising our intended path for any hidden surprises along the way. I didn't expect to make it out at the first attempt and decided on a trial run to see how it felt.

With preparations complete, we said our goodbyes, stressing that everyone *must* stay well back with children and animals kept on leads until we were either airborne or shut down again, which the announcer then relayed to the crowd over the PA system. Firing up and fingers crossed, I taxied Delta-J as close to the hedge as possible without trimming it, and pointed her nose down towards the opposite corner. Suddenly the field looked very small. I took my time over power checks, making sure that everything was doing what it ought to be doing and all systems were go. Now it depends on the rotor blades: how will they react? Engaging the pre-rotator, I tuned in to what the rotors were saying, and they agreed that we wouldn't be getting out first time. I don't like driving them mechanically like that, but aerodynamic spin-up alone was not going to get us over that hedge. Employing a modified Italian technique, I drove them hard until they had a nice beat going, then let Delta-J off the leash, accelerating to the halfway point to feel how quickly the rotors responded and how much more we were going to need. I sensed consternation among the crowd as I closed the throttle, braked with the rotor disc and swiftly turned back uphill to keep the momentum going. The surface of the field was actually better than expected and it felt safe to accelerate faster.

Back to the top again, swing around in our corner and engage pre-rotator, this time driving it a bit harder. Delta-J edged forward as the airframe pulsed to the beat of the rotors, her little drum brake struggling gallantly against the thrust of the propeller. It couldn't take much more. With rapid dexterity I released the pre-rotator and parking brake, steadied the throttle and we shot forward. This was much better, I could feel the rotors gathering lift, and the nose wheel popped up well before my point of no return. A quick glance at the gauges confirmed the engine was good to go, so power on and we soared over the hedge in fine style. No worries! A couple of slow passes around the field for the waving crowd, then wagging our tail in farewell we set course for the north coast.

It was a gorgeous evening to fly: visibility still good and we had the remains of a tail wind to play with, but the long day was beginning to take its toll as Perranporth came in to view. We whistled into a deserted airfield against a glowing western sky, air-taxiing straight in and shutting down with a sigh of relief. Time was getting on. I didn't fancy another detour around the clay pits when home was only fifteen minutes away on the other side of the MATZ. It's already 20:00 – is it worth a shot? They didn't hear me this morning: if that happens again we'll have no choice but to take the scenic route. But this was 1999, and modern technology had finally crept into the far south-west. A quick stroll around the airfield managed to intercept a tenuous bar of signal for the chunky mobile phone in my pocket. A brief conversation with St Mawgan tower explained my plight, and yes, we can go straight through the zone non-radio, provided we were above 2,000 feet to clear scheduled traffic departing in twenty minutes. Result!

Dwarfed by the silent runways, we climbed up into a perfect setting, sending foraging rabbits dashing for cover. On our left, the peaceful Atlantic waters glistened like burnished metal, rippled by a gentle swell. The deepening haze lent a soft filter to the range of headlands stretching out to the west, guiding us home like pointing fingers. St Mawgan tower poked out of the dusk inland as we reached 2,500 feet and eased off to let the engine catch its breath. It was cold up there. The tower came on frequency with departure clearance for the outbound traffic, and I spotted the movement of a large aircraft below on Mawgan's runway. The pattern of nav lights took up position and made their way ponderously into the air, straight over the cliffs and out to sea, watched by a tiny rotorcraft hidden high above. A pincushion of radio masts twinkled with red obstruction lights, marking neighbouring St Eval with a string of rubies against the evening sky. St Merryn wasn't far and we were much too high, but Delta-J was happy where she was. We drifted out over the estuary, trickling down in gentle descent and savouring the glorious prelude to sunset before turning for home. That was a very long day. Unfortunately we proved so popular that they asked us back again the following year, and we did it another five times after that. I didn't like it, but they were so appreciative and I'm such a doormat...

A local farmer offered the use of a bigger field along from the show ground, and so began the routine of towing Delta-J down for static display, then flying a demonstration at a given time. This proved to be more user friendly although the new field was also rough and far from ideal, sharing it as we did with a herd of bullocks who were generous with the gifts they left in our path. Careful taxiing was required or it really would've hit the fan! The first time that we used this particular field nearly ended in disaster – it was entirely my fault and only pure luck stopped us from going home in a wheelbarrow. Something had gone awry with the program and I was asked to fly an hour earlier than expected, leaving little time to trailer down to the field, negotiate the gate, unload, pre-flight and pick out a take off run. Stupidly, I agreed to do my best so as not to disrupt their revised schedule. What I *should've* said was sorry, but no can do.

Having got Delta-J ready in the bullock field, I was very conscious of time ticking away as I planned our take off path into wind, grateful that it took us well away from where the herd was quietly grazing. The rough grass ranged from thick tufty clumps to tall stringy stalks and marsh reeds, sprouting from a churned up mass of hoof prints interspersed with a minefield of ripe cow pats. A moderate wind of no real use wafted lazily across the countryside ruffling the foliage around us. I chose an aiming point at the far side and drove my van slowly towards it, avoiding the cow pats as best I could. With time constraints foremost in my mind (*wrong!*) I stopped a little farther on from where I thought we should be airborne, and walked back between the tyre tracks to check for debris on our makeshift runway. Had I been less worried about other peoples' time scales and more concerned for my own neck, I would have continued driving to shortly discover a hidden gully that ran across the width of the field like a crease, dropping abruptly into a dry ditch about three feet deep.

Instead it was only by chance that I spotted it just ahead of Delta-J's nose as we jolted our way painfully across the bumps and ruts, trying to achieve escape velocity. No time for rational thought, it was one of those moments when instinct takes over and it's in the lap of the gods. The nose wheel was just beginning to lift as I caught a glimpse of the ditch that we were seconds from ploughing into and rammed open the throttle. My guardian spirits were working overtime that day. The engine roared and shoved us over the drop like a kick in the pants. Thankfully the rotors took the abuse and clutched at the air, holding us as the ground fell away with our wheels skimming the tips of the reeds. I kept her low over the field to build airspeed and let the rotors settle down before climbing away to safety. Curving back on ourselves and gaining height, we arrived at the show on time to do our stuff. Everyone was delighted. Only I knew how close we had come to disaster, and I was furious with myself.

TOULOUSE, LONG TREK

You won't see this at home!

Entering the gyroplane world brought several landmarks to my life, but this particular trip was monumental for discovering a parallel universe where gyronauts enjoyed unimaginable freedom to evolve. It sowed a seed that would grow into a strong friendship with a group of people who are as important to me now as those of old at St Merryn. They too have helped to spread my wings.

*

Apart from some short visits to Italy and Austria, I had hardly been outside of the British Isles at all, but in 2005 everything changed. It was a huge adventure for me to be part of a road trip down through France, travelling in a converted Chevrolet ambulance with three gyro pals, Rusty, Will and Ron, culminating at the annual gyroplane meeting near Toulouse. I was ridiculously excited! First the ferry to Dunkirk and all that history, fascinating to see those famous beaches at first hand. Despite reading many books about the world wars, it was startling to see just how close all the unimaginable horror and heroism of that brutal occupation had been to our island. Road signs showed evocative place names synonymous with both major conflicts, but we were on a tight schedule with no time to stand and stare.

The terrain was remarkably flat with wide-open countryside and few apparent boundaries, very different to the rugged hills of Cornwall, criss-crossed by meandering hedges and dry-stone walls. We motored long into the evening, lit by a golden glow on the western horizon, finally coming to roost in a lay-by south of Paris after driving through the city at midnight. Struggling hard to stay awake for my first visit to Paris, I caught a dreamlike glimpse of the Eiffel Tower before we were swallowed up by an underpass. Thousands of light bulbs set the iconic shape ablaze against the night sky, a large tricolour crowning its peak – is this *really* real?

Thursday morning dawned fresh and clear, the dew sparkling in expansive fields that stretched as far as the eye could see. It's perfect airfield country. Only in Lincolnshire have I seen fields anything like this size at home. It made Cornwall seem really small and compact, as did the roads, running arrow straight for miles on end and disappearing into the distance like switchbacks. A vast panorama dotted with ancient communities of narrow streets and wooden-shuttered windows, teasing glimpses of imposing châteaux peeping between the trees. I didn't know where to look first, gawking in amazement at the scale of it all. The French take their lunch breaks very seriously (as I would learn in years to come!) and traffic all but disappeared between midday and two in the afternoon. The sky grew overcast as we rolled further south, the flatlands giving way to gentle slopes that grew increasingly hilly as we wove between ancient volcanic heights.

It was raining hard by the time we pulled in to a hypermarket on the outskirts of Limoges. This was a voyage of discovery in itself: a mammoth structure that could swallow a jumbo jet, the place was so big that the assistants whizzed around on roller skates. The shelves were crammed with an unbelievable variety of consumer goods and every kind of comestible imaginable. Thick wheels of cheese the size of hub caps; glossy apples bigger than cricket balls, and bananas on steroids – I swear they were a foot long. Row upon colourful row of weird and exotic fruit and veg, some wreathed in a fine mist of cooling spray. Live crabs and lobsters destined for a boiling pot clambered helplessly against the sides of glass tanks, their powerful claws tightly bound. I felt sad for the poor creatures, surely there was a kinder way to dispatch them. Below the tanks lay a kaleidoscope of fresh fish, glassy-eyed on sacrificial slabs of crushed ice, mouths agape as if in silent plea. One aisle left me particularly nonplussed, being dedicated to different kinds of mustard – a *whole aisle* of mustard – surely that can't be necessary. And so much food! It was fascinating yet strangely disturbing. Do we really need such incredible diversity to keep us satisfied when half the world is starving? It felt almost shameful.

Moving on late in to the night through heavy rain, we could see nothing of the sodden landscape in the pitch black, aware only of the steeply increasing gradient of a road that was slick with running water. It was somewhere near Montauban where we eventually stopped to rest, but we could've been anywhere lost in that sightless void. Awake early next morning on Friday the thirteenth, I wriggled my sleeping bag between the front seats to watch a pale orange sun ascend into an ashen sky. Plump round hills filled the windscreen, pastel colours in a morning mist, and somewhere in the distance a clock tower struck five. Not a sound from my companions. We were deep in France with an unimaginable weekend of gyroplane action ahead of us. I squirmed back to my bunk, quietly thrilled by the wonder of it all.

Around two hours later, a tousled head appeared over the edge of the top bunk, swiftly followed by the rest of its body which bounced down off the foot of my bed on to the floor. I can honestly say that I'd never been greeted by a dawn chorus of 'Happy Birthday' from two Belgian lads standing at the foot of my bed in their underpants! It's the thought that counts. The rain had cleared through the night and a bright fresh morning revealed the full lush green of the surrounding hills. We celebrated with breakfast outside at a picnic bench, accompanied by the soft chimes of sheep bells (presumably smaller than cow bells but equally charming). Later we rejoined the main road and carried on south, reaching Toulouse around midday. Safely through the chaos of the ring road and back out in to the sticks, we stopped to collect bread and croissants for a fine picnic lunch, which we enjoyed under the shade of a willow tree beside the lake at Peyssies. Fresh French bread is out of this world, nothing like the over-processed cotton wool that passes for bread at home. I was still struggling to believe that this was all real.

And so on to Bois de la Pierre, barely five minutes away: a tiny community with the obligatory church and town hall, little more than an intersection of narrow streets lined by rows of typically higgledy-piggledy houses. The road crossed the end of a long grass runway and we looked eagerly down its length to see several low hangars clustered along the far side, where a hive of activity was in progress. The air was heavy and humid as if a storm was brewing so we hurried to set up the tents, including one for our friend John who was joining us from Wales via Squeezy Jet. Several gyroplanes were being prepared on the other side of the runway which was most distracting, so fortified with another round of coffee and croissants we headed for the flight line where people were hard at work putting up stalls and barriers.

Xavier Averso, veteran pioneer of French autorotation was flying his twin seat open-frame machine, leaving the two watching Brits gaping in amazement. By pre-spinning the rotors up to what seemed like a furious rate, he took off with barely any forward roll, it was the closest thing we had ever seen to an actual gyroplane jump take off. Circling the airfield, he touched back down and used the inertia stored in the rotor disc to take straight off again, powering into the sky. An impressive performance for a standard 80 hp engine, with two people on board. A sporty looking gyroplane with two seats arranged tandem-style was a German copy of the Spanish version of the Italian M16, a clone not yet seen in Britain. It looked all right from a distance until Rusty pointed out the poor standard of engineering and low quality materials. As the asking price was comparable to that of a four-seat aeroplane with better range and payload, I managed to restrain myself from placing an order. The only other 'standard' gyroplane was a Magni M14, again a rare bird to British eyes. Everything else was a taste of what was in store for us over the weekend – nothing was standard! They appeared to build and fly anything they liked, a marvellous mix of rotary-winged diversity that Ron and I found hard to believe as we wandered down the flight line, staring in wonder.

Xavier zoomed down the runway with another passenger: the French really do have flair, a certain style. Rusty remarked that he didn't think I would like to fly with Xavier, and of course I said no, I would hate that! Time was getting on and soon we had to collect John from the airport back in Toulouse, so it was all a bit of a blur. Xavier didn't speak English and I barely spoke French, but Rusty handled the niceties and I was soon being installed in the left seat, amused by Xavier handing me a hair net to put on. My only experience of a completely open-framed gyroplane was on the east coast of Scotland, when I flew from the back seat, squeezed between the twin masts of a very underpowered Parsons tandem, which flogged every bit from its 65 horses just to maintain level flight. A considerably larger gyronaut occupied the front seat, his bulk providing welcome relief from the blast of frigid North Sea air as I huddled behind him, tightly sandwiched between the masts.

The side-by-side seating in Xavier's machine is much more comfortable, but there's nothing between you and 70 mph blasting up your trouser legs, which even in the temperate climes of southern France is rather bracing. The short take off was every bit as thrilling as it looked, Xavier spun the blades really hard with the pre-rotator and poured on the power. We were off the ground within a few feet and he immediately handed it over to me – I wasn't expecting that! The big rotor blades felt heavy on the control stick, but the machine was very stable despite sitting in a roaring gale. My borrowed crash helmet was much too big, and the slippery hair net beneath it didn't help: the wind kept pushing it back off my head and forcing the headphones down over my ears, which was quite distracting. Poor visibility gave no clue that we were so close to the Pyrenees, only forty miles away yet completely obscured in a pale sepia haze. Xavier let me play with the controls for a few minutes then directed me to fly towards base leg, where he took control again. *Did he take control!* I glanced to my left, staring straight at the ground in an almost vertical bank as we chased our tail in tight figure-eights, accompanied by a delicious *whop* from the hard working rotors. Awesome! After that it was around the trees (we weren't overly high) and in for a perfect touch down. Rusty was right, I didn't enjoy that at all! I thanked Xavier as best I could, and Ron said he'd never seen such a big grin on my face.

There was no time to catch my breath, the afternoon had quite literally flown by and now we had to go and fetch John from the airport. The weather was really closing in. Lightning flickered in the scowling overcast and a steady drizzle intensified as we drove back to the city, where John was already waiting at the terminal. Happy to see him again, I struggled to collect my thoughts, not wanting to lose a moment of the brilliant flight with Xavier, and all the sights on the journey down. So much to take in and the weekend had only just begun.

It was almost dark by the time we got back to the airfield, where several more motor homes had joined our cluster of tents in the pouring rain. It didn't look too hopeful and I wondered if we were in for a repeat of the deluge at Magni Days. The Gyro Club had arranged an informal hangar meal for the early birds, to which we were kindly invited along with around thirty other people. Heavy rain drummed on the roof, a few leaks dripping through in places and splashing onto the table. I was feeling very full and increasingly weary after the excitement of another long day, when suddenly veteran Gyro Club member Pierre Cena picked up a microphone and announced something unintelligible in French, and my name was on the end of it. *Uh oh...* Bottles of champagne appeared as if by magic and the whole gathering burst into a hearty rendition of Happy Birthday, toasting me with bubbly – and we'd only just met! Rusty produced an elaborate cake which I was tasked to cut while being kissed by various lovely French people. Stitched up a treat. It was quite overwhelming and little could I have imagined what a precedent that would be in years to come.

Splashing back to camp later in the dark, there followed a final piece of lunacy which had us doubled up with laughter. John had brought a couple of inflatable mattresses and insisted that I took one. These things were 6 feet long by 2.5 feet wide, and the foot pump squeaked and parped like an asthmatic donkey. It must've been close to midnight. Shut inside the van, trying to pump up these monsters without disturbing our neighbours, after finally getting one fully inflated we couldn't get it out of the door! Wrestling it outside with barely stifled giggles, John still wanted me to take it, despite the obviously inadequate dimensions of my tent. He meant well but as the old adage goes, *you can't get a quart into a pint pot.* Pitch black and raining, trying to stuff a giant inflatable mattress through the little porch without snagging the guy ropes – what a comedy! – I wish we'd had a video. Struggling inside the confines of damp fabric walls, tangled in the darkness with luggage and bedding, it was like trying to fight my way out of a shopping bag. The mattress would not fit. I tried to manoeuvre it out through the porch, but John standing unaware outside in the rain kept shoving it back in! I was laughing so hard I could barely breathe.

Eventually with some difficulty I managed to get the darn thing out and we pushed it inside John's big tent, stopping Will from pumping up the other one. But I wasn't off the hook: no, you must have a mattress, try it partially inflated instead. First I had to straighten my battered home, fumbling through the rain to tighten wet guy ropes in a feeble beam of torchlight. I love camping! It must've taken a good hour to resolve this nonsense, finally cramming a damp and saggy mattress into the wreckage of my sleeping quarters, but when at last I lay down, all the air squeezed up either end with a motion somewhat akin to a waterbed and it didn't support me at all.

A beautiful morning greeted us with a chilly wind and no sign of any mountains. I woke to the song of cuckoos, who sound exactly the same in French. John and Ron were already up, so we went to the clubhouse to partake of what appeared to be cereal bowls of black coffee before heading for the flight line. More rotorcraft were already arriving, some by air and some by road: exotic gyroplanes in varying states of construction, some of them more like works of art than flying machines, so creatively sculpted were they. We wandered among them open-mouthed in disbelief. Gyroplanes, more gyroplanes, and *even more* gyroplanes, never had we seen so many and such diversity. What sorcery was this?

Very few machines were close to centre line thrust (regarded as the optimum safe configuration for a gyroplane) but every single one of them wore a horizontal tail plane of some description - begging the question why can't we do things like this at home? One pilot showed us photos of his machine which featured an unusually tall and tapered mast, fashioned from a discarded lamp post! One particular single-seat gyroplane was made from mild steel, and the pilot told us that after every few hours of flying he had to weld up the cracks. A big Lycoming-powered enclosed two-seater was doing a lot of flying. It had an individually sprung undercarriage which looked quite comical taxiing over the grass, legs twitching independently like a robotic insect. It's a different world over there.

We walked the flight line from end to end and back again in amazement. Coming from a gyroplane scene that had barely progressed since the 1980s, this was an autorotational feast of unimaginable proportions. I didn't know where to look first, greedily filling my camera with memories - please sir, can we have some more? A group of three open-frame single-seat gyroplanes flown by veteran Gyro Club members, Jean Marie Varga, Pierre Cena and Xavier Averso, put on a lovely formation display as the afternoon drew to a close. Collectively known as the *Patrouille,* they have flown together for more than two decades, performing routines at events all over the country. It was a fine way to end a most enjoyable and enlightening day.

Everyone gathered around the clubhouse ready for the evening meal. Long rows of trestle tables filled the main hangar where we joined the throng, greeted by smiling faces and absorbed into the community spirit. It was fascinating to watch hundreds of restaurant quality meals being prepared in giant pans on what was basically an open-air field-kitchen. Five courses later, we waddled to our beds beneath a luminous sky filled with starlight, so clear in the pure mountain air. A nocturnal chorus of insects and amphibians echoed all around, lulling us to sleep.

Next morning, I joined John and Ron for an early stroll through the quiet village, the day already warm and full of birdsong, and suddenly – there on the horizon stood the Pyrenees! Beautiful proper mountains with snow and everything, as if pulled like a rabbit from a hat and placed there overnight. How does that happen? I couldn't stop gazing at them. Returning to the clubhouse intent on coffee, we were waylaid by the sight of an intriguing craft being prepared for flight. Shaped like an airship, it was inflated like a balloon (presumably with gas), and driven by a pusher engine. A small gondola hung beneath, and the tail of the envelope actually worked as a rudder, albeit a floppy one. The temperature was stoking up rapidly and we took shelter from the blazing sun to watch events from the side of the runway. Around a dozen machines left for a local trip before returning en masse to the field, a sky full of gyroplanes against the mighty backdrop of the mountains – a spectacular sight. I could never have believed that one day I would be a part of it too.

The Patrouille did their full display, complete with a synchronised release of a weighted flag from each machine as they did a final fly-past along the runway – something else never to be seen at home! Sporadic flying continued through the evening with both local and visiting gyronauts making the most of beautiful conditions, and possibly delaying the moment of departure. But we still had the evening meal to enjoy together and it was an absolute epic. Everyone was in festive mood: paper place mats folded into aeroplanes sailed past our ears, and explosive pops fired champagne corks into the rafters. Six courses, gallons of wine and yet more champagne lubricated a seemingly endless prize raffle draw, but I was in complete sensory overload by then and really too tired to care. We stumbled to our beds at a very late hour beneath a wondrous array of stars, brilliant against the night sky. What a day.

And then it was all over. Monday morning dawned grey

and overcast, and so was the weather. Rent-a-Mountain had taken the Pyrenees away again, much to my disgust. It's amazing how such a massive mountain range can vanish so completely. A melancholy mood overtook us as we reluctantly dismantled the tents and repacked the camper van, taking perverse delight in squashing John's giant mattresses in to submission. We had looked forward to this weekend for such a long time, and now it was over in a heartbeat. Only a few machines remained on the flight line - where did it all go? I went to say goodbye to the Club members, and got hugged and kissed from all directions, such a lovely bunch of people. It was a very subdued bunch of campers that headed back to Toulouse to drop John off at the airport, before making our way north to Dunkirk and the ferry.

But a fuse had been lit and it was burning merrily. I'd tasted forbidden fruit and seen a world of autorotational freedom that British gyronauts could only dream of. It was a major pivotal moment in the evolution of a Rotormouse.

How Not to Win Friends and Influence People

Ken Wallis often said that 'Those who never make a mistake, never make anything'. Most pilots experience the odd near miss now and again: maybe some mechanical defect that was overlooked, or an error of judgement that could have escalated but fortunately didn't. Even something completely beyond our control like almost being mown down from behind by an inattentive Dash 8 (been there, done that!). Such events merely add a shiver to the spine if we stop to consider what might have been, casting a nod of thanks to our lucky stars and we strive to do better next time. On this particular day, a series of errors escalated into the biggest fubar of all my flight time. Never have I made so many bad decisions – and never have my actions brought me so close to carnage.

*

In 2007, Grenfell and I trailered up to Henstridge airfield where we were to be part of a flight of six gyroplanes leaving for RNAS Yeovilton Air Day. My radio wasn't transmitting properly, although it received perfectly well, so I could at least hear other traffic even if I couldn't talk to them. However, I was assured that it wouldn't be a problem as we were all going together, with one aircraft handling communication for the whole group. We got up early on Saturday morning to make ready in what we believed to be ample time, only to find that the instructions had changed. Instead of the expected group take off, we were now to leave at delayed intervals and assemble to the north-west to await our slot time. We had to get moving straight away to take up a holding pattern as the Red Arrows were due to arrive – jeez, what could go wrong? Pretty much everything as it turned out.

I like to preflight quietly and take my time over checks to be sure that I haven't missed anything. Rushing went against the grain, and stress levels were rising rapidly, compounded by the thought of nine Hawk jets sharing the same piece of sky. I didn't want my tiny vulnerable gyroplane anywhere near them. Being unfamiliar with the area (an area of controlled airspace that would shortly be hosting a major air show!) I'd expected instructions to be a little more specific than a general 'head north-west', but we'd come all this way specially, and the other gyronauts didn't seem particularly concerned as they buckled themselves in and started their engines. Why do I do these things to myself? The four two-seat machines went on ahead to take off in relays, leaving the Crickets to fly as a pair, the newly qualified Grenfell handling radio calls until we rejoined the others.

But on reaching the holding point, an angry voice in my headphones made it clear that Henstridge Radio wasn't receiving Grenfell's transmissions, and were repeatedly trying to contact him as he taxied straight out across the runway. I could see the airfield manager getting quite agitated through the ops room window, and tried a call on frequency, only to be told that it was 'carrier wave only'. He urgently insisted that if I was receiving him, I must prevent Grenfell from taking off as he had already back-tracked to the threshold and was spinning up. Not the most auspicious of starts. Taking Delta-J out in front of my errant leader, I managed to herd him back to the parking area to investigate the problem. A loose connector was identified which Grenfell duly tightened, but we were now behind schedule and I was reluctant to go on. The Red Arrows were inbound and would be there to the minute whether we were in their way or not, and a diminutive gyroplane gives a poor radar return. The airfield manager phoned Yeovilton Air Traffic, and Grenfell explained that we'd become separated from our group who were now somewhere to the north-west. Permission was given to continue, much to my dismay, and I scrambled back on board feeling that this was a very bad idea as Grenfell made a clear strength 5 transmission and taxied for take off.

Now in the years that I'd come to know him after Chris's accident, it became increasingly obvious that Grenfell wasn't lacking in self confidence. I taught him everything I knew on the gyro-glider, then helped him through the early stages of powered training with Bob's Cricket, the same machine he was using for this trip. Despite repeated assurances that the problem was fixed, I was very concerned that we had no back up plan in the event of another communications failure, but Grenfell was typically confident. He knew the area (having completed his training at Henstridge); he had a GPS on board, and he'd flown into Yeovilton twice before. I really should have known better. I really should have stayed on the ground.

In the air, we tracked north-west as previously agreed and I heard Grenfell contact Yeovilton LARS, who told him that the rest of the group were holding in our three o'clock position. Visibility was good yet neither of us could spot them (we later learned that two machines had gone on ahead after also failing to join up). Yeovilton came back on frequency asking Grenfell for the number of souls on board, and although his reply was muffled I heard him say 'One on board,' but failed to tell them that we were a flight of two. That left me in limbo, unaccounted for in controlled airspace with no way to communicate. It took a couple of minutes to catch up and get his attention, trying to make him understand that they needed to know *two* gyroplanes were inbound. It's embarrassing just thinking about it. We were wandering around all over the place.

At last the penny dropped. Grenfell called again to update our status, adding that we couldn't find the rest of our group: Yeovilton asked if we wanted a straight-in approach for runway 27, and told him to contact the tower. We were now in a very bad position, completely out of the pattern and much too close to the airfield boundary. The huge white numbers on the threshold of runway 22 were dead ahead, with crowds of spectators lining the barriers alongside, but Grenfell didn't deviate from his track and appeared to be on final approach. I was stressed to hell, totally convinced that he was going to land on 22 and there was nothing I could do about it. In hindsight, perhaps it would've been the lesser of two evils to have just turned around and got the heck out of there, but I was scared of being adrift in controlled airspace with an air display imminent and no means of talking to Air Traffic Control. Why do I do these things to myself...

By now we were only a couple of fields away from the perimeter fence. I stayed at 900 feet as Grenfell continued down towards 22 (wondering what the merry hell I was going to do if he landed), when the tower came back on frequency making us number two behind the aircraft on final for 27. I breathed a sigh of relief as Grenfell suddenly broke left and headed in at right angles to the active runway, confirming visual contact with the aircraft landing ahead. I was sure that Air Traffic didn't know where we were. At long last we took up the correct heading of 270, but I deliberately stayed above 600 feet, thinking that fixed-wings generally turn base leg at 500 feet and much further out. I couldn't see anything coming as we turned towards the runway, but less than half a minute passed before another voice in my headphones called final for 27. Oh God. We *are* number two, aren't we?

Grenfell was ahead and descending on approach. Anxiety went off the scale. Craning my neck and searching desperately for the aircraft that had just called, I slid Delta-J to the right of the centre line as a precaution, grateful for her instant agility. Seconds later the large shadow of a fixed-wing appeared to my right, moving sedately over the ground and closing in from behind. Quickly checking all round, I found myself staring down into the cockpit of a silver Chipmunk as it passed about 50 feet beneath our left axle. I immediately applied power and slid further to the right to keep the Chipmunk in view, stopping briefly to give him space before continuing in to land. I heard the startled pilot call that a gyroplane (Grenfell) had landed directly in front of him. It was a whisker away from carnage. None of us had seen the other, and it was only because of the shadow that I saw the Chipmunk, who had no reason to suspect that anyone was above or below him. A typical build up of errors right from the very start, and a minimal difference in timing would have been catastrophic. Quite rightly, a pair of very sorry gyronauts were hauled up to the tower for a serious dressing down. It wasn't our finest hour. (And yes, I did file a report.)

Taking the Plunge

Three visits to the annual gyroplane meeting at Bois de la Pierre had left me seriously inspired to attend with Delta-J, but I wasn't at all sure of being up to the task.

Perched on a wall overlooking Falmouth harbour one day, I pondered the complexities of getting my precious flying machine safely to the South of France in one piece. Could I really undertake such a quest or was I just kidding myself? Deep down I already knew the answer to that one. Towing my gyroplane 600 miles on the 'wrong' side of the road. That was *six hundred miles* worth of potential mechanical problems to deal with, alone in a foreign language. Would I even be able to find my way? And what if we did get there: was I really good enough to fly with the best in Europe? I knew the answer to that one – hell no! But should we survive that far, another 600 miles lay in wait to get back to the ferry, and whichever way you cut it, I had zero confidence in my ability to do any single part of it. But I *really* wanted to take Delta-J...

Across the water, berthed alongside the harbour wall was a large white ship with a sort of dolphin-esque silhouette painted on the superstructure. Lost in my reverie I hadn't paid much attention. It was just another vessel, one of several in the background of the docks until the fluttering tricolour of a French flag suddenly permeated my brain. Looking up and noticing the ship properly for the first time, the letters stencilled on her bow seemed to cry out to me in a fanfare of trumpets. *Pourquoi Pas?* was her name – *Why Not?* I couldn't believe it! If ever there was a sign.

And so the following year (4 May 2008, to be exact), I first ventured over to foreign shores under my own steam. Bois de la Pierre is heck of a long way down, and never having driven abroad in a language I can barely speak, I thought it best to see if I was actually capable of making the trip before exposing my vulnerable gyroplane to continental traffic. This is how it went...

*

After leaving Portsmouth at 23:00 for an exceptionally smooth Channel crossing, the *Norman Spirit* arrived bang on time in a sunny Le Havre at 08:00 on Sunday. Having passed a restless night repeatedly sliding out of my reclining seat, I was a confusion of nervous excitement as I watched the ship manoeuvring herself into the dock. The nagging thought occurred as I took in my first view of the deserted city, that here I was, alone on a huge continent hundreds of miles from home, and still many hundreds more from the few people I knew in the country – none of whom spoke English! Reunited with my faithful old van down in the bowels of the ship, matters were not improved when I tried to get a fix on the satnav to help us find our way back in twelve days' time. Not surprisingly, deep inside the hull shielded by several tons of steel, not a single satellite made itself known before we were unceremoniously swept into France on a tide of disembarking vehicles. Customs and immigration were conspicuous by their absence, not a solitary gendarme to be seen: *it is Sunday morning, do not bother us with your passports!*

It took all my concentration to drive on the opposite side of the road and avoid any turnings that could potentially lead to a motorway. I had no clue where to go, my carefully prepared route out of the city bore no relation to anything that I could see. Momentum and fear alone took us through empty streets, until by chance I spotted a nearby park and headed towards it with the desperation of a drowning man to a straw. We were only a matter of minutes from the docks but already I felt completely wrung out and seriously doubting my ability to make this trip. A few people were starting to appear on the streets, and dog walkers strolled through the park in the early sunlight. I felt strangely conspicuous, an obvious foreigner with British plates and right-hand drive, but thousands of Brits pour through the town every week via the ferry terminal, and the locals weren't the slightest bit interested in yet another one.

I tried to calm down, mentally taking myself by the scruff of the neck to either sort it out or spend two weeks in Le Havre and miss the best gyroplane event of the year. We were close to a major road and I could see a big sign from which I deduced that we were in a suburb called Harfleur. The satnav tried again to find some satellites to talk to, and after a worryingly blank few minutes finally locked on to some healthy signals. I gathered what remained of my shattered wits and began to pick out a route on the map. Given the mind-bogglingly massive size of France along with its metric measurements, I had no clear idea of time scale other than attempting to arrive at Bois de la Pierre on Thursday evening, preferably via Millau to see the new bridge – if I could find it. It looked heck of a long metric way away.

Somewhat reassured with satellite assistance, I took inspiration from a certain book and decided to take it stage by stage (or rather page by page) and tackle the journey in short hops, giving wide berth to any area that looked large, urban and complicated. Three years earlier as a passenger along with my companions, we'd followed a mainly motorway, almost due south route which I still basically remembered, but now I was pilot in command I wanted to stick to quieter roads and take a more easterly track towards Millau. Still, we had to start somewhere. I programmed the satnav for a Rouen direction, avoiding motorways like the plague (the actual option available was somewhat less explicit, unfortunately), took a deep breath and turned the van back towards civilisation.

My first time driving outside of the British Isles was also my first experience of using a satnav, which only added to my apprehension of remembering to drive on the other side of the road. However, after the initial terror of disembarking I surprised myself by settling relatively quickly in to the new regime and snuggled the offside wheels into the right hand kerb with determined intimacy. There were plenty of other hazards to worry about. The satnav was purely an audio aid, being fully occupied concentrating on the barely readable inner dial of the speedometer and not lapse into miles per hour, I didn't dare risk the distraction of trying to follow the visual display. Overhead traffic lights were a new and startling concept, not expecting to see them up there and frequently didn't! It was a good thing that the roads were still quiet as I began to learn about continental driving the hard way.

We threaded our way through a housing estate, bouncing over speed ramps and gradually emerged in to open country, a huge concrete bridge towering above us carrying the motorway towards Paris. I began to feel a bit better as we left the 'burbs behind, going steady and totally dependent on the satnav to guide us. So it was about an hour later that we found ourselves directed into a small and lifeless industrial estate and ordered to 'Take the ferry' - to which the immediate response was *what ferry?* Driving round the units in all possible directions revealed a distinct lack of water and no indication of anything remotely nautical, so I pulled over next to a cluster of recycling bins to have words with my navigator. Further requests for a Rouen orientated heading were stubbornly resisted with repeated instructions to 'Take the ferry' yet devoid of any clue as to the whereabouts of this mythical vessel. Faced with implacable computer logic, I studied the map once again and chose a different aiming point in the same direction, and just like magic, the obsession with ferries was gone.

It wasn't yet mid-morning but even with both windows down and all three vents open, the temperature inside the van climbed rapidly. It could only get worse as we dropped further south. Driving through a narrow deserted town, I stopped at a T-junction where the main traffic lights had been replaced by a temporary set. A red light was showing and suddenly a flashing amber lit up beneath it. There was no green light. I remembered that flashing amber meant proceed with caution - but red for stop and flashing amber at the same time could seriously confuse a stupid person! Fortunately, the only other car on the road made a timely appearance behind us, and its impatient beep was encouragement enough to proceed.

A love/hate relationship began to develop with the satnav after being directed the wrong way up several one way streets, and catapulted on to a toll road when I'd specifically asked it to avoid them. My stress levels rocketed as we were funnelled into a long row of automated barriers from which there was no escape, and all naturally arranged for the convenience of left-hand drive vehicles. Pulling up at the barrier and stretching across to the passenger window, I couldn't see what I was supposed to do. Grabbing the keys, I bailed out and ran round to face the machine hoping there would be some kind of clue on the panel. Traffic was streaming through on all sides, barely pausing as the row of automated arms oscillated wildly in a demented Mexican wave (what would a demented Mexican do?). Round at the passenger side the machine showed its contempt by sticking out its tongue. Aha! A ticket protruded from a low slot, cunningly positioned beneath the eye-line of the passenger door. I plucked it delicately between finger and thumb, which immediately raised the barrier. *Aaaargh!* Scuttling back to the van, I threw myself into the seat, looping safety belt over one arm while slamming the door and starting the engine, expecting a karate chop through the roof in punishment for my tardiness as we squeaked through. I don't know how those things work, are they on a timer or use sensors to tell them when a vehicle is clear? I was just glad that Delta-J wasn't following along behind to be decapitated.

Now I had to find a way off this impressively smooth and scarily fast stretch of road, that effectively concealed all of the interesting countryside it blasted through. There were no pleasant shady trees and the temperature rose alarmingly as the sun reached its zenith, blazing through the windscreen at me. *Jeez, it was hot!* Already tired from the ferry crossing and stressed by uncertainty, a growing headache was beginning to pound my overworked brain as the heat sapped energy and added dehydration to my discomfort. Finally a rest area appeared and I drove gratefully in to a cheerless expanse of car park, scattered with concrete benches among barren patches of dry grass. A torpid mix of heat and carbon monoxide lay heavy in the air as traffic thundered by, melting tarmac sticky underfoot. There were no trees, no shade and no respite. You would have to be desperate to stop there, and I was.

It felt like a microwave inside the van as the sun beat down on the thin metal shell. Leaving the windows open, I crawled into the back and flopped out on the bunk, sucking from a bottle of tepid water that did little to ease my thumping headache. But exhausted though I was, sleep just wouldn't oblige and drifted teasingly at the edge of my consciousness. I lay there roasting for a couple of hours, too hot to sleep yet too tired to move on, finally being roused by the call of nature and plodded over to the toilet block, which had clearly been modelled on the Black Hole of Calcutta. I've seen cow sheds cleaner than that! Suffice to say, the filthy squat hole did nothing to improve my fragile state of mind. Back on the tropical boredom of the toll road, we headed in a Chartres, Orleans, Bourges kind of direction, eventually escaping its clutches somewhere around Vierzon, where I hung out of the passenger window to be mugged of twelve euros by the ticket machine.

It was a great relief to be back on country roads fringed in leafy shade, a delicious reprieve from the brutal heat of the motorway. I began to perk up considerably as the landscape grew more curvaceous and inspiring, threading our way over hill and vale studded with ancient towns and villages, rich with character. This was more like it! Evening was drawing in and soon I would have to find somewhere to spend the night. Not being completely au fait with my satnav, I didn't realise it could direct me to such useful places as campsites, fuel stations and supermarkets if requested, but life is nothing if not a learning curve. By happy chance a picnic area appeared as we rolled down a long and heavily forested hill, so I stopped for a break and to find exactly whereabouts we were on the map. A thick hedge screened the lay-by from the road, and small trees provided pleasant shade for the few picnic tables set among them, overlooking a river valley. Wearied by stress and uncertainty, 300 miles had elapsed fuelled by fear and momentum alone, and this simple lay-by provided an oasis of calm that was most gratefully received. The sun's rays were gentle after the searing heat of the day, and I stretched out barefoot in T-shirt and shorts to bask in the mellow evening glow. It was the perfect spot to spend the night.

I woke from an excellent sleep at 07:00 and parted the curtains to view the new day. The sun was still hidden below the horizon, and thin veils of mist hung softly between the contours of the hills. Not a ripple disturbed the course of the river Cher, shining like a mirror in perfect reflection of the pale light of dawn. It was cold inside the van. I snuggled back into my sleeping bag and snoozed again, but an hour later my little tin house was cooking as the sun's rays beamed in full effect against our hillside. Time to get up! Savouring the modest triumph of 300 miles unscathed, I rewarded myself with a leisurely breakfast at the picnic table, and reviewed the route of yesterday's nightmare on the map. Later, standing at the back of the van brushing my teeth, a car pulled in behind us and after a brief pause continued abruptly on its way. I had to laugh, imagining the poor monsieur confronted by a skinny barefoot foreigner apparently foaming at the mouth.

Fully rested and revitalised after a good night's sleep, I was in much better shape to deal with whatever lay before us, and at least I had some idea of what to expect now – unlike yesterday. I almost chickened out in Le Havre, I was so scared. It'd been a major test of my resolve, and surviving the first stage completely clueless was now a confidence boost – things could only get better! I tidied my living quarters then attended to the business end of my heroic little van, topping up oil and water and checking the tyres. And thus we set out in search of Millau.

Diversions and street markets (of which there are many in France), completely flummoxed the satnav, eliciting repeated demands of *Turn around when possible* in a tone that seemed to grow increasingly irate. The stubborn device was determined to herd us through the barricades, but I soon learned to head off in the nearest available direction until the querulous voice fell silent and grudgingly worked out a new route. No doubt the total mileage was substantially increased by frequent unplanned excursions into the wilds, trusting to the whims of my electronic companion – I didn't know where we were most of the time – but I couldn't have made it by map reading alone. My poor van has been in places it was never meant to go!

Driving in busy urban areas is a real pet hate of mine, even when I know where I'm going. After being directed through heavy traffic in the stifling heat of several town centres, I developed a new method of navigation to allay my growing anxiety. The satnav was merely fulfilling the instructions it received. It couldn't know that the bag of nerves in the driving seat only wished to head in the *direction* of large towns en route, and definitely not plough straight through the middle. Picking our way south on the map, I aimed instead for small villages in the general vicinity, hoping to stop quietly and plan evasive action for the upcoming conurbations. If nowhere suitable was available, I tried to stop on the outskirts and re-route to avoid being sucked into the manic queues of traffic ahead. It didn't always work but at least I was growing accustomed to the foibles of my navigator.

We edged our way south through the Dordogne and Limousin on quiet back roads dripping in mist, snaking through a rising landscape of densely wooded hills and dark pine forests where tiny communities appeared at random with never a soul to be seen. Rugged volcanic heights gave way to flowing slopes of vineyards, ascending anew into the overcast as directions for Millau began to appear at the road side. Driving down a steep approach road towards the town spread at the foot of a massive vertical rock face, there up ahead in the murk twinkled a delicate web spun across the valley – the *Viaduc de Millau* – YES!

France is a great country for touring. Most towns have well-equipped municipal campsites, and Millau being a tourist centre for the spectacular Tarn gorge provided an embarrassment of riches for the weary traveller. There were many signs for *Campings*, which I followed to the edge of town and over a wide bridge above the river. The commercial-looking family orientated sites with garishly coloured play parks, pools and bars were definitely not my idea of fun, driving on by to shortly discover a quiet site on the riverbank, a spacious plot among the trees where ducks waddled freely in the grass. Perfect. I chose a spot near the water's edge as an evening drizzle began to close in, but I really didn't care. We were here, safe in Millau. I'd actually done it.

Water rats swam powerfully, ploughing furrows across the current (*water rats* being a general term for these stocky brown-furred aquatic rodents, considerably larger than the average rat). A squadron of small white storks came gliding overhead, inbound to a thick reed bed forming an island in mid-stream where assorted wildfowl were gathering to roost. I prepared my own roost in the back of the van, doors propped open to accommodate the riverside view, and stretched out on my bunk wallowing in a rare sense of achievement. A pan of beans and sausages bubbled disrespectfully on the gas, my typically English *cordon-bleugh* somewhat shameful in this land of haute cuisine. I promised to do better tomorrow. The grey mizzle softly deepened into dusk, bringing with it a flight of bats easily as big as my hand. I stood on the bank watching enthralled as they skimmed the surface of the water, zipping round at speed on a silent flicker of dark wings, and coming so close as to almost brush me as they whizzed by. How cool is this!

A rustic outbuilding housing the wash room was the next port of call, where I enjoyed a long tepid shower by torchlight as heavy rain pattered on the roof. It was so wet outside by the time I'd finished, that I left my shirt and jeans in the bag and paddled back semi-clad in jacket and trainers. A water rat was putting in a late shift, a dark head just visible at the apex of ripples marking its course. The occasional *plop* echoed from the river: a leaping fish or the dive of a hidden rodent, it was impossible to tell, but I stopped to watch until it grew too dark to see. Lights glowed softly from the windows of elaborate motor homes parked among the trees, their occupants safely sealed inside with all the comforts of home, satellite dishes pointing at the heavens.

And there was me out in the night with my scruffy old van, standing half-dressed in the rain and loving every minute.

FRATERNISER
(MINGLING – IN FRENCH)

The following morning, I woke late from an excellent sleep and pulled back the curtains to find a grey overcast crowning my riverside view, but the rain had stopped and there were signs of a brighter day to come. Taking time out to look around was just what I needed after the long drive down; having been in France for two whole days with minimal interaction, now it was time to mingle. There's no denying that mingling is not my strong point. I'm one of those who hangs back from the crowd leaving the uninhibited and less socially inadequate to take centre stage, while I remain unheeded on the fringe. Yet despite my ingrained reticence and poor command of the French language, I felt remarkably perky as I walked over the bridge towards the town centre, keen to experience whatever the day had to offer.

Tree-lined avenues filled with lively market stalls awaited, thronged by a buzzing melting pot of humanity. Alone in the depths of France, I wallowed in a cosmopolitan sea of dialects and cultures, surrounded by cheerful faces of ebony to ivory and every shade in between. Expecting nothing more than to immerse myself in ordinary every-day French life, the diverse reality of Millau came as a total surprise. My lack of linguistic ability was of no great consequence after all, and a hesitant gambit garnered friendly smiles – this was terrific! Flowers adorned the town with colour, spilling from baskets, window boxes and planters, vivid blooms of subtle perfume that added to the sense of vitality. A sheer cliff face rose for several thousand feet on the far side of the river, crowned by a tall mast on its brow that was clearly visible between the streets, an excellent landmark with which to get my bearings. The day was growing uncomfortably hot, and some primeval island instinct kicked in, pulling me back towards the soothing flow of the river. Scrambling over an embankment below the busy road, I entered another world.

Yards away from bustling suburban streets, a quiet footpath followed the banks of the Tarn where the local wildlife went about their business undisturbed. The air was still and the heat grew heavy as I strolled beside the peaceful river envying the ducks and swans gliding through its cool waters, and I longed for the Atlantic breeze. In the distance, the elegant *Viaduc* spanned the valley above the town, yet no matter how far I walked, like a mirage it remained tauntingly beyond my reach. Time had flown by. Outpaced by an inanimate object, I had to admit defeat and followed the next set of steps back to the pavement above, emerging at the foot of a bridge crossing the weir. A supermarket peeped between the trees on the other side of the river, and suddenly feeling hot and thirsty I made a spur of the moment decision to pick up some supplies. A dark loaf of locally made walnut bread, fresh ham and a tub of apple ice cream crammed into my small backpack, seemed like a good idea at the time. My knees were beginning to complain, and reality whacked me round the head with a loaf of walnut bread as I crossed the weir towards the town – and realised just how far I had to walk back!

Fatigue had kicked in when about an hour later I found myself staring stupidly at my van parked on the opposite bank, having traipsed all the way back along the river and completely missed the bridge! I don't usually swear. My lapse in concentration added another hour by the time I retraced my steps and crossed the big-wide-blatantly-obvious bridge back to the campsite. Footsore and weary, I flopped gratefully in the back of the van and made myself a late lunch of melted ice cream mopped up with chunks of walnut bread.

A mallard couple, a duck and a drake, waddled up the sandbank from the river and settled themselves companionably by the back tyre, beneath my balcony. They were experienced operators wise to the ways of visiting tourists, and happy to exploit their aquatic charm in the hope of some edible reward – they knew an easy target when they saw one! Tired from the heat and my extended walk, I was honoured by their company and only too pleased to pass the time with them. We shared the ham and walnut bread (crusty and deliciously nutty, but enough about me). My feathered friends conversed sporadically with soft quacks and mutual preening, until overcome by the languid heat of the afternoon, they rested their heads on their backs to snooze peacefully in the grass. The river flowed by on its timeless course, and the distant rumble of traffic faded into the background of a lazy afternoon. Evening crept in. Madame et Monsieur Mallard roused themselves and after graciously accepting a final titbit in appreciation of their visit, waddled off and slid into the water with a comical waggling of tail feathers. Having been stuck in the van for several hours not wishing to disturb them, I could now unfold my legs and follow my guests (or had I been theirs?) to where a patch of pale sand formed a modest beach in the shallows.

A mother mallard sailed by, pursued by a large brood of ducklings: a flotilla of delightful fluffy bundles, little legs paddling like fury to keep pace with mum's effortless glide. I grabbed my camera from the van and sat barefoot on the sand, thrilled when they returned to clamber up the beach and check me out. How could I resist! The remains of bread and ham were well received and they kept me company until the sun dipped below the mountains. Mother duck returned to the water and sailed serenely towards the island, trailing a ragged line of frantically paddling fluff-balls cheeping plaintively in her wake. The sky was so clear after last night's rain, the fresh mountain chill in the air made a welcome relief from the soporific heat of the day. I sat on the riverbank supremely content, dangling my feet in the water as light began to fade on a magical day that wasn't over yet, as frogs began to trill and the bats arrived to catch their evening meal. Who needs television.

My mission for the following day was to get up close and personal with the town's famous *viaduc*. As luck would have it, I arrived with unexpected ease at a large tourist information centre (I'm not a large tourist but I hoped they wouldn't mind), outside of which stood a special bus stop for guided tours of the *viaduc*. I managed to say something coherent to the helpful lady inside, and she exchanged my proffered euros for a ticket on the next scheduled departure. It was all going great so far! At the appointed hour, I joined my fellow tourists boarding a smart open-topped bus for a pleasant ride through the centre of Millau, before ascending along a steeply twisting road to the top of the gorge. Teasing glimpses of the *viaduc* between the hills gave the impression of sneaking up on it from behind, as if we might scare it away. The delicate web grew steadily in stature, ultimately revealed in all its glory as a mighty beast of engineering construction that dwarfed the town and river, 800 feet below. Its size deceived all sense of distance – no wonder I couldn't get near it on foot!

The bus stopped on a raw plateau carved at the foot of the motorway, a future rest area in the making. Following our guide, we crowded round the edge of a precipice to view the road stretching out towards the first giant pillar rooted deep in to the earth, a ribbon of tarmac curving gracefully across the void towards the flank of the Causse Rouge, 2,460 metres away. Built to withstand wind speeds in excess of 150 mph, the sheer strength of this massive structure was now plain to see, yet from a distance its simple elegance belies such magnitude. It's magnificent. We goggled at a wide panorama of distant mountain tops, and the miniature Millau nestling in the valley beside the river Tarn, all crowned by a tiara of engineering triumph. Who would have thought that a motorway could be so interesting! I was very surprised to learn that the large birds which I'd assumed to be buzzards soaring on the afternoon thermals, were actually vultures. All too soon we were rounded up and herded back to the bus, but instead of heading back to town as expected, it turned down a steep narrow track through a security gate beneath the road, taking us to the foot of the nearest gigantic pylon. We craned our necks to grab photos of the road suspended high above, a most imposing sight from this unique perspective. While my limited translation skills had no hope of keeping pace with the commentary, the visual spectacle of the tour surpassed all expectation and I was thrilled.

Safely deposited back in the centre of town, a celebratory

ice cream was in order. A park bench provided the perfect spot to enjoy a large chocolate cone amidst a colourful fusion of flowers, freshened by plumes of water jetting from a nearby fountain. Among the change from my purchase was an exceptionally shiny ten cent piece, which I've kept in my pocket ever since. It reminds me of that marvellous day on my first solo trip abroad, and the rare sense of achievement in doing something that I hadn't believed I could do.

Leaving Millau the next day for another long day's drive through spectacular scenery, the satnav guided my gallant little van to Bois de la Pierre where we received an amazing welcome from the Gyro Club. They really are the nicest people. Great effort was made to ensure the lone Anglaise was well taken care of for the whole weekend, and I had to promise to take Delta-J with me next time. After successfully returning to Le Havre and completing my practice run with both wing mirrors still intact, I had no excuse. She shall go to the ball.

Turn Around When Possible...

Sometime during that first solo run to the south of France, my original old satnav became known as Ethel. With a lifelong habit of talking to inanimate objects, having one that actually answered back (after a fashion) was most appealing to my offbeat sense of humour. Satnavs are predominantly an audio aid and I rarely look at the screen while driving. My new navigator possessed a variety of voices available for verbal instruction, and experimenting with its vocal chords proved that a lower-pitched female tone was the most audible while on the move, but there was nothing premeditated about how Ethel got her name. Six hundred miles of terse navigational demands delivered in a stern headmistress type manner began to make me feel somewhat delinquent at every wrong turn or missed junction – and there were a few! A random snippet from an old novelty song surfaced from the depths of ancient memory and slotted itself into the internal music system of my brain. It was *The Streak* by Ray Stevens, which includes the line 'Don't look, Ethel!' Why on earth had that been retained in my memory banks? For some inexplicable reason, the previously forgotten refrain now played constantly in reply to every impatient command from my navigator, and so the name stuck.

Subsequent episodes over multiple hundreds of miles had showcased Ethel's more eccentric side, hence the eventual purchase of Satnav-2. Fully aware of what chaos would ensue if I had to negotiate my way through France by map reading alone, I thought it wise to invest in a backup. Despite the arrival of this upstart younger model, Ethel still reigned supreme in the navigator's chair. Eight years of technological global positioning progress since her manufacture had seen fit to remove my favoured *limited speed* option, meaning that my streamlined super-hot new satnav only looked for the shortest or fastest routes. Where's the fun in that, and what the heck is an *Eco-route,* anyway?

Over a decade later and having grown increasingly erratic, Ethel is now languishing in semi-retirement, relegated to the reserves as a backup. Oddly, the newer version hasn't developed a personality, despite guiding us over several thousand miles since the day that Ethel had to be substituted en route – and what a début that was! With my gyroplane in tow, we were deep inside wine country of the Dordogne, sweltering in a humid torpor that hung heavily over an endless wave of vine covered hills. Up ahead, a solid mass of thundercloud darkened the horizon, topped with towering sunlit peaks that boiled high into the heavens on a maelstrom of violent energy. Lightning cracked silently in the distance, cleaving the bruise-coloured sky with bolts of jagged heat. There was a sense of growing pressure, as if the weight of gathering fury was squeezing the very life from the air. Something wicked this way comes...

Ethel chose her moment with perfection, suddenly diverging from what seemed to be a reasonable course and shot us further out into the sticks along narrow lanes too insignificant for classification. I had no choice but to trust her. No matter how random the routes seemed to be, she always delivered in the end, smugly announcing 'You have reached your destination' as if to say *I told you so!* But this time she'd totally lost the plot. Daylight dimmed to an ominous gloom as I stuck cautiously to the convoluted twists and turns demanded by my navigator, suspicion rising with every increasingly familiar junction that reappeared through the rain. We were definitely going round in circles. Given the surging mass of static swamping the signal and tickling her circuits, I couldn't really blame Ethel, but this was pointless – we had to stop and regroup. Providence supplied an empty lay-by which I almost missed in the downpour, the headlights catching it just in time and we stopped abruptly, grateful for any port in the storm. It was wild out there! Poor Delta-J was barely visible behind and I wondered if her prominent mast would bring the lightning, but in any case there was nothing to be done. It was in the lap of the gods and four pairs of rubber tyres to keep us from being fried.

All the usual tricks and even the last resort of the reset button failed to bring Ethel out of her flat spin, so there was nothing for it but to bring on the substitute. A sad moment for my faithful old navigator – but would the younger model be able to function any better with a raging storm overhead? Stuck in the middle of nowhere, alone in the depths of France on an anonymous back road being pounded by a monsoon wouldn't have been my first choice scenario for testing a new satnav, quite frankly, but there we were. Satnav-2 was out to impress, speedily firing up as advertised and duly locked on to a healthy signal, much to my surprise. We'd lost about two hours thanks to inclement weather and Ethel's circular deviations, so as there was no clue as to what exactly an *eco*-route might be, my choice was limited to the shortest or the fastest, neither of which were particularly appealing but needs must.

Consequently we were guided out from under the storm through dark and dripping countryside to emerge some hours later in cheerful sunshine, the sodden tarmac steaming in its warmth. I can't recall which option I went for, but as it produced a most tortuous path of twists and turns that ate up six hours and a whole tank of diesel to cover a mere 200 miles, I guess it wasn't the fastest! My old van is economically excellent, even with a gyroplane on the back. One year, when France was in the grip of another strike with national fuel reserves seriously depleted, I managed a sedate drive (without the trailer) all the way from south of Toulouse back up to the north coast of Brittany on 38 litres. I love my van.

Back to Satnav-2's inaugural run. Having spent all day meandering giddily through deserted countryside, the last thing I expected was to be rudely catapulted off a pleasant and relatively quiet D road straight into three lanes of heaving rush hour traffic. Suddenly we were in the midst of mayhem on the Toulouse ring road at ten past four on a Friday afternoon before an extended weekend break – mon dieu! (OMG in French). There were only half a dozen junctions to negotiate to pick up our road going south, but it was well past six o'clock before we managed to break free. Endless streams of traffic converged on us from all sides, horns blaring in the gridlock as hundreds of impatient vehicles tried to muscle their way out of the city, eager to begin the long weekend. I gripped the steering wheel in terror as enormous lorries squeezed by with millimetres to spare, praying they wouldn't clip my vulnerable trailer. Stress! Crawling around the edge of Blagnac airport brought some welcome distraction as we inched on by, with a good view of a beautiful Air France Concorde parked outside a hangar. Then another distinctive shape appeared among the queue of passenger jets passing low overhead: the bloated body of a Beluga heavy-lift transporter, an unusual sight for my eyes.

Suffice to say, we arrived at the Gyro Club absolutely shattered and soaking wet, but gratefully still intact. Satnav-2 had saved the day but I was going to have to modify my approach with this one, and find a way to replicate the missing limited speed option. Towing Delta-J through the middle of motorway rush hour at the start of a bank holiday weekend, is not an experience that I want to repeat!

*

Apart from retaining more than a modicum of the French language between my ears, another frustrating mental block is my complete inability to reverse a trailer. Anything other than backing up in a more or less straightish line, I'm absolutely useless. I can get the trailer in the right place or I can get the van in the right place, but both together, not a hope. It's quicker to unhitch and push the darn thing to where I want it. I can handle five-ton forklift trucks of various configurations, and manoeuvre large pieces of multi-million pound aircraft safely through crowded hangars. I can shift Merlin main rotor blades stowed in containers 28 feet long by 5 feet wide, and stack them up 12 feet high – yet I can't reverse a simple trailer to save my life.

This rather serious deficiency in my skill set makes me very wary when towing down unfamiliar roads, especially when being led by a satnav that has no concept of vehicle size or driver incompetence. Here's your route, deal with it! Normally I don't mind getting a bit lost and discovering unexpected places off the beaten track, but not when my ability to *turn around when possible* is severely hampered by a gyroplane and trailer. We've been tied in some proper knots. The other drawback to being attached to gyroplane and trailer is that everybody stares. There's no stealth mode with this baby following along behind – *Oooh, what's that!* To be fair, I'd be exactly the same if I saw a flying machine in the high street, but it doesn't help matters when you've been directed through a busy town centre and fooled in to turning in to what appears to be a dead end.

This exact scenario happened in Saint-Pol-de-Léon, just a few miles from Roscoff. Driving through the town after a short detour for diesel, we arrived alongside a pedestrian square at the foot of a large and ancient church (which, with apologies to the good people of Brittany, I've since learned is actually a small thirteenth-century cathedral). 'Turn right' repeated my navigator, insistently. Slowing to a crawl reluctant to commit myself, I craned over the tops of parked cars at a row of shops that appeared to form an impenetrable right angle with the side of the church. Er? A quick glance at Ethel's screen confirmed that she did indeed want me to turn in to what looked like a pedestrianised square. A row of silver bollards denoted the edge of the road, which had otherwise disappeared beneath an open expanse of intricately laid flagstones merging with the pedestrian area. A stout transept protruded from the side of the church into the confines of the square, further reducing room to manoeuvre between the parked cars and regimented row of small trees. Surely this isn't right? My hesitation was causing something of a logjam behind my miniature convoy. I should have driven straight on and let Ethel catch up, but in a mild panic and not wishing to further delay those stuck behind, I pulled the trailer clear of the road to stop in the square, neatly blocking a line of parked cars. A narrow gap was now visible between the end of the shops and the church, along with some black and white version of a *no entry* sign planted at the end of the transept. There was no chance of turning round without unhitching the trailer, which was attracting some attention as usual. Why do I do these things to myself!

I could imagine a video appearing on the Internet in weeks

to come: *crazy-foreigner-causes-havoc-with-microlight-in-town-square!* Nothing is sacred these days. It's a sad world when first instinct is to stand idly by and record the misfortune of others, I don't understand the mentality. But anyhoo, there we were basically stuck, the van, the trailer and me. I grabbed Ethel and quickly reprogrammed for another route back to Roscoff, but no, she was determined to shoehorn us through that inadequate looking gap in the corner beyond what looked like a no entry sign. Just as I was about to unhitch the trailer and drag us out of there, a car pulled in alongside and without slowing, proceeded to vanish into the impossible gap in the corner, a bit like Hogwarts' platform nine-and-three-quarters. Where did he go? Steering warily towards the corner revealed a most convincing optical illusion, which now dissolved at our approach. The buildings parted like the Red Sea, exposing a narrow lane just wide enough to admit a single car - or a small van and trailer - which I now carefully threaded through the tight junction and headed back to Roscoff with a sigh of relief. Ethel was right as usual: it was nervous Nellie in the driving seat causing all the trouble.

Such is my fear when towing that I'm my own worst enemy. Early excursions trusting Ethel through the mountains had me barely managing to extract the van at times, and it would've been impossible with the trailer as well. Being fully aware of my pathetic reversing abilities when towing, I'm therefore very cautious about getting in to potential predicaments like the magic corner in cathedral square. To be fair, the satnavs have always got us to our destination - sometimes by the most tortuous and improbable of routes! - but we get there. So I've learned to adapt accordingly during our travels over the years. Now with a better understanding of my navigator's implacable computer logic, the responsibility for going 'off piste' is more apportioned around the 90/10 mark in its favour. *Turn around when possible...*

IT HAD TO BE DONE

Locked and loaded

And so my fifth visit to the annual meeting of the Gyro Club Toulouse, became a first for Delta-J. You can't carry a great deal in a Cricket, and sleeping under the wing is difficult so my trusty old van made a return trip to provide accommodation and do the donkey work. The rotor assembly had to be dismantled and packed in its box on the trailer, a lengthy process which has to be done in situ as I can't lift the box once the blades are in it! Once everything was loaded and strapped down, I assaulted Delta-J with an industrial sized roll of cling film, covering the engine and rotor head to protect them from the elements. Three weeks of adventure lay ahead of us, the plan being to leave her at the airfield after the event and tour around a bit by road, so we were heavily loaded with flying kit, various spares, tool boxes and fuel cans.

Now, it may seem a bit strange not to sightsee from the air after all that effort to get her down there, but the main objective was to keep the promise I'd made and take part in the festivities with Delta-J. I was perfectly happy to do a few flights with my new friends, and not push my luck by inadvertently infringing any unfamiliar regulations. While English is the globally accepted language in mainstream aviation circles, at the other end of the scale on the microlight frequencies of France, they naturally talk to each other in French. This is quite beyond me. Anyone listening would think Inspector Clouseau had arrived.

My little convoy was the source of great interest queuing for the ferry at Millbay docks. A short officer of advancing years arrived at the door as we waited our turn at security. With my rather extensive and unusual load I'd been expecting an inquisition, but not quite along the lines of what happened next. The back doors were opened to reveal just how much can be stuffed into a Vauxhall Combo, as I answered questions about hidden knives, fuel cans or gas bottles by indicating the stove and cutlery buried inside, and the empty fuel cans strapped to the trailer. That was all fine, it was the next bit that threw me. 'Are you carrying any tools or chainsaws?' I went back to the cab and dragged my toolbox out from behind the seat to display the contents, which he regarded with an overwhelming lack of enthusiasm. 'Any power tools or chainsaws?' he repeated hopefully. Trying to be helpful, I selected the extent of my lethal weaponry from the box, an admittedly pathetic offering of Stanley knife, tin snips and a junior hacksaw, but they just didn't cut it. 'No angle grinders, chainsaws...?' Nope! I almost wished I could produce a chainsaw for him and felt guilty for failing to pack any hardcore cutting equipment. He paid no attention to the trailer or what could be hidden inside my gyroplane (like a chainsaw!) and seemed quite deflated by my lack of destructive capability as he waved us through.

Another restless night was spent sliding out of my allotted seat, woken at intervals by complaining limbs to find myself wedged above the foot well. Vinyl covers may be practical for cleaning purposes, but they're not the best when trying to sleep on a slope! It seemed like no time at all before the lights came on and the shutters over the bow windows raised to reveal a new dawn. (That's *bow* as in front end of a ship by the way, not a bow-window. That would be weird, yet strangely appealing.) Ahead in the pale light lay the rocky coast of Brittany. The *Armorique* slipped easily through a gentle swell, gliding back to her home port from which several large trawlers were already heading out, white moustaches foaming at their bows.

A handful of passengers gathered to watch, among them a lone elderly gentleman whose journey was unbearably sad. Chatting to his neighbours the bewildered old chap asked for advice, and gradually the unhappy tale unfolded. Two weeks earlier he had lost his wife of almost fifty years, and after her funeral couldn't bear to return to their empty home. By now everyone was listening in sympathetic silence as he related how he had gone to a local travel agent and bought a ferry ticket for a two-week excursion. He knew nothing about the country, couldn't speak the language and didn't know where to go or what to do, yet that was preferable to being at home without his beloved wife. Bless that old man! I often wonder what happened to him, especially when we're sailing into Roscoff. I hope he found peace.

One really excellent way of spotting your vehicle parked among hundreds of others is to have a gyroplane fastened on the back. We followed the conga line of cars around the decks, down one ramp and up another, and there we were in France – *almost*. A group of gendarmes on the prowl between the disembarking vehicles immediately homed in on the trailer and surrounded it, gesturing eagerly at my gyroplane. 'ULM?' (the French microlight class, which includes gyroplanes) Oui, un autogire. 'Ah! Rotax?' Oui. 'Bon! You fly?' – this in English accompanied by vigorous flapping motions. Oui, bien sûr! They spent several minutes passing round the photos that I cunningly kept in the cab for such an eventuality, showing Delta-J in all her unwrapped and fully-assembled glory. The Gyro Club Toulouse sticker on the back of the van helped to establish that I was indeed heading south with only mechanical companions, which appeared to cause some concern and we gravely shook hands all round.

Mindful of their collective gaze, I steered carefully out of the docks grateful that they hadn't spotted the lack of headlight adjusters (which I'd forgotten to fit after the comedy with the chainsaw enthusiast), and in a mild panic managed not to turn left around the roundabout. Before we went any further I needed to check the trailer straps hadn't worked loose, and then attend to the headlights. British vehicles drive on the left, therefore our headlights aim to the left to avoid dazzling oncoming traffic on the right. This doesn't work in Europe where oncoming traffic is on the left, hence the need – quite a serious and important need – to deflect British headlight beams from dazzling oncoming European traffic. Correcting this potentially dangerous alignment is unbelievably hit and miss. Two semi-transparent vinyl stickers come with several yards of diagrams and instructions enough to cover every make and model of every vehicle on the road, and none of which is any help! With the best will in the world, there's no way of knowing if you've stuck them in the right place until nightfall, when the blaring horns and angrily flashing lights of oncoming traffic suggest that all may not be well. Getting it wrong can also impede your own illuminations, as I've found to my cost on several dark nights crawling through the wilds of France, eyes out on stalks trying to follow the edge of the road. Back in the car park, a helpful truck driver spotted me knelt in front of the headlights puzzling over a mass of diagrams, and came over to advise that putting the stickers in a seven o'clock position under the main bulbs would pretty much do the trick.

I really have to concentrate for the first hour after arriving in France. Wrong-side-of-the-road-mode comes surprisingly easy and I don't have a problem with it – except on foot! It's bonkers. Even now, all these years later, as soon as my feet touch a French pavement, I'm incapable of crossing the road without looking the wrong way. What makes it worse is that I *know* I'm going to do it. Is it so ingrained from Sixties childhood and the repeated chanting of Kerb Drill (Look right, look left, look right again, if all clear, quick march) that looking left before I look right defies all of my adult concentration. Analyse that...

Thankfully I've no such confusion at the wheel, what requires my full attention is driving in *kilometres* per hour instead of miles. The universal speed limit through every French town and village is 50 kph (which handily equates to 30 mph), displayed on a big circular sign with a big number 50 on it. Do not forget that we're now on the metric scale and blast through the charming petite ville at 50 miles per hour, scattering grandma's baguettes and toppling grandpa off his bike into the vegetable patch. It doesn't leave a good impression. Ironically, no matter where I go as I carefully adhere to the speed limit, everyone goes tearing past, no doubt cursing the lazy foreigner for holding them up. (In the years since I wrote up this trip, the fashionable curse of the 20 mph limit with its rash of infuriating speed bumps has infected both British and French towns alike.)

Approaching uphill to a T junction about an hour out of Roscoff, directly in front on the other side of the road is a big lay-by. Several box vans were parked there and the crews were standing around smoking and chatting casually to a couple of gendarmes. Ethel demanded a left turn as we pulled up at the junction, poised on the brow of the hill. All eyes turned towards the van and the strange projection half hidden behind it, as we waited to cross. Arms began waving and smiling faces called for us to stop. I thought it best to oblige as gendarmes were present, unsure if this was something official to be complied with – happily my headlights were legal now! I pulled in behind the box vans wreathed in a strong aroma of fish, and hopped out. The excitable group converged upon my trailer all talking at once, and after the obligatory hand shakes, the conversation went much the same way as it had at the docks. *What was it, did I fly it, where were we going,* etc. I removed the cover so they could see the cockpit, and once again the Rotax engine was correctly identified, suggesting a wider familiarity with microlight aviation. One chap climbed up on the trailer especially to point at the spark plugs, telling me that the French word was 'bougie'. That's one of the few I can remember! It was getting on for half an hour by the time the photos had been handed round, and we all needed to make a move, Delta-J's admirers being on their way back from delivering the morning's catch, which explained the fishy perfume. We all shook hands again and went our separate ways, leaving the big lay-by that's now become one of my landmarks on the journey south, namely *Fish Van Junction.*

Keeping a wary eye out for potential ambush by toll road, we took a leisurely drive in to the heat of the day, tracking parallel to the coast with the occasional glimpse of distant ocean. Road signs indicated famous names from those terrible years of the U-boat war: Brest, Lorient, La Rochelle, and of course St Nazaire and the courageous sacrifice of HMS *Campbeltown*, a suicide mission that sailed from Falmouth, near my Cornish home. Centuries of fascinating history in every direction. We stopped halfway down to camp overnight at Saintes, on the river Charente, and tomorrow we turn inland. From here on, the scenery gets more interesting after the relatively bland landscape of the Vendée and Charente-Maritime. The terrain grows increasingly hilly through the woods and vineyards of Dordogne and Aquitaine, before we drop due south, eager for that first glimpse of Pyrenean skyline.

France is such a refreshingly air-minded country, and for a gyronaut in particular, Bois de la Pierre is the icing on the cake. To actually be there with my own gyroplane was a whole other level, and I couldn't quite believe it as I pushed the trailer back between the hangar and the clubhouse to make camp for the night. Who would've thought, me and Delta-J *in the South of France!* And thus we were discovered later the following day, as I untied multiple straps and covers, unwrapped yards of grimy cling film, and sorted through a mound of kit. What a welcome, they were so delighted we had made it – and so was I! They hadn't seen a British designed single-seat gyroplane in the flesh, and without fail she drew the same three reactions in exactly the same order. First impression, invariably 'How small and cute she is!' French gyroplanes have big wheels for rough ground handling, and tall masts to accommodate large propellers. A second glance, and the glaring deficiency is all too obvious: 'Why do you not have a tail plane?' I have yet to see a French *autogire* without a tail plane, and our distinct lack of tail feathers caused great consternation among our new friends, a fire that continued to burn unabated until we were later able to join them in the twenty-first century.

The third (and inevitable!) reaction to my petite red bird was that the British are quite insane – and who could argue? Fastened inside the pod of my tiny single-seat open cockpit flying machine, as per British regulations is a *No smoking* sign. The hilarity was absolute. They do not allow a horizontal tail plane, yet you must have a *No smoking* sign! I couldn't explain it either. Jean Marie was keen for us to fly together so he could show me his home and village, but I still had some work left to finish before we could join him. Thierry very kindly (and very insistently!) insisted that I stay with him and his family for the duration so with Delta-J safely installed inside the hangar, we called it a day.

The blustery grey humidity of Saturday gave way to the much brighter humidity of Sunday. The countryside is just fantastic, so much open space everywhere and the majesty of the Pyrenees on the horizon. They were the clearest I had ever seen them during that first week, and I couldn't take my eyes off them as Thierry drove us back to the airfield. He had some adjustments to do on his own single-seat gyroplane, which involved removing the top cog of the pre-rotator shaft with an angle grinder. It was best not to look. Xavier pulled out the AX05 and treated us to a joyful beat up in the stiff breeze, almost achieving vertical take off and having a great time zooming all over the field.

Later that evening he switched to his single-seat machine, joined by Jean Marie and Pierre to practice their routine for the forthcoming festival. A comical exchange followed as Pierre's concerns about an engine problem were apparently dismissed, and he reluctantly trundled out as leader. It's always a pleasure to watch these three fly, a lovely demonstration of skill and experience in half a dozen passes and position changes, but it soon became clear that Pierre's machine wasn't performing as it should. Xavier and Jean Marie were struggling to stay in position above him, and a low downwind pass along the runway saw Pierre land abruptly while his wingmen carried on around the circuit. His engine lost power (fortunately in a good spot), and willing hands helped push the machine back to the hangar. Later everyone gathered in the clubhouse for one of those spontaneous moments that are such an integral part of the Gyro Club. Mario and his wife brought champagne and nibbles to share in celebration of his newly completed gyroplane, and a genial hour was spent in honour of his achievement.

During the winter, I'd given Delta-J a bit of an overhaul, including a rework of the instrument panel to fit another gauge.

I wanted to double check everything before we fired up, and make sure nothing had dropped off en route – not that I would be going back to look for it! First there was a small matter of 680 miles worth of road grime to be scrubbed off, *tedious* being the appropriate word for that one. Next up: put the finishing touches to the wiring, install a new four-point harness, and change her tyres for a lightweight pair. Having confirmed that all requisite hardware was still present and correct and suitably torqued, I assembled the rotor blades ready to be bolted on to the head (the last bit requires muscles that I don't have), and we were almost good to go. The traditional male and female roles are still much in evidence among the older generations, and the sight of a female wielding a spanner seemed to be quite a novelty, causing some good-natured amusement. Armand and Jean Marie appeared in the afternoons to continue preparing the field, aided by Gaby who took charge of strimming the verges. Tough brambles along the driveway were quickly dispatched with a can of petrol and a match. A huge lorry arrived and deposited a beast of a road roller, with which they spent hour upon hour lumbering up and down the runway. Hangars trembled and the ground literally shook with the weight of the thing. What a whopper.

By Wednesday evening, I was ready to test fly. There was a heavy overcast and feisty wind, the portents of a predicted storm but I only needed a few circuits to check the instruments worked correctly and ensure that nothing important fell off. Instead, the air ambulance arrived ('That's service!' I thought) and proceeded to practice circuits and engine-outs over the runway for the next hour, by which time the darkening cloud base had lowered with ominous intent. The wind blasted across the airfield, rattling hangars and battering the windsock, which writhed and flapped against its pole like a fish on a hook. I do love a good wind through my rotors, but this was just a little excessive. With Delta-J safely tucked up in the hangar, I drove back to Thierry's house under a dramatic purple sky, accompanied by deep rumblings as distant lightning flickered angrily around the mountains.

Thursday was scorchio. Final preparations were about to begin in earnest for the fête, and I needed to get Delta-J checked out as Jean Marie wanted us to fly with him in the evening. It was lunchtime. The sweet fragrance of cut grass hung in the air, and all was quiet except for the constant trilling of insects, and a light breeze rustling through the corn. The sky had recovered its composure from the turmoil of the night, and the Pyrenees shimmered in the heat beneath an infinity of clearest blue. I worried about the humidity. My carburettors were perfectly tuned for fresh Atlantic air, and I didn't trust myself to meddle with their settings. Just as I feared, the engine temperature rose rapidly as we taxied to the far end of the runway, our four-inch wheels bouncing painfully over the hard baked earth. We took off in a confetti of grass cuttings and I kept her low along the runway, fixated on the engine gauges before pulling up into the circuit – and what a spectacular view! When I flew with Xavier a few years earlier, the mountains had been completely hidden in the prelude to another storm. Not today! It was hard to concentrate on the job in hand and not gaze at the amazing panorama to the south.

Three tentative circuits later, we jolted our way back to the parking area and shut down. The exhaust gas temperature gauge wasn't fully operational, but that was an easy fix with only one combination of connections left to try. Regardless of whatever I'm doing, when several options are available it's a sure-fire bet that I'll only discover the right one after first trying all the wrong ones. I'm consistent if nothing else. Coolant temperature was on the high side as expected, the conditions being considerably warmer than anything experienced at home. Propeller pitch seemed a bit too fine and she needed more roll trim on the right, but generally all was good. I removed the instrument panel and swapped the connections around, then pulled the roll trim up another link on the rotor head. Back to the end of the runway and off we went again: this was much better, although the propeller definitely needed more bite. We flew another three circuits and a hands-off pass just for the hell of it, mindful that it was lunchtime and the villagers may not be so delighted.

Jeannine had appeared, the first of the volunteers for the afternoon's toil, and she was comically thrilled to have seen us in the air. I parked Delta-J in the shade of the hangar and left her to cool, putting my tools away ready to start work when the boss arrived. I joined Jeannine for a sunny stroll along the runway while we waited, picking up the odd stone from the grass and flinging it aside. Jean Marie turned up shortly after, berating me in jest that he'd missed seeing us fly - he hadn't missed much. And so we set to work. All the wooden stakes needed repainting, slapping on whitewash and propping them against the wall to dry, which didn't take long in the afternoon heat. I was roasting inside my pair of borrowed overalls. The gigantic road roller continued rumbling back and forth along the runway, while Xavier's crew prepared the flagpoles on the far side. We fetched and carried and lifted and shifted as directed by Jean Marie, and the blazing afternoon passed quickly in a flurry of activity. An impromptu hangar meal was arranged for the workers that evening, Louis and Jean Louis being dispatched to town for supplies.

At 18:30 I stopped work to scrub dirt and paint from grimy paws and prepare Delta-J for action - Jean Marie was eager to fly and 19:00 was zero hour. Armand was coming with us in his BMW powered Air Copter, although he would take a different route on return. I was nervous: these guys are very experienced and I didn't want to let them down. With no map or radio, we deciphered a flight briefing between us using a combination of Jean Louis's few words of broken English and my shattered French. It was a gorgeous evening to fly, a warm breeze gently wafted the windsock and the mellowing sun bathed the countryside in golden hues. We three lined up on the runway, Jean Marie leading with me in the middle, and away we went.

Pulling into a hard climbing turn, we formed up on him downwind before swooping back in a low pass along the runway for everyone who had gathered to watch. A wider turn-out at the end and we settled into an easy cruise towards the east and the village of Montesquieu Volvestre. The scenery was breathtaking: a vast carpet of countryside spread to the horizon for as far as the eye could see, towns and villages widely scattered among its contours, colours vivid in the evening sun. Lakes gleamed like mirrors, and above it all rose the pastel peaks of the Pyrenees, a colossal barrier across the southern sky. *Am I really doing this?!* Delta-J was alive in my hands, skittish in the thermals that lifted us on an invisible swell, the busy flutter of the rotors singing in my ears. Armand was on our left, his yellow Air Copter easily keeping pace with the two smaller machines. Jean Marie bravely beckoned me in to fly closer alongside, holding his thumb aloft in mute enquiry which I happily returned in reply. We crossed a cluster of artificial lakes beside a long and impressively straight length of motorway that cut through the landscape like a fold in a map. Flying rather too low for my liking over a curving loop of river, we skirted the edge of a small town cradled at the foot of a range of hills that rose up to meet us on the other side of the plain.

Jean Marie dropped lower as we followed a tree-lined avenue running parallel to the hills on our left, the orange and white bands on his rotor blades made the disc superbly visible. He pointed ahead to what I assumed to be our target area and swooped even lower - it looked about 200 feet - we weren't going down there! Remembering the photos that he'd shown me previously, I suddenly recognised the house, set back from the road and perched halfway up a steep hill. The neighbours must be accustomed to dive-bombing as he zoomed all over the property at what seemed like roof top height, following the contours of the hill. Circling above with Armand, I stayed at 600 feet, which still felt uncomfortably low as the high ground reared up beneath our wheels. With a final roof-rattling pass across the gardens, Jean Marie popped out of the trees and climbed up in a wide spiral to meet us. Armand waved farewell and peeled away to the south-west, his yellow gyroplane brilliantly framed against the mountains in the sunlight.

Jean Marie's machine is lightweight and simple with an air-cooled Rotax 503 driving a tall two-bladed propeller, and he was steaming along with the wind now on our tails. My Dragon Wings were a handful at anything over 60 mph and I had to be delicate on the controls as we raced to keep up. I would loved to have taken some photos but at that speed I didn't dare let go of the stick! After twenty minutes or so we crossed the trees at the end of the runway and roared down its length, curving back into a tight circuit and landing line astern in a flurry of cut grass. Parking up and securing our rotor blades we grinned at each other like loons, Jean Marie beaming from ear to ear - he was as excited as I was - that was awesome!

A Coyote microlight stood idling on the grass as I stowed my flight gear back in the van, and Jeannine was calling me: Gérard was waiting to take me flying. I squirmed up into the boxy fabric-covered high-wing and off we went again, Gérard handing me the controls and pointing out local landmarks to help me learn the area. The two-stroke powered Coyote whirred along like a little lawnmower, very light on the controls, it responded nicely to my touch. Gérard took us out along the river Garonne, flying low above the water and chasing its contours through the fields. The mountains looked spectacular in the evening light, shadowy crags and ridges accentuated in stark relief by the brightness of the snow. The twin fishing lakes at Peyssies make a useful landmark for returning to the airfield, as Gérard showed me the way to go home. Coming in on final approach, the wind had dropped to a whisper, but the low sun dazzled us with crazed patterns through the distortion of the windscreen, so Gérard made a wise decision to land on the reciprocal heading. A most enjoyable and unexpected treat, and very kind of Gérard to share his aircraft with me.

Everyone had worked hard all afternoon and while the lucky ones took their toys out of the hangar to play, the others relaxed around the clubhouse watching the action. The sun was low in the west, its gentle rays like warm honey as the last engine faded into silence and we took our places at the table, set outside the main hangar. There was half a melon each, followed by a huge platter of sausages, fresh bread, tomatoes, cheeses, crisps and plenty of wine, followed by chocolate mousse and coffee for dessert. Still buzzing from the flights, I sat comfortably full of food, surrounded by good friends on a beautiful evening, and felt a profound sense of contentment.

Friday was HOT in capital letters (this is a relative term by the way. I'm English - anything over 18°C is hot!). Several motor homes were already in residence and a steady stream of visitors arrived during the day, some with gyroplanes in tow. My first job was to coarsen the propeller by a degree and give it a bit more bite. It was only ten o'clock but already stifling inside the hangar, not a breath of air. I pushed Delta-J outside in the shade, not that it made much difference, and people kept coming over to greet us, which was lovely but distracting! Many of us only see each other at this time of year. The Club's extended family arrives from all over Europe, and there's much to catch up on in a short intense weekend as old friends are reunited, and new friendships forged.

Again we were busy working all day, putting the finishing touches to the airfield under the eagle eye of Jean Marie. A heavy old farm wagon was dragged out and placed beside the runway, wrapped in tarpaulins and disguised with briefing boards to act as commentary position. The dozen or so resident gyroplanes were pushed and pulled across the runway to form the beginnings of a flight line, while the now empty hangar was filled with long rows of tables and chairs. A steady flow of motor homes arranged themselves sociably in the camping area, and there was much laughter as friends old and new welcomed each other. By evening there were about thirty gyroplanes on the flight line, with the promise of more to come as the weekend forecast was excellent. Everything was looking good. The light was exquisite on a perfect evening to fly but I didn't feel particularly good by then: how daft can you get – 32°C and I'd caught a cold!

Tired, hot and filthy, we sat down to another hangar meal with everyone in high spirits and the banter in full flow. The sound of approaching rotor blades grew louder and a landing light appeared suspended in the heavy dusk as a small helicopter somehow picked out the airfield from the surrounding darkness and settled on to the runway. Jean Marie shot out to greet the crew and bring them to the hangar, while chairs were shuffled around and two extra meals prepared with typical Gyro Club hospitality. The crew looked tired, but walked round the table shaking hands with everyone before sitting down to eat, recounting their journey to an appreciative audience. It was getting on for midnight when I crawled into the back of the van and found my bed.

I Can't Believe I Did That!

The early morning haze soon burned off as the sun returned with a vengeance. Armand and Jean Marie were out early as usual, organising every detail and dispensing hospitality with fresh coffee waiting in the clubhouse. My little van was now surrounded by a hamlet of tents and motor homes, slowly coming to life as the rattle of an idling Rotax issued a wake-up call from the other end of the runway. Returning from the flight line with Delta-J's covers, I was accosted by Jean Marie and herded into the clubhouse for a breakfast of coffee and cake. Some Belgian lads took the opportunity of a light breeze to practice two-wheel-balancing with their single-seat Guepards, and another unique single-seat machine took off for a wander round the plain. A spirited arrival from veteran gyronaut Jean Pierre Doleac blasting down the runway in his red Air Copter, got things under way in fine style. Ground marshals controlled the runway with coloured bats: green, you go – red, you don't. Simple, and it worked.

The flight line continued to grow with a brightly coloured droolfest of rotary-winged originality. It was a nice mix of amateur and commercially built machines, too. Jean Marie Enfissi provided some entertainment with his original Lycoming powered two-seater, although the heat was obviously affecting its performance – it wasn't doing mine much good either! Delta-J looked extremely petite tucked between the AX05 and another of Jean Pierre's Air Copter creations, my little bird the only one on the field not sporting any tail plumage. I spotted a familiar face having a crafty smoke in the back of a car, delighted to find John, Colin and Peter safely arrived courtesy of Squeezy Jet. The sun was blazing and we sheltered by the car from the relentless heat of a cloudless sky, happy to have found each other many miles from home.

Lunchtime was upon us but we decided to give it a miss, knowing full well that our stomachs would need all their spare capacity for the evening meal. The crowds began to disperse, either to dine in the hangar, or to picnic beside commodious motor homes. Some of those vans are so big that I could easily live in it and keep Delta-J in there as well, not that I'd fancy driving such a monster. I very much doubt they're getting fifty miles to the gallon! It was quite funny how everyone vanished as if on cue, so we took the opportunity to photograph the flight line while things were quiet. Spot the foreigners: mad dogs and English gyronauts out in the midday sun. *Les anglais sont fou...*

The afternoon passed without a great deal of activity compared to previous years, and even the locals admitted it was too hot! I covered Delta-J's fuel tank as a precaution against vapour lock (a condition that rarely concerned me at home), but the minimal shading made little difference in the afternoon heat. Petrol vaporises in high temperature and weakens the mixture in the carburettors, yet the French machines didn't seem to be affected and typically no one else appeared to worry. I had no intention of flying before such a large crowd anyway, happy just to watch and enjoy the music of free-spinning rotor blades. We spent most of the afternoon flopped out on the grass behind John's hire car, and it was here that Jean Marie dug me out of hiding, keen for his visitors to see the little red English machine in action. It was 17:00 but not discernibly cooler and I was reluctant to fly, yet equally reluctant to disappoint the friends who are so good to me. Only *cinq minutes,* he coaxed, and I found myself perched behind him on the quad bike, ferried over to the van to get my electric hat and swiftly deposited back beside my gyroplane.

I really hate doing displays. I never know what to do, so we just fly around aimlessly doing mundane manoeuvres as I refuse to risk Delta-J for entertainment value. John helped me to push her over to the far side next to the cornfield that marks the display area, where one of the Brakos was flying overhead. *Cinq minutes* seemed like an awful long time, and the coolant temperature climbed rapidly as we bumped our way to the threshold. Air traffic control had vanished, no coloured bats to be seen: I guessed they'd all run for cover, and who could blame them. A clearing turn showed the Brako away off to the right, nothing on approach and an empty runway ahead. Let's get it over with. I powered up, the rotor blades responding sluggishly as we jolted forward – there's a lot to be said for suspension – that road roller wasn't nearly big enough! We hammered over the grass and scrambled into the air, feeling the rotors losing their bite as we slid downwind over the cornfield. It was most uncomfortable, my attention divided between watching for traffic and the engine temperature gauge, which quivered disturbingly close to the red zone. Any gyrations we performed were purely for damage limitation, and probably too high for the watching crowd who were looking directly in to sun. I skidded Delta-J on to approach as soon as was polite, relieved to throttle back and remembering just in time to land on the far side, dropping short to clear the runway and shut her down as quickly as possible. Stress!

Then came the professionals. Xavier, Pierre and Jean Marie flying as the Patrouille did their formation take off and treated the attentive crowd to their special routine, albeit without the flag release. They landed together and taxied to the centre, facing the flight line to take their applause. Several more machines ventured up as afternoon faded into evening, including a pair of single-seat Mosquito helicopters driven by Rotax 503s, one open-framed and one enclosed; they displayed impressive agility with some very accurate flying. Not to be outdone, the Alouette screwed itself into the air, sandblasting everything in its path and gave us a twirl, looking large and ungainly after the dainty Mosquitoes. Proceedings began to wind down as evening drew in, the engines switched off and rotor blades tethered for the night. A tired crowd of happy people drifted back towards the hangar ready for dinner, the clubhouse bar doing a roaring trade. Seated in the midst of the voluble gathering, we four Brits chatted with difficulty to our neighbours, resorting to scribbling on the paper tablecloth when a particular word escaped us. A lot of fun and another late night.

Sunday dawned a smidgen cooler but just as bright and gorgeous. I started out for the flight line to unwrap Delta-J, waylaid en route by friendly people and diverted by Jean Marie waving the coffee pot at me. It was some time later when I emerged from the clubhouse perky with caffeine and lightly dusted in cake crumbs, to tend to my neglected bird. Then Francis appeared along with Jean Marie, asking us to take part in the mass fly out to another airfield that morning. *Er...* While it's an undeniably impressive sight watching safely from the ground, can I really trust myself to fly among ten other gyroplanes? It seemed I was about to find out. The field buzzed with activity and a new sense of purpose as they tried to round up the participants, and we were already half an hour behind schedule when everyone had been gathered for the flight briefing. I was exceedingly nervous: this was well out of my league, but Jean Marie had it all worked out. I would stay close to him as number two, while Pierre flying at number three would guard our tail, and duly sandwiched between the two veterans we would be shepherded to Cazères and back. I was very glad that I'd re-pitched the propeller.

We lined up on the runway, the first three in order and a free for all behind, a late addition taxiing rapidly to join on the end. Jean Marie looked across enquiringly - I held up my thumb and we were away. Stealing some extra lift from his prop wash I caught him in the turn and moved in on his left, Pierre and Daniel behind us as promised in the Subaru tandem, and a ragged string of gyroplanes taking off below. We took a wide circuit as the last few got airborne, turning in for a runway pass which must have looked spectacular with eleven machines in flight. Again I had no map and no clue of where we were going, trusting them completely and caught up in the moment, my fears forgotten with the thrill of it all. Rotor discs shimmered all around, left and right, above and below, the big machines weaving to keep pace with the little ones - what a fantastic sight! I kept us close to Jean Marie, periodically exchanging thumbs as we sailed through the fresh morning sky towards the imperious bulk of the mountains.

Having tracked south-west along the motorway we now

crossed over and headed for a cluster of artificial lakes, beyond which a range of darkly forested hills reared up from the plain to perhaps a thousand feet or more. As we approached the lakes, I spotted the cranked wings of a Jodel descending on our left, and Jean Marie was leading us on a parallel course, following it down. Imagine finding yourself suddenly pursued by a swarm of gyroplanes! Ahead at the foot of the hills lay a wide grass runway, tucked between the Garonne and a narrow man-made waterway. Keeping formation on Jean Marie we landed short and close to the edge of the spacious runway, making a rapid exit stage left as the others came in hot on our heels. I saw Xavier zoom past to land further down, with Yvan and Gilles bringing up the rear in the camera ship. Club members Eric and André had gone by car to meet us there, and they said it was like something out of Vietnam! Everyone was very excited. Personally, I couldn't believe what we'd just been part of, staring at tiny Delta-J parked among the line of exotic gyroplanes, mentally pinching myself and struggling with reality a million miles out of our comfort zone. If Chris and Tony could see us now...

After a group photo and some rather potent looking refreshment which I declined, we prepared to take up position on the runway, and with ten machines burning and turning ready to launch, Delta-J wouldn't start - *aaargh!* Something had shaken loose. Jean Marie was out of his seat and by our side in an instant, unhitching the recoil starter to fire her up with the lawnmower method, and we were off again. Chasing him down the runway and pulling a right hand climb out over a grassy embankment, we found ourselves flying across the middle of a lake at 200 feet - *jeez!* If the elastic had snapped we'd have been right in it. Whether it was the effect of refreshments or just keen to get back for lunch, our rotary-winged swarm was a little less cohesive on the way back, everyone having a wonderful time as Yvan and Gilles whizzed back and forth filming it all. The Gyro Club was easy to spot with its coloured flags and hamlet of motor homes, sunlight glinting on a forest of rotor blades lining the runway like a guard of honour. We followed Jean Marie in the obligatory low pass and swooped back over the cornfield to see a chaos of gyroplanes funnelling into the circuit and chasing us down - *woah!* Pierre and Daniel overtook us in the turn, and Armand appeared from nowhere on my right. I held back to make space for Pierre, and Armand swung wide to let us go first, the bigger machines starting to crowd us. Jean Marie landed at the far end closely followed by Pierre, I tucked us in behind and likewise landed long, faithfully shadowed by Armand. Two in front and eight up your rudder certainly focusses the concentration!

Somehow we all squeezed in and taxied quickly in single file along the edge of the runway as the others landed and tagged on in turn. We were now caught in an uncomfortable situation, trapped in the wake of Pierre's big Subaru. I watched anxiously as my rotors lost inertia, hoping he wouldn't need to rev up as a blast of prop wash could easily set them flapping. Boosting them with the pre-rotator wasn't an option with Armand close behind, and the extra load of driving the rotors was the last thing my engine needed. This slow conga line crawl was cooking it, pushing the temperature towards the red zone and inevitably the warning light came on, leaving me no choice but to shut down. I hopped out to secure the rotors, dragging Delta-J to her place in the centre of the runway as Jean Marie turned the line to face the crowd. That was awesome - *scary* - but awesome.

John and Colin were waiting for us as we slotted back in to the flight line: a quick perusal of engine and electrics showed nothing obviously adrift, but I was too happy to worry about it right then. Everyone had dispersed for lunch so we took the opportunity to photograph the eclectic mix of machines before flopping out on the grass under a blazing sky. Aerial activity was again quite subdued in the wearying heat of the afternoon. Jean Pierre flew a nice display with one of his Air Copter creations, and Xavier gave a polished performance in the AX05, their expertise and harmony with their gyroplanes a real pleasure to watch. The lazy afternoon passed all too quickly and the Patrouille were airborne once again to crown the weekend with their full routine. The trio of orange and silver gyroplanes headed down the flight line at about 50 feet in a triangle formation, each trailing the Tricolour, European stars and the Cross of the Midi respectively. Vibrant colours streamed proudly in the breeze as they flew steadily down the runway to drop the flags at the end, a fitting conclusion to a most excellent weekend.

The stalls began to pack away and machines loaded on to their trailers, some beginning the flight home with farewell passes along the runway, waving madly as they whizzed by. I put Delta-J to bed, wrapping her up for a last night outside on the flight line as everyone converged on the hangar ready for the main feast, followed by the tombola. The hangar resonated with hundreds of cheerful voices, making conversation difficult regardless of language complications, but no one seemed to mind. I've always found the French very accommodating and they appreciate the effort even if it is unintelligible! As the meal drew to a close, I was startled by Jean Marie and Xavier calling me out to stand with them at the front. Pierre gave a speech (none of which I understood!) and produced a heavy gold medal on a tricolour ribbon, which he placed around my neck to huge applause. Thoroughly embarrassed I didn't know what was going on, but as Thierry later explained, it was an official French honour. I really didn't deserve that. All I did was go flying.

Now for the climax of the weekend with the tombola. The prizes (all donated by Club members, families and friends) are displayed at the back of the hangar during the weekend, and the star prize is always a television generously provided by Club president, Jean Marie. The draw generally begins around 22:00 at the end of the evening meal and lasts for a couple of hours, depending on how raucous things become! Sunday is always a late night or an early Monday morning, but it's great fun. Children pull the tickets from the box as Xavier calls out the numbers, Jean Marie selecting a prize from the shelf which Pierre delivered to the lucky recipient, accompanied by enthusiastic cheers, banter and catcalls depending on the popularity of the winner.

On my third visit in 2007 via Air France, I won a smart brushed aluminium briefcase which I thought contained a tool kit. It was only on opening it the following day that I discovered somewhat to my alarm, that it was actually a comprehensive set of thirty-six extremely sharp (and some extremely large) kitchen knives, which I would somehow have to negotiate through airport security! Luckily I had my camping gear in checked baggage and not just a backpack, as there was no way that would've got on board otherwise. It took some re-arranging to fit the briefcase in with my tent and sleeping bag, wondering what the x-ray machine was going to make of that lot, so it was with great trepidation that I presented my luggage at security. They didn't bat an eyelid. Got to love the French! It was a beautiful set of knives, top chef's quality and completely wasted on me. I gave it to Cornwall Air Ambulance for fund raising.

*

The Monday of Whitsun weekend is always tinged with a little sadness: the extended family begins to go its separate ways for another year, and the airfield returned to its normal modest state. After a leisurely breakfast we all swung into gear, uprooting fences and flagpoles, packing amplifiers and electrics, stacking chairs and tables, collecting rubbish and sorting the recycling. A playful wind snatched at the canopy untied from the framework of the hangar extension, giant tarpaulins fighting back as we struggled to fold them into submission in the heat of another scorching day. Peter, John and Colin arrived from their lodgings to bid farewell before leaving to catch their flight from Blagnac. It'd been great to see them again and share the fun, our paths rarely cross at home and generally we only meet in France.

Everyone was in high spirits as we gathered round for a last hangar meal at lunchtime, delighted with the success of the weekend. I was thrilled to have taken part with Delta-J, happy to have kept up with far more experienced gyronauts and thankful that I hadn't disgraced myself. It couldn't get any better than that. Finally we tidied the hangars and retrieved the resident machines from the flight line, pushing them back to their nests. It was like one of those time lapse films of a flower blooming, and by the evening everything was gone. No one would guess that hundreds of visitors and around fifty unique and diverse rotorcraft had just enjoyed a marvellous festival of flying on this sleepy little airstrip.

I stayed on for a few more days, returning to the Club with Thierry and Vincent to watch them training with Pierre, and I took Delta-J up for a last wander round, courtesy of Vincent on the pull-start. The weather deteriorated steadily all week, the mountains now lost in a muggy haze but the air was wonderfully still as we floated lazily above the vast expanse of countryside, feeling exceptionally mellow and content. There was a flash of colour across the woods below as Pierre and Thierry passed beneath us in the tandem trainer, heading back from their exercise. Time was up. I drifted Delta-J slowly around to follow them down for the last time, the pale western sky streaked in pastel shades of pink and grey providing a faded backdrop for our final curtain.

It was a sombre two-day haul back north to catch the ferry – I did not want to go! But as they always say on the day of my departure, *to return, you must first have to leave.* Wise words indeed. Everyone lined up to wave us off, pointing to the right and yelling 'à droite, à droite!' in subtle reminder not to revert to British mode and drive on the left! It's another good-natured ribbing that continues through the years and even follows me into the air, as the English only fly on the left. Torrential rain followed us for much of the route back to Brittany, heart frequently in mouth as huge lorries thundered past in a curtain of spray. It was like driving through a car wash at times. The wipers batted impotently against the deluge that poured over the windscreen, yet an endless line of traffic sped past at crazy rate of knots, drowning us in a wall of water. How could they even see? I was genuinely scared that some idiot would fail to spot the light-board low down in the flying surface water, and ram the back of the trailer. Somehow we made it back to Roscoff late in the evening after a very long and stressful couple of days. Everything on the trailer was thoroughly saturated including the rotor box, despite being wrapped in cling film. I shunted it into the far corner of the car park above the docks and locked everything down for the night.

The rain had cleared by morning and I spent a couple of hours wringing out Delta-J's covers, mopping filthy water from trailer and strapping everything down again, leaving just enough time to scrub up and re-arrange my mobile home to a more presentable state of affairs. Ready for inspection, we headed down to the docks where *Armorique* was waiting alongside. The footprint of my trailer is no bigger than the small van that tows it, which partly conceals the low-riding gyroplane hitched on behind. Parked a couple of rows away was a big expensive car attached to a very large and powerful looking speedboat, that stuck out like a sore thumb above the assembled ranks of vehicles. A movement of gun-toting uniforms appeared from the terminal. Lunchtime was over: the gendarmes were coming, and almost as one they homed in on the big shiny speedboat. I immediately felt sorry for the owner. All eyes were on him as he obediently removed and opened every possible hatch, cupboard and cover from the gleaming vessel, while the officers went at it like terriers down a rat hole. Failing to unearth anything of interest, they abandoned the boat in disarray with its fixtures and fittings strewn around the tarmac and turned their attention to the big posh car instead. Doors were thrown open and the remaining occupants made to unload their luggage as a couple of officers ferreted through the vehicle and frowned over a wad of proffered documents.

I was growing ever more nervous as this went on – what on earth were they going to do to us? Given their persistence with the hapless speedboat, the screwed down lid of the ten foot long rotor box securely wrapped and strapped to my trailer was an obvious target for potential contraband. To undo that lot would take a good twenty minutes, and at least another forty to put it all back together again. If my fellow passengers had been entertained by the hapless Speedboat Man's discomfort, they were in for a real treat if my rotor box had to come off!

Apparently satisfied with the scene of devastation surrounding the speedboat and finding nothing left to dismantle, several of the gendarmes ambled away, leaving a mortified Speedboat Man and his companions to gather their belongings and reassemble their vessel. Wait for it... I glimpsed a pair of uniforms in the wing mirror, pointing at my gyroplane. Here we go. An officer arrived at the door, framed in the open window he politely requested my presence outside, and I duly followed him to the back of the van. Ever felt you're being watched? Please, not the rotor box...

But it couldn't have been more different. The gendarmes were relaxed and smiling behind their aviator shades, admiring my little flying machine with genuine fascination. I undid the cockpit cover for them to see the controls and tried my best to answer questions about how everything worked, grateful that they seemed to understand. Photos of a fully assembled Delta-J helped with the explanation and were viewed with pleasure. They were charming, I couldn't believe it. They didn't even want to check inside the van!

CLOSE ENCOUNTERS

Plotting a course on the map one page at a time as we motor along does little to convey the colossal scale of France in relation to the British Isles, and hours on the road equate to minimal progress down the page. People remark on how brave I am to cover such distances alone, yet the mileage doesn't occur to me at the time and being alone is just a normal state of affairs. Returning to Plymouth in 2009 onboard the *Armorique* is when it first struck me what a mammoth excursion it'd been. Outside on the aft deck, affixed to the ship's structure is a very large map of France in its entirety, and there in front of me was my whole journey in one giant hit. Ye gods, it was terrifying! Had I seen that map on the outbound crossing to Roscoff, I very likely would've been a lot more scared than I already was. It took three years and one test run before I was 'brave' enough to take Delta-J to Bois de la Pierre, but as the pioneering lady gyronaut Marion Springer used to say, if you're going to eat an elephant, you have to take it a bit at a time.

I've found that I can cover greater distances across the Channel without experiencing the same level of fatigue as in Britain. My limit when driving at home is around five to six hours or about 300 miles, yet in France I've covered Roscoff to Thénac in a very long day, which (depending on satnav eccentricities) is a distance of around 400 miles. Logic would dictate the opposite, being on the wrong side of the road with a right-hand drive vehicle, using metric measures in a language that's not my own – what could go wrong! But many roads are so long and straight as if someone put two marks on a map and simply drew a line in between, the miles are gobbled up with ease. They have plenty of room for it though, unlike my overcrowded little island where the roads sort of amble almost apologetically in the general direction of a destination and will eventually arrive somewhere at some point. Hey, it's home.

We don't have the same sizzling temperatures either, which is what knocks the stuffing out of me the further south we get. Personally, 15-18°C is perfect, preferably with a nice sea breeze to make it comfortable. Driving down the huge landmass of France in mid-May, sun glaring through the windscreen and heat radiating from the baking earth is more than my Anglo Saxon blood can bear. With timing dictated by Whitsun weekend, mid-June is the latest that I've stayed in the South and temperatures are regularly up in the thirties by then. It really isn't comfortable. There's a limit to how many clothes you can decently remove without being arrested, and even then it wouldn't be enough! A brief visit to Thénac with John one August saw the mercury hit 38°C with not a breath of wind. We could barely function – it completely flattened us.

*

One of my personal landmarks that won't be found on any map is *Stupid Dog Corner,* a tight bend on the back roads through the flowing hills of the Gers between Bois de la Pierre and Samatan. It approaches a sharp right hander before dropping steeply down into the valley, opposite which sits a large property with an unfenced garden alongside the road. Roaming this homestead was some kind of matted off-white canine the size of a sheep with brains to match, that might've been vaguely related to a Pyrenean mountain dog. I've seen *real* Pyreneans living and working alone with their flocks deep in the mountains, and to associate these gentle intelligent animals with this four-legged numbskull is quite an insult to the breed. Let's just say it was a *very* distant relation.

Thierry and Chantal had kindly adopted me during this particular visit, so I was staying at their lovely farmhouse in the hills near the village of Lombez. I had already encountered the gormless mutt, having had to brake hard as it lumbered straight out in to the road in front of my van, barking moronically and rushing at the wheels. There was no sign of its owners. We were coming from the other direction the next time it charged us. I was following Thierry back to the airfield, pulling up from the valley towards the tight bend with the large house in front of us and a stunning view of the mountains beyond. I saw the grubby animal appear from the garden and launch itself at Thierry's car, which veered sharply, horn blaring as the idiot creature hurled itself against the wheels. Now the thing was in the middle of the road, squaring up for an argument with the next ton of metal heading towards it. I slowed to a crawl, afraid of catching its paws under the wheels as it persisted in crowding the van, lumbering alongside and barking its silly head off.

Thierry had some choice words to say when I caught up with him at the airfield, 'stupid dog' being about all I can repeat in polite company! We met the beast several more times after that, a repeat performance of blundering out in to the road and doing its best to cause an accident. At no time did the owners appear and the dog was never restrained or confined. It made me very wary when approaching that bend, the damn thing was as big as a sheep and just as foolish, it could make a real mess of the van. Then suddenly it was gone. Whether someone did eventually hit it (which was only a matter of time) or whether someone complained, I don't know. Whatever fate befell the shaggy menace, it's forever immortalised as we approach the hairpin bend, which is now known in the exasperated words of Thierry as *Stupid Dog Corner.*

*

Returning home after a second trip down with Delta-J in tow produced another moment of comedy. For reasons I can't remember, it was a morning docking at Plymouth instead of my usual late evening arrival. Filtering back through passport control, a customs officer separated my little convoy from the line and waved us over to the cavernous grey shed, which for once was wide open. This was new. Normally when disembarking in the evening, everywhere except the passport booths are shut tight with not a soul to be seen. I could have a rugby team crammed in the back of my van for all the interest that's been shown, which makes me angry at how sloppy we our with this country's security.

Anyway, I steered into the shed as directed, followed by the customs man who informed me in a very serious manner that my vehicles had triggered a radiation sensor and was I carrying any radioactive isotopes? As conversation stoppers go, that takes some beating! I wouldn't know an isotope if it came up and introduced itself, never mind how to carry one. Questions were asked as to where I had been, why I had been, how long for, etc, while another officer circled van and trailer wielding an ominously clicking device that may have been a Geiger counter. What on earth...? How long had I owned the van: where did I buy it from, and had anyone borrowed it, questioned the officer, maintaining a stony demeanour appropriate to the gravitas of radioactive substances. Apparently satisfied with my response, he picked up another sensory gadget and I watched with interest as he joined his colleague in a lengthy examination of my vehicles. I was rather keen to discover the source of aggravation myself: how in the hell had we become radioactive? The socks from my Pyrenean hike were festering in the laundry bag, and there was a rather ripe portion of goat's cheese found forgotten in a jacket pocket while tidying up yesterday – dangerous definitely – but *radioactive?*

A thorough scanning of gyroplane and trailer failed to reveal anything untoward and they were given the all clear, the finger of suspicion now pointing firmly at my miniature motor home. The doors were flung wide and I began pulling everything out as directed by the officer, who scanned each bag, box and container in turn and piled them to one side. It's quite impressive how much can be crammed into a Combo! Meanwhile, the second officer was on hands and knees examining the underside with a large mirror. Half an hour had passed: the ominous clicking continued and seemed to be concentrated around the nearside rear wheel in particular. The second officer now back on his feet having failed to find any covert nuclear warheads, wandered off and left us to it, perhaps disappointed that there was actually nothing to see here. Well, I'd brought a little excitement to his daily routine and it was good practice if nothing else.

Time went on and it was becoming increasingly difficult to take this seriously as my over-developed sense of the ridiculous kicked in. Having removed and inspected all the clutter onboard, including flight gear, toolbox and gyroplane spares to no avail, my remaining officer was also loosening up, even veering towards the sheepish at the distinct lack of radioactive isotopes. My little van stood naked, bonnet open and doors thrown wide as if baring its innocence, yet still the Geiger counter sang its song. Up came the mats, revealing nothing more sinister than a plywood floor. There was nowhere left to look unless he wanted to rip out the wooden panelling as well. The poor chap was rather embarrassed, having literally pulled us apart for over an hour with nothing to show for it except a stubbornly clicking radiation sensor.

We recounted how long I'd owned the van and no, the panels hadn't been removed, but desperation was beginning to creep in when he asked if I ate bananas. Apparently a decomposing banana skin can emit gases with a similar signature to radioactive isotopes: could a banana skin have slipped down somewhere? Every day's a school day. Unfortunately bananas are one of the few fruits I'm not particularly fond of, so by the process of elimination only one possibility remained. I felt bad for the poor guy, who was only doing his job and growing more apologetic by the minute. We had a nice chat about gyroplanes and our travels in France as he helped me to shovel a mound of kit back into the van, laughing at the absurdity of mighty-mouse-me smuggling radioactive substances! It was a good two hours since we had driven off the ferry and the place was now deserted. Finally with everything tidied away, my new friend squatted down by the rear wheel and pointed to a lump of dried mud stuck under the arch, concluding that this was the only possible source of trouble. *Cabbages!* In the weeks leading up to our trip, the local roads had been thick with mud flung from tractors crossing between cabbage fields, and the Cornish peninsula is known to harbour radon gas, which (he informed me) was enough to tickle a Geiger counter. Well, who'd have thought.

A short postscript to that episode followed a couple of

years later. Queuing once again at the docks on return from Roscoff, the customs officer in the passport booth returned my document with a beaming smile and cheery greeting. It was my radioactive friend! I hadn't recognised him, but he remembered me - even before he saw Delta-J behind on her trailer. Or maybe I'm on file somewhere at international borders...

*

After a tedious dash up from the South leaving friends and gyroplanes far behind, it's always a welcome relief to see the comforting white bulk of the *Armorique* waiting at the dockside, signifying the successful completion of yet another marathon. It's literally plain sailing from here on, time to chill out and reflect for a while as we head back to my native isle and months of flightless reality. It comes as a bit of a shock to hear English voices again after the lilting fluidity of the French accent, our hard consonants sound so harsh and clumsy, they really grate in my ears. The long drive leaves me feeling very scruffy on eventual return to civilisation, invariably clad in favourite old flying jacket over a rumpled T-shirt, and the least disreputable pair of jeans left from my clean laundry. Despite best efforts to polish myself up before boarding, suffice to say I am not the picture of sartorial elegance.

Settled on board in my favourite front seat one year, watching the scenery drift by as the ship extracted herself from the port, my reverie was interrupted by the arrival of a well-spoken and smartly dressed elderly couple. Laden with bags and paraphernalia enough to pass the time of a lengthy sea crossing, they alighted in the adjoining window seats and I found myself in the company of Mr and Mrs Verri-Nice. A gentle fussing of baggage, magazines, jackets and cardigans arranged in suitable order, accompanied by earnest enquiries as to each other's comfort, which never failed to include the phrase *Very nice, dear*. They were sweet, it went on all afternoon. A waft of perfume drifted over after a visit to the Duty Free: 'That's nice, dear.' 'Yes it is, dear. Very nice, dear.' Later, being despatched for refreshments, the old gentleman returned bearing a tray of tea and cake for his beloved: 'Is that nice, dear?' 'Very nice, dear. Is yours nice, dear?' They kept me amused for hours until evening came and it was time to dine. The courtly old souls collected their belongings, making sure everything was correctly in its place, and arm in arm made steadily for the restaurant on the upper deck. I could almost hear them settling down to enjoy their meal: 'Is it nice, dear?' 'Very nice, dear.' Bless!

*

One year at the Gyro Club tombola, Colin won a large rose bush that was almost as big as Pierre, causing much hilarity as he struggled between the tables, enveloped in foliage. Having flown down with John for the weekend, Colin rather optimistically thought he might take it home with him on Squeezy Jet but it wasn't really practical, so I offered to take it for him. That was a marathon trip for a rose bush. From the Haute Garonne to Cornwall, where it stayed for some months in the back garden until I was able to reunite it with Colin up in Gloucester, over 1,000 miles in total. It's amazing that it survived what began with a tropical two day drive in the foot-well of my van, where it just about fitted perfectly. The pot was completely hidden below the seat and it looked quite comical apparently sprouting from the floor, foliage and delicate pink blooms spreading over the seat and rising above the dashboard.

Waiting in line to board the ferry, a local Breton lady was working her way along the queue doing a survey for the Brittany tourist board. She arrived at my side in due course and we conversed in a genial mix of French and English as she noted my response against her list of questions. On enquiring as to the type of accommodation used during my visit, I gestured to the back of the van and replied 'Dans mon camping-car' (in my camper van). By outward appearance it's nothing more remarkable than an ordinary little common-or-garden pallet van, so the lady's look of surprise was quite understandable as she peered over my shoulder beyond the curtains of my covert mobile home. And then the centime dropped: 'Oh!' she cried 'C'est un petit camping-car! C'est charment!'

No sign of movement at the front of the queue, so I opened the back doors to reveal my accommodation: the bunk bed, the fairy lights, the larder, the gas stove, the bathroom (wash bowl). She was delighted, the questionnaire forgotten as she cooed with pleasure over each new discovery. Souvenirs of our travels adorn the walls and she enthused at all the postcards and stickers, impressed that I travel alone. When at last we returned to the cab to complete the questionnaire, she spotted Colin's rose seemingly rooted in the foot-well of the passenger seat. 'Oh!' she exclaimed in English, 'You even have a garden!'

The Unfathomable Power of Emotion

Although my fixed-wing days are well and truly over, I still enjoy historic, vintage, or just beautifully designed aircraft, especially those pertaining to the exploits of the pioneers and the heroic struggles of war. Never did I imagine that I might see *two* Avro Lancasters in the air, but in 2014 it actually happened. Canada's painstaking restoration of *Vera* had graced the world with a second airworthy example of Britain's famous wartime bomber, her crew making an epic flight from Ontario to bring Vera back to her paternal shores. Now in company with our own Battle of Britain Memorial Flight's *City of Lincoln,* they would make a series of unique appearances across the country. It was an opportunity not to be missed.

Leaving home at 06:15, I stood for more than three hours squashed inside crowded trains converging on the seaside town of Dawlish. Normally a popular annual air show, this year was exceptional for the inclusion of a fly past by the only two airworthy Lancaster bombers in the world, a once in a lifetime event. The place was stuffed to the gills, swarming with people vying for the best positions to view the upcoming spectacle. I didn't know where to go on my first visit to the town and traipsed for what felt like miles back and forth along the seafront, searching for a space with a decent view of the action. Discovering a steep cliff path behind some houses, I plodded upwards, dodging flocks of holidaymakers and spotters alike. Halfway up was a viewing area offset in front of the path with a few benches overlooking the bay, and crammed with people like everywhere else. I'd been on my feet for over four hours and fatigue was kicking in. The chance of finding a better spot was highly unlikely: there was just room for a little one on the edge of the path above the viewing area, to which I staked my claim. It would be another eight hours before I could sit down again!

The weather gods had smiled on the town and conditions were perfect on this lovely summer's day. Sunshine blazed from a cloudless sky, looking out over the crowded sands to colourful boats bobbing around in the bay, masts adorned with festive bunting and decks full of people waiting for the show to begin. There wasn't much of interest in the programme, to be honest – noisy aerobatics don't wag my tail at all. A small glow of pride as our local 771 Squadron displayed their search and rescue expertise, but nothing mattered to me more than the pair of Lancasters.

It seemed like an interminable wait. Exposed to the full glare of the sun, I teetered awkwardly on the steep slope unable to ease complaining muscles, and praying that it wouldn't be in vain. Both Lancs were sixty-nine years old. *Vera* had suffered mechanical problems after her epic transatlantic trip, leading to the cancellation of several appearances scheduled during the course of her tour. Or what if *Lincoln* had a problem! So many variables for vintage aircraft to contend with, any one of which could ruin the day. Two was the magic number, there had to be *two* Avro Lancasters! Tired and sore, squirming uncomfortably on my little patch of tarmac being fried by the afternoon sun, it seemed almost too much to hope that it would actually happen. But finally at long last – at ten minutes past five – it did.

Words are painfully inadequate to express the emotions these two venerable old aircraft aroused as they flew sedately into view along the coast at cliff top height, flanked by a Spitfire and Hurricane. The wave of spontaneous applause that echoed respectfully around the bay from 70,000 spectators cannot be captured on paper. An actual *pair* of Avro Lancasters! So proud they looked flying in perfect formation above the red Devonian cliffs, sunlight gleaming on their wings and shimmering propellers. A marvellous symphony of eight Merlin engines proclaimed the triumph of *Vera's* momentous journey across the North Atlantic to join us. It was overwhelming and tears streamed down my face. After several passes en masse, the two bombers cleared the display area to fly a holding pattern while the fighters did their party piece across the bay. I didn't think it possible to ignore the sight of a Spitfire and Hurricane, or to think the unthinkable and wish they would stop wasting precious time and make way for the two superstars, the rarest of rarities. But this was a moment that wouldn't come again in my lifetime and I only had eyes for the circling Lancasters. The unique and all too brief sight and sound of our beloved *City of Lincoln* in company with the noble *Vera*, manoeuvring as one in perfect harmony as if they had always been together. It was a beautiful piece of flying, a fitting tribute to the brave aircrews of Bomber Command. And then they were gone. Wow. Just *wow*.

Ten hours I had been on my feet by then, but there were still three more to endure as tens of thousands of people queued to leave the town. It was 20:15 before a vacant seat appeared on the crowded train, into which I gratefully slumped, ultimately crawling into bed around 22:50 utterly exhausted and grateful that tomorrow was Sunday. Limp and feeble like a old lettuce forgotten at the back of the fridge, I slept the entire day and night, drained to the very last drop of energy. Forty-eight hours dedicated and condensed into ten minutes of absolute sensory perfection. The imprint of my sunglasses left a comical white mask on my irradiated skin, but the price of my raccoon face and every aching muscle, bone and sinew was more than worth it. I had seen *two* Avro Lancasters together in the air.

*

Back in 1997, the accident that took the lives of Chris Julian and Bob Bond altered something deep in my psyche. I wasn't a particularly emotional person in an expressive sense, but the floodgates opened that day and remain ridiculously sensitive ever since. It's bizarre, I have no control over it whatsoever: my inner self looks on aghast thinking *what the hell are you crying for!* The sound of eight Merlin engines and the iconic shape of the Lancasters bathed in sunshine against the summer sky was a most powerful and inspiring sight. I was so incredibly happy, yet I cried like a baby (thankfully without the vocal accompaniment, it's embarrassing enough as it is).

The human mind is such a bewilderingly complex and unpredictable piece of biological engineering. I've seen a dear friend reduced to a vacant shell, outwardly fit and healthy yet completely devoid of all the memory and experience of his eighty plus years. Everything that made him who he was had been purged from his mind. Another friend suffered a gradual mental decline that was marked by a radical change in personality. Over the course of several years, this popular good-natured chap turned into an increasingly belligerent and argumentative character, before he too succumbed to memory loss. It was a sad transformation to witness, a sorry feeling of impotence knowing there was nothing you could do to help. And my poor old dad: a series of falls caused one blow to the head too many, leaving him paralysed, unable to communicate and struggling for breath until five days later his body finally surrendered and set him free.

How fragile is our central processor. What is it among this extraordinary interaction of organic matter and electrical impulses inside our skulls that makes us who we are, an individual among billions of others. So much goes on beneath the surface of our shallow consciousness where subtle tweaks and permutations go unnoticed. I guess it was trauma that blanked out those bleak months following the double fatality at Kemble. I have vague recollection of an all-consuming grief that deprived me of sleep and appetite, moving zombie-like through the motions of a daily routine that would never be the same again, numb and uncaring. But I clearly remember sitting dazed from the sucker punch of shock at past one o'clock in the morning of 18 May, when Mark Hayward arrived at the door. This good man should've been leaving for a family holiday in America, but having heard snippets of the terrible news, came 60 miles out of his way in the small hours, hoping to find that it wasn't true. That's a real friend right there, not the one who turned up days later to see what pickings might be going.

Other hidden memories have trickled back into my

consciousness over the years, things that I didn't know had been stored away. How can you not know that you know something? Two decades on, my employers decided that their minions should be uniformly clad in red T-shirts. Something as innocuous as a red T-shirt caused memories that I didn't know I had to come flooding back on an unexpected wave of sadness.

I'd been a bearer at Chris Julian's funeral, a last resort volunteer to make up the numbers along with a fellow gyronaut and four ex-speedway stars of advancing years. Chris was a hefty chap for four elderly bearers, one bad back and an eight-stone wafer, so his coffin was transported from the hearse on a wheeled trolley rather than borne aloft in the traditional manner. All went well until we arrived at the narrow door of the ancient church. Six of us trying to squeeze through with our unwieldy burden and negotiate the angled steps inside was pure slapstick as we promptly got stuck. Chris would've loved it! A brief moment of levity on that miserable day, a brief moment completely lost in the fog of grief, yet weirdly resurrected twenty years later by a simple red T-shirt. By special request from Judy, I escorted the coffin conspicuously clad in my bright red flying suit. Sorrow numbed the embarrassment of sticking out like a sore thumb among the sombrely dressed gathering, clinging tightly to a small crumb of comfort with the knowledge that beside me, my late friend and mentor was being laid to rest draped in his own red flying suit. I never wore mine again.

La Joi de Vivre

I could quite happily spend the rest of my life exploring the French countryside in my dear old van, following my nose and going where the fancy takes me. It's such a big country that a wandering camper can stop practically anywhere and spend the night, whereas in most parts of Britain 'wild camping' is actually illegal. Greedy ticket machines adorned with *No overnight parking* signs lurk in every potential ad-hoc camping spot – beaches, woods, picnic areas – even a modest field will likely conjure someone awaiting payment for the pleasure of your company. Roaming the vastness of France is such a refreshing change from the negativity that infiltrates every aspect of British life these days. It's the curse of litigation, presumably: the fear of being sued or plastered all over social media by attention-seeking idiots. Our wonderful Nanny State has spawned several generations incapable of taking responsibility for themselves, quick to blame anyone and anything rather than admit to their own stupidity. Couple that with the fame hungry desperation of social media, and welcome to the dumbed-down mess that we're in. Thankfully, the French are more independent of spirit and don't appear to slavishly follow the American way. Long may it continue.

*

One year I based myself at the picturesque Pyrenean spa town of Bagnères-de-Luchon to tour around and absorb the magnificent scenery. Darkness fell as I settled down after a long day of ambulatory exploration. The air hung heavy and humid like a thick wet blanket draped across the valley, and it was uncomfortably hot inside my pocket-sized home. Parked within the relative safety of the campsite, I decided to leave the back doors open and sleep *on the balcony,* as it were. Space is at a premium in the confines of the van. Its internal dimensions are those of a standard wooden pallet, and accommodates kitchen, bedroom and bathroom in rotation as required, sometimes with my mountain bike in there as well! It's a bit snug, so I'd hooked the bin bag over the tow hitch to gain a few inches of space. The bass notes and tenors of an amphibian chorus tuned up for their nightly recital, with crickets and grasshoppers adding a counterpoint of high-pitched vibrato. I lay back on my bunk, looking up at the night sky between the trees. The few campers in residence were well spread out across the site and all was peaceful as I slipped in to an easy slumber.

Sometime later a strange rustling permeated my dreams. Keeping still, I tuned my ears towards the soft scuffling that seemed to be coming from beneath my bunk. Intriguing! I reached for a torch and quietly rolled over to shine it into the grass. Something rustled very close – it sounded like a plastic bag. Aha! Gently moving the torch around to illuminate the bin bag, a pair of bright black eyes stared back at me from a pointed snout. Halfway up the bag was my burglar, a young hedgehog the size of a grapefruit, caught in the act. We regarded each other for a few moments while he assessed the situation, evidently deciding that I posed no threat and resumed his activity unperturbed.

Tiny hands clawed at the plastic intent on finding a way in. I dearly wanted to get my camera but couldn't reach it without disturbing my charming visitor, so I just lay there and watched as he continued to rummage. There was nothing particularly appetising in the bin, a few yoghurt pots and empty soup packets that wouldn't make him a meal. Neither could I offer anything in reward for his charming persistence, my larder being tightly packed in a box beneath the bunk. So there I stayed, torch in hand until the little guy lost interest, probably deciding that this was too much like hard work and shuffled off into the night in search of easier pickings, leaving me with another special moment to keep.

On an early visit to the Gyro Club before instant adoption became the norm, I was to camp alone on the field that night, which wasn't a problem for me at all. As usual everyone gathered in the clubhouse for drinks and nibbles before going their separate ways, which on this particular evening included a large bowl of freshly warmed popcorn. A sprinkling of these puffy corns made a bid for freedom as the bowl was passed around, rolling unnoticed on the floor between the chairs. Jean Marie decided that it was better for me to stay in the clubhouse, and handed me his own set of keys. Picking our way through the crowded hangar dodging tail fins, ducking propeller blades and clambering over axles, he showed me how to set and deactivate the shrieking alarm system – I really didn't want to mess that up! Back inside after a demonstration of television, fridge and gas stove, he left me to it with the obligatory kisses and instructions to help myself to anything that I wanted. Imagine that level of trust in Britain. I should also sleep inside as it will be warmer, he added kindly.

It didn't take much to prepare a tin of soup on my little stove, so suitably armed with book and baguette, I carried the steaming bowl back inside to settle at the table for a while. I had no intention of spending the night when there was a comfortable warm bunk in my miniature motor home – a bone of contention that continues to this day! My kind-hearted friends don't understand how I can possibly enjoy living in my van, small but perfectly formed though it is. It's cosy and I love it. Jean Marie and Claudine in particular get quite perplexed any time I mention spending a night at the airfield, and are most tenacious in their efforts to keep me at home. Bless 'em, it must be like having a space alien as a pet. Anyway, all was quiet back in the clubhouse where it was dark and bit chilly with all the shutters closed. I washed bowl and spoon in the sink which took all of thirty seconds, then sat down to read for a while so that I could honestly say I'd made use of their generous hospitality.

A movement in the shadows caught my eye as a mouse appeared from beneath the fireplace and stopped in its tracks.

Whiskers twitching he watched me intently as if weighing up the risk, but the discarded popcorn proved too much of a temptation and suddenly the little rodent threw caution to the wind and shot across the floor to claim a morsel, sitting back on his haunches to munch greedily. And then there were two. A smaller mouse peeped timidly around the brickwork of the fireplace. Drat, caught without my camera again! The pull of the popcorn was irresistible and after a moment's hesitation, mini mouse scuttled out along the skirting board and under the chairs to scout a suitable target. Another pause to assess the situation and off he went to grab his prize and drag it to safety under a chair, demonstrating a more prudent sense of self-preservation than his pal who remained feasting in the middle of the floor. They obviously owned the place when no one was around.

The next day when my friends returned, asking if I'd slept well (and where), I told them about my little companions, so the story went round that I hadn't stayed in the clubhouse because I was scared of the mice! I didn't mind them one bit, after all it was their home. However, my tolerance level would've extended only to the limits of my sleeping bag. It didn't need extra ventilation holes.

*

During another early visit down South, I went exploring along the edge of the Pyrenees – not that I realised it at the time. Channelled through a valley by dark muscular slopes vanishing into the cloud base, I followed a road that snaked interminably round tight narrow bends, climbing through a dank grey mist. Only the low gears and rising note of the engine gave any clue as to the increasingly precipitous incline up which we crawled, eventually reaching the summit at just under 5,000 feet to park on the bleak shoulder of the Col d'Aspin. A moist hike to the top of a steeply forested rise added another few hundred feet that failed to break through the cloying mist, yet it was strangely beautiful all the same.

I stood on a fragment of deserted woodland, wrapped in cloud and cast adrift in the heavens. Beyond the mournful trees that surrounded me there was nothing, the landscape erased by an ashen void that caressed the skin with an icy touch. The keen mountain air carried a fresh earthy scent, infusing a calming sense of purity as the clouds softened the world around me, a gentle patter of raindrops enhancing an almost Zen-like tranquillity. There was not the remotest hint that a magnificent panorama of the Pic du Midi and the Pyrenean range were right there in front of me. I couldn't see a thing!

Evidently conditions wouldn't improve anytime soon, which curtailed my hopes of further off piste adventure, the daylight being pretty dismal and already beginning to fade. Despite the gloom I was reluctant to go back having ventured this far in to unknown territory, and pulled out the map to consider my options. The spa town of Bagnères-de-Bigorre looked a likely place to find a campsite, so I continued down the other side of the pass in search of civilisation and a place to stop for the night. The town duly obliged with a pleasant site set in a converted orchard, and I gratefully booked in, keen to curl up in my little tin home and shut out the depressing drizzle.

The cloud lifted slightly by daybreak, not enough to reveal my close proximity to the mountains, but patches of watery sunlight had begun to break through the mist here and there. Encouraged by favourable signs of a better day, I gathered soap and towel ready for an assault on the shower block and leapt out of the back door, startling a fellow camper walking by with his dog. From the outside my Vauxhall Combo is nothing more than an ordinary white van similar to many such popular utility vehicles in France, so the last thing the poor gentleman expected was for someone to pop out of the back like a jack in the box. I apologised for scaring him, and after recovering his composure he enquired if I had stayed the night, immediately answering himself that I couldn't possibly have slept in there! I opened the back doors in reply and invited him to view my compact but perfectly serviceable accommodation. He couldn't believe it, and was so delighted that he went back to his considerably more spacious vehicle to fetch his wife. I don't think she was quite so enamoured, to be honest, but they did return a little later to present me with a couple of fresh croissants for breakfast. What a nice thing to do.

This Way Up

*

Arriving at my target area near Puyguilhem in the small hours, it was far too late to disturb Marie and Martial, who were expecting me at some point on my way down to the Gyro Club, so I decided to make camp on the outskirts of their farm. It was a beautifully clear moonless night, the landscape rendered in starlight a vivid relief of silver and ash against dusky shadows of midnight hues. A pair of luminous eyes shone from the darkness as I turned through the gate, and suddenly a fox shot out from the trees, a brief flash of russet in the headlights streaking away among the vines. Jolting slowly down a pale ribbon of rough chalk track, I drove into a Disney film. A tawny owl drifted low across a thick field of maize alongside, brushing the cobs with silent wings and perfectly framed in the window beside me. A pair of hedgehogs spooked by my approach, hitched up their skirts to reveal some surprisingly long legs as they scuttled into the forest of maize. Their swift exit alarmed a group of rabbits who also quickly vanished. It was enchanting.

I stopped the van beside the maize and steered onto the grass, relieved to finally switch off and park for the night. The stillness was absolute. I couldn't resist stepping outside for a last look around on a night so wonderfully clear, stretching tired limbs beneath a sky full of stars. The pure night air cleansed my mind from the cobwebs of a long drive, refreshing weary bones with each breath as I leaned against the van, grateful to have arrived safely once more. The dew on the grass sparkled like jewels in the starlight, a modest homage to the diamond-studded firmament above. Then to my delight, the nocturnal residents began emerging from cover to resume the activities I had so rudely interrupted. Rabbits crept back into view, keeping a watchful eye on the strange object that had arrived in their midst. Another hedgehog, a big one, shuffled through the grass between the rows of vines growing opposite, a prickly challenge for the lurking fox. Owls called to one another across distant fields, a haunting sound that floated through the clarity of silence like a skein of oil on water. And bats! Dark alien shapes skimmed past with incredible speed and agility, diving, twisting and jinking on a rubbery slap of wings. It was a fascinating glimpse into a whole other aspect of life quietly existing in parallel – and a gentle reminder that the Earth doesn't belong to us.

*

Staying at Amboise one year during a road trip, John and I were camped at the municipal site on an island in the middle of the river Loire, a pretty spot looking across the water to the historic town and château standing tall above the opposite bank. Hot air balloons operate from the adjacent playing field, making an impressive sight as they rise slowly above the trees. The roar of gas burners became a regular wake-up call to grab the camera before the giant balloons came drifting low over the campsite in the early light of dawn. One such morning after watching the colourful departure, as there was no sign of John yet, I decided to have my shower before making the coffee. Like many campsites in France, it had a mixed shower block. Installed in my cubicle I was greatly amused by the arrival of a foreign gentleman next door, a cheerful soul who proceeded to accompany his ablutions with a loud baritone humming. I'd never been serenaded in the shower and it was most entertaining, he could certainly hold a tune! The partitions terminated just below knee height, and suddenly the concert stopped in mid-flow with a grunt of surprise as a bar of soap plopped on to the floor and came skidding into my cubicle, followed by a tanned and rather hirsute arm reaching blindly around in pursuit. I retrieved the soap and slid it back underneath, receiving a joyful cry of what presumably was thanks in a Germanic sounding accent, which once again broke in to hearty song. What a happy chap – and why not!

THE BEST PARTY *EVER!*

One of the most vivacious events I've ever had the pleasure to experience is the acclaimed festival of free flight, *le Coupe Icare,* held annually near Grenoble in the French Alps. It's a huge celebration of all types of minimalist and alternative ways of getting airborne, including ingenious battery and solar powered aircraft, balloons, airships, all kinds of gliders, wing suits and paramotors to name but a few. Based around two alpine villages, Lumbin on the valley floor, and far above separated by a vertical rock face of over 2,200 feet, the mountain community of St Hilaire du Touvet. For me, it perfectly encapsulates the French community spirit and joi de vivre. A panoramic backdrop of mountain ranges beneath a sky dotted with multicoloured wings, where thousands of people of all ages and nationalities enjoy a wide variety of creative workshops and entertainment, wrapped up in a lively carnival vibe. It's so much fun! It was John, my good friend from Wales who discovered this marvellous event and suggested that we join forces to check it out. And so we did.

While there are many excellent roads running north to south down the length of France, driving across the country is rather more challenging. After camping overnight near Angoulême, we planned to head directly east from Périgueux using a network of minor roads, but Ethel had other ideas. After a couple of hours it was becoming apparent that all roads led to Clermont-Ferrand, despite repeated efforts to divert her and regardless of whatever small backwater was chosen in the desired direction. So we took a long detour back to Clermont-Ferrand whether we liked it or not! The scenery in that ancient volcanic region is most impressive, an area that I'd like to explore more thoroughly when time allows, but for now it was getting dark and we were many miles adrift of our intended target. John found us a place to stay for the night in the town of Merlines, which appeared to be on the Plateau of a Thousand Cows. There's something you don't see every day.

A dull wet morning set the scene as we continued on steep and winding roads cutting through spectacular forests and extinct volcanoes, all depressingly hidden under a sodden cloak of mist. With previous experience of the terrifying motorway traffic around Lyon, I planned a route for Tournon-sur-Rhone, thinking to drop short and slightly south of Grenoble while encouraging Ethel to avoid Lyon at all costs. Instead, we visited Valence, followed by a brief but interesting glimpse of Maquis country around Vercors as we headed back up to Grenoble via the scenic route. It'd been another long and tiring day trying to work our way down to the south-east, and we managed to hit the city just as everyone came piling out of work. John had booked rooms for the night at the university campus in the suburb of Gieres, but with the impeccable timing of which only satnavs are capable, Ethel had another mid-life crisis.

She sent us on repeated orbits of the same stretch of dual carriageway, varying only to include all points of the compass and sampling every junction and every available set of traffic lights amid the heaving rush hour traffic. Stress! I couldn't decide if she has a sense of humour or an evil twin, yet later in to the trip I began to find John's interpretation of her instructions left something to be desired, so it might not have been entirely Ethel's fault! For twenty minutes we bounced merrily between junctions somewhat akin to a pinball, before diving gratefully into an elusive parking space to stop and have words with the mischievous gadget. Using the old s*witch-it-off-and-on-again* ploy, I reprogrammed for Gieres and nervously rejoined the busy carriageway, braced for another grand tour of the traffic lights – and we arrived at the campus a mere five minutes later. C'est la vie.

The next day we made an early start and set out for Lumbin, corralled along the valley floor by towering rock faces on either side. A group of hot air balloons were already rising through the morning mist, drifting serenely overhead as we approached the village. Once again our British conditioning was shocked by the lack of parking and entrance fees, leaving the van all day for free in a large field of stubble. A similar sized event at home would cost at least twenty-five pounds each. More balloons were inflating from a roped off area next to the car park, so we hurried around a large cluster of marquees and static displays to watch. An intriguing one-man airship floated 20 feet above the ground. Completely transparent, this miniature Zeppelin-shaped envelope had a single seat fastened beneath it, and was driven by what looked like a pair of electric fans fitted on either end of a pole, which was simply rotated in the required direction by the pilot. A see-through sister ship used a spherical envelope like a giant soap bubble, again with two electric fans on a pole held across the pilot's lap. They looked quite fragile just hanging there, emitting nothing more than a soft purring noise, much nicer on the ears than the hypersonic whine of a drone. If only gyroplanes could be made as quiet.

A scattering of paragliders began to trickle down from the launch site at St Hilaire, so we decided to visit the upper half of the festival via the beautifully restored funicular. Originally built in 1924, these wooden-clad stepped wagons ascend steeply on an increasingly vertical railway track, hauled up over 2,000 feet on cables by an engine at the top. It's quite a feat of engineering, but this is not a ride for the faint hearted! People with a fear of heights are often surprised that flying doesn't induce the same sense of distance as looking down from a tall building, for example. It's a completely different perspective. I'm not particularly fond of heights when wobbling up a ladder, yet have no problem at all sitting in a plastic tub hanging from a rotor blade. Looking down the vertiginous track of the funicular as it dropped away hundreds of feet below is a another matter entirely. I recommend concentrating on the stunning alpine scenery that opens up between the trees, and not speculate on the condition of the brakes or structural integrity of the cables!

Of course we arrived safely at the top, to find ourselves up in the clouds. A chill morning mist swirled through the flag bedecked village of St Hilaire, where party mode was already in full swing. An energetic steel band rocked Caribbean rhythms to help warm things up, and costumed jugglers, roving acrobats and theatre groups cavorted among the smiling crowds to entertain. Dance troupes and musicians of every genre bounced and swayed through the narrow streets, filling the air with melody in a genial upbeat vibe. It wasn't long before the mist began to fade and the temperature rose rapidly as the sun broke through the clouds to join the party.

A huge part of the attraction is the amazing spectacle of the Masquerade, or fancy dress in English terminology, but it's nothing like any fancy dress to be seen on these shores. The launch site is a short steep run at the top of the cliff that ends in an abrupt drop of 2,200 feet. Throughout the course of the day a steady stream of paragliders sailed into the air clad in a variety of crazy and ingenious costumes. Willing helpers assisted the more elaborate constructions through their take off runs, some pilots being completely engulfed by their creations and a few of which barely got airborne in time, sending their helpers tumbling alarmingly over the edge as momentum spilled them into the trees below. There were flying houses, cars, animals, rockets, steam trains, ships and submarines, and all manner of cartoon characters. One towel-clad pilot was dispatched down the ramp in a wheeled shower unit, complete with curtain and spraying water! Chinese dragons and mythical beasts trailed many yards of colourful ribbons and streamers that billowed out behind them. A lycra-clad couple on a tandem cycled over the edge, and a stork ran off the mountain with a grinning youngster hung in a giant nappy from its beak. I had to draw the line at one competitor who ran off the top of the cliff with a terrified dog strapped to his harness, the poor animal clearly distressed as it was rushed towards an apparent doom.

I was surprised to see dozens of tiny children from local primary schools happily running around unattended in the vicinity of some readily accessible drops of considerable height. No one was in the least bit concerned and the kids were having a great time! I guess being born and raised in such a lofty environment instils a suitable sense of caution, yet I couldn't imagine such casual freedom from Health and Safety being allowed at home, in fact I doubt very much that an event like the Coupe Icare is even possible in Britain. Risk assessments alone would fill enough paper to decimate another rain forest, and insurance costs would be horrendous, spawning extortionate parking and entry fees to recover expenses. The site would be heavily fenced off and plastered in warning signs, patrolled by an army of hi-viz jackets brandishing walkie-talkies, eyes peeled ready to curtail any outbreak of fun. What a miserable country we've become! *No ball games, No cycling, No skateboards, No swimming, No dogs, No parking* - the list of negativity is endless. In France they just get on with life, as we once did before the Nanny State smothered the bulldog spirit and wrapped it safely in cotton wool. During a break in proceedings at the launch site, a French boomerang champion gave a demonstration of his art by flinging multiple whirling projectiles that scythed closely above our heads. Only one went astray and nobody sued. It was brilliant!

Back down in Lumbin for the evening, one of the Patrouille de France pilots flew a solo aerobatic display in the valley below the cloud base (which was now below the mountain tops) doing things with an Extra that looked to be aerodynamically impossible. One particular manoeuvre left us gaping when he barrelled straight in towards the mountain and instead of the expected - not to mention rational - vertical pull up into the clouds, he bunted the aircraft *down* over its nose *towards* the rocks and trees and flew back out inverted! We couldn't believe it, fantastic flying and what a nutter! We waited as darkness fell to see the thousand paper lanterns released from St Hilaire: presumably a magical sight up there on the mountain top, but marginally less spectacular from the valley floor and all we could see was a trail of cinders on the wind.

Sunday afternoon was uncomfortably hot (a recurring theme as you may have noticed). After an enjoyable morning filled with airships, wing suits, radio-controlled models and kite flying demonstrations, John decided to go back to the launch site, so we split for the day. I stayed in Lumbin to watch the Masquerade participants coming down to land, something we hadn't been able to see from St Hilaire once they disappeared over the edge. It was just as entertaining. Target rings on a massive inflatable mattress in the landing zone encouraged the more competitive pilots to test their precision. The couple riding their tandem managed to land it upright and still pedalling until their collapsing canopy toppled them to the ground, getting huge applause from the crowd. A whole group of giant Avatar characters floated down wearing stilts, all successfully landing upright to more boisterous applause. A pair of hang gliders did a very enthusiastic beat up as they descended from the launch site, and a wide variety of 'eco-friendly' flying machines were put through their paces in spectacular fashion. The mountain rescue helicopter gave a nice compact display, then had to do it for real when a paraglider collapsed his canopy after one pirouette too many. His reserve chute didn't seem to slow him down very much, dropping him in the trees halfway down the mountain from where he was successfully retrieved on the end of a winch. It was an isolated incident in a spirited weekend of quite intense aerial activity. Curiosity piqued, I was keen to try paragliding for myself.

Monday morning was perfection, bathed in sunlight and crisp alpine air. We packed up and wandered in a vaguely northerly direction, marvelling at the lofty grandeur of the countryside against a sky of almost luminous clarity. An hour or so later we chanced upon the stunning vista of Lake Annecy – the wow-factor went off the scale! Stopping in the ridiculously pretty town that shares its name, we left the van and followed a wide pedestrian area through some pleasant lakeside gardens. We weren't wide pedestrians but no one seemed to mind. Fountains jetted near the shore, casting fleeting rainbows in the sunlight. Rows of small boats, yachts and pleasure craft nestled against wooden jetties lining the banks, and further along, several enormous pleasure boats of barge-like proportions squatted beside the town quay.

Spurning the unsightly behemoths, we returned along the path to join a boat trip of more modest dimensions on board the *Arc en Ciel*, a jaunty little vessel with a chunky posterior, possibly inspired by Tupperware. Comfortably seated on her broad derrière, we gorged on a wide panorama of leafy slopes and rocky summits, dazzled by the sun sparkling on the water. It was surprisingly choppy away from the shelter of the shore, an indication of how deceptively large the lake actually is, and the temperature dropped accordingly. Distant paragliders clustered around craggy limestone peaks, tiny slivers of colour drifting thousands of feet above. This was the place to be: I couldn't wish for a better setting, and fortune duly obliged. Come evening as we drove around the lake in search of lodgings, we discovered several paragliding schools nearby. John had done it some years ago when he was launched from the slopes of Mont Blanc and thoroughly enjoyed it, but he didn't feel the need to do it again. Well, he was in his seventies! Incidentally, a few years later, I arranged for him to fly in a paraplane (something he'd always wanted to do), which he absolutely loved. After a perfect touchdown, the collapsing canopy rolled the little buggy over on to its side - almost in slow motion - gently coming to rest with wheels in the air as John roared with laughter from the front seat! My dad was of a similar vintage, and I often wished that he could have had just a fraction of John's zest for life.

Returning next morning and despite the short notice, I was lucky to procure an afternoon flight in a tandem paraglider, so we spent an idyllic few hours wandering round the lake and nosing through pretty wooded villages, until it was time to go. Back at the school, I joined a young French lad who was taking his first ever flight in anything, and clambered into a beefy-looking 4x4 along with our respective pilots, to be taken up to the launch site. The pleasant prospect of a scenic mountain drive was rudely shattered as it soon became apparent that we were in the hands of a complete and utter maniac. Thankfully he wasn't one of our pilots. The bulky 4x4 raced up a vertiginous single-track road, somehow muscling its way past several vehicles in front. We clung to the seats with nails dug deep into the upholstery, the lunatic speeding around narrow hairpin bends at an insane velocity, carnage being the only possible outcome had we met someone coming down. I felt sorry for the poor lad beside me who was already nervous enough for his first flight. More by luck than judgement, we screeched to a halt at the launch site and tumbled gratefully from the clutches of our demon driver, who leaned casually against the bonnet and lit a cigarette, supremely unconcerned by his display of appalling road sense. I seriously wonder if he's still alive. Perhaps it was some kind of perverse reverse psychology:

scare the pants off the punters on the way up, thus negating any qualms about sailing into thin air suspended from a piece of rip-stop nylon – unquestionably safer than descending by road!

We lugged the equipment over to a short grassy slope which looked to be about halfway up the mountain, revealing the true magnitude of the lake, a spill of molten pewter glistening some 2,000 feet below. My pilot arranged our canopy, spreading it out on the grass behind us while I was helped into a webbing seat and clipped on to the front of his harness. And that was it. In just a few steps we literally jogged off the edge and soared out over the treetops, almost brushing them with our feet – *spectacular!* Steep forests of pine and fir clung to the upper reaches, beyond which the last vestiges of determined flora fell away and a wall of pale rock rose vertically to the sky. Normally I wouldn't dream of flying so close to such large and unyielding obstructions, but there were no worries of engine failure today. It was intriguing to be in a flexible 'flying machine' for want of a better term. The lack of rigid airframe made for quite a wild ride at times: the harness bucked and twisted in a boisterous wind tumbling in from the high peaks of the Mont Blanc range, hidden from view just beyond the clouds. I was loving my first flight without the racket of internal combustion – a marvellous sense of peace suspended far above the chaos of humanity.

Paragliders decorated the stark ridge of the Dents de Lanfon with crescents of colour, several swooping by in close proximity as we steered within ten feet of the sheer rock face, everyone searching for thermals. I could have done with some thermals myself as we levelled out at a chilly 6,070 feet, brushing the cloud base just above the summit of the Dents. It surprised me that they fly so close to the big cumulus given the turbulence these clouds can generate, so presumably the canopies are more robust than they appear, although I did have a very experienced pilot pulling the strings. He let me take control after descending to slightly warmer levels, sailing out across the water making gentle turns before steering back inland, slowly losing height. We skimmed across a busy road and set down on a nearby playing field, where the lunatic was waiting with the 4x4. Thankfully it was just a short ride back to the school.

I really enjoyed that. There's something very appealing

about stuffing your aircraft into a rucksack and taking it home at the end of the day. Inflatable gyroplanes – I wonder...

The End of an Era

St Merryn airfield will always be very special to me, one of the few hallowed places where autorotation first began in this country. Back in the early 1960s, Charlie Force made a set of wooden rotor blades and fitted them to a gyro-glider built from exhaust pipe tubing. Charlie taught himself to fly and so became one of the very first gyroplane pilots in the British Isles. Later, up at the bleak wartime airfield on Davidstow moor, he shared both his knowledge and home-made flying machine with David Bazeley. Because of Charlie and David, Chris Julian got involved and the rest is autorotational history. Erratic and deafening McCulloch engines gave way to heavy and temperamental Volkswagens, which in turn were superseded by the Rotax two-strokes. Home-made wooden rotor blades evolved into self-assembly aluminium blade kits, which in turn gave way to mass produced ready-to-fly metal rotors, and St Merryn was at the heart of it all.

Every weekend rain or shine, we were out there swapping parts, tweaking rotors, propellers and engines, trying anything to improve our tiny rotorcraft. It was so much fun! The old airfield embraced the spirit of the pioneers and we lived it to the max. Flying was everything. Chris knew no fear and Tony was the consummate accomplice, driven by a mutual thirst to discover *what if...* There's a photograph of Chris dangling in mid-air beneath an enormous hang-glider wing, a rope around his middle tied to the back of Tony's car, being towed aloft like a giant kite. I remember him saying how relieved he was when it finally began to lift, as he hadn't been able to run any faster! Such experiments were commonplace. The only way to prove something was to try it out, like the day we towed a pair of gyro-gliders on the same hitch to settle a difference of opinion as to whether it would work. I was crouched in the back of the car watching in horrified fascination as two whirling rotor discs were drawn irresistibly closer together by the apex of the tow hitch, even before Tony had changed out of first gear. The indisputable conclusion was right there for all to see, and the cable release quickly activated before things got *too* exciting, but like everything else it was a conundrum to be tackled with an open mind. Grass roots flying at its best.

Some modern-day gyro pilots just can't get their heads around it. Imagine flying without all the facts and figures instantly available at your finger tips – imagine having no option but to try something out and see what happens! Those old school gyronauts were a breed apart and their skills have kept me alive. Sadly those were the last of the halcyon days before Health and Safety went mad and our once great country succumbed to the ambulance-chasing litigation of American society, with all the resultant paranoia.

So it may seem a little odd (and I'm nothing if not a little odd), to base my gyroplane 700 road miles away in a foreign land. After the duplicitous Grenfell plotted to have St Merryn airfield all to himself, Delta-J spent several months wrapped up outside while I searched for a new home. Perranporth offered to cram her in to their already packed hangar for the price of an arm and a leg, considering the modest dimensions of my miniature rotorcraft, but the airfield was up for sale at the time and facing an uncertain future of its own. Nor was I overly keen to have her tangled up behind a load of aeroplanes as I would struggle to get her out, which is why she was eventually housed in the cavernous overflow hangar of Culdrose Gliding Club – and I couldn't get her out of there either! The problem in this case was the weight of the massive sliding doors, I couldn't budge them an inch. Add to that the frequent evictions as visiting military types like Chinooks and Apaches took priority for hangar space, so Delta-J was wrapped up and pushed outside again. There was one time when she was the sole civilian left in the hangar when the Chinooks arrived. She's so tiny that a Chinook could swallow her with ease and still have room for coffee and dessert, so she was allowed to stay.

The situation was far from ideal. My poor bird was spending too much time outside in all weathers, and when I *did* want her outside I couldn't open the doors. The gliding club were friendly enough but they just didn't understand what sheer unadulterated joy it is to fly a wind-powered rotor blade - w*ho would go up in such an eccentric contraption as that!* They had no idea and regarded us like some strange curiosity you might find tucked away at the back of the mantelpiece. We really didn't belong. It was so frustrating: all we needed was a reasonably level bit of field with somewhere to put a small shipping container, but no one wanted a potential risk of liability on their land. The carefree days of the barnstormer are well and truly over. The ever-present possibility of engine failure raised another problem. My few real friends all live hundreds of miles away and there's no one to ask for help should we become stuck in some remote field, unable to fetch the trailer.

St Merryn was our home, the heart of everything, the roots from where it all began - now after nineteen marvellous years it'd been sullied by a narcissist's greed. He is remarkably self-absorbed. I kick myself for not seeing the signs as there were enough of them over the years. On hearing of an accident to a fellow pilot, a decent person is first and foremost concerned for their welfare: a decent person does not immediately respond to the news of a wrecked aircraft with the words 'Has he got any bits?' Ironically, 'bits' were all that the poor guy had left of his machine (a nice tandem gyroplane that he had flown to St Merryn only a few weeks earlier) and the selfish lack of concern was another red flag that I failed to heed. To continue flying around the Cornish coast and look down on our former home knowing the door was closed, was too painful to contemplate. The selfish one put paid to over forty years of St Merryn tradition, passing on the skills handed down from the pioneers of autorotational flight. Even the decades of dedicated instruction by Chris and Tony who did their utmost to keep us all safe on that historic ground, have been glossed over with sycophantic intent.

Anyway, on our next visit to the Gyro Club Toulouse and learning of our homeless plight, the response was immediate -

you must stay here! Having towed Delta-J down there pretty much every Whitsun since 2009, it would certainly save on fuel and ferry costs. She would be safely housed with friends who truly appreciate our special way of flying, and thus we are family. Admittedly there's a minor inconvenience of the English Channel and a small matter of 600 miles to go on the other side! There was no longer anyone within 300 miles of home to do the annual permit inspection, and even with her based at nearby Culdrose we still couldn't fly, so I had little left to lose. In 2014 we joined our new squadron permanently, and I returned to Cornwall alone. It would be quality not quantity from then on, and both Delta-J and I began an evolution that wouldn't have been possible in the British Isles.

*

Jean Marie Varga is the heart of the Gyro Club: he's the driving force just as Chris was at St Merryn. They share several mannerisms and I can't help but notice how alike they are in many ways. Everyone knows Jean Marie and he's the first port of call for many in the event of a problem. He'll do anything for anyone, just as Chris would do back in the day. Weirdly they have the exact same distracted manner when driving: the seat belt inevitably forgotten until a sudden one-handed grab to attach it as they swerve down the road, minds occupied with other matters. Thankfully Jean Marie isn't quite the speed demon that Chris was – at least not while he's on the ground! Rooting around in skips looking for salvage is another mutually favoured activity, repairing televisions and in Jean Marie's case, all kinds of computers and electronic gadgetry that hadn't been invented in Chris's time. Likewise, they both struggle with excess weight around the middle, although Jean Marie's intake of fresh French produce is considerably more healthy than Chris's favourite fare of fish, chips and pasties! And last but not least, they both fly like the dickens, veteran virtuosos who have performed many an autorotational display at events all around their respective countries over the years. I count myself very fortunate to have had them both as friends.

Renaissance

She'll always be Delta-J...

Flying as an 'ULMiste' in the south of France is very different to being a gyronaut in Britain. Gyroplanes are a class apart under British regulations: a very special class that automatically excludes them from any concession granted to other flavours of homebuilt aircraft, and always for a very good reason that no one can actually explain. Things couldn't be more different across the English Channel, thanks in particular to the tenacity of Gyro Clubs Toulouse and Gascon, whose founder members fought long and hard for such freedom. Because of their determination, gyroplanes are now included in the microlight (ULM) category - even the big factory-built machines. What a world of opportunity this presents! The freedom to investigate and explore: to nip down the local hardware store and gather all you need without certificates and batch numbers, and the inflated aviation prices that come with them. It took me a long time to get used this new approach after more than twenty years of negativity, restricted to the very few aged and over-engineered designs that British gyronauts are allowed to construct. I couldn't believe it was all so simple. Surely there was going to come a point when somebody would say *'Non,'* yet no one has. (Actually to be fair, we *can* build anything we like in Britain – just don't expect to fly it.)

Horizontal stabilisers for example: only in the last few years have British homebuilt gyroplanes been permitted to fit basic tail planes to improve stability. It's just the way things are, even when safety is compromised. On that first memorable visit to Bois de la Pierre in 2005, the immediately obvious glaring difference (apart from the unbelievable variety) was that every single machine wore a horizontal tail plane of some description. When I took Delta-J down there for the first time, everyone was most concerned for my safety due to her lack of tail feathers, and assumed that I must be some kind of hot pilot to fly without them, which couldn't be further from the truth.

The colossal gulf in attitude became even more apparent when we officially completed our adoption at the Gyro Club and made more progress in three weeks than in twenty-three years at home. Fill in a few basic forms and the French ULM system issues a tail number prefixed with W to denote an experimental aircraft. You then have twelve months in which to test, modify and refine your machine to your heart's content (including major structural changes) and should the time allotted prove insufficient, you merely apply for another year's extension. I'm told this can go on indefinitely. Having achieved your ultimate flying machine, all it takes are a couple more forms and a small amount of euros to remove the W designation from the tail number, and that's it. Sadly, the vast majority of the British Isles and its airspace are just too crowded for such liberty to operate in safety, so Delta-J and I have gone from one extreme to the other, but I'd prefer a middle ground, to be honest. It's all very well pilots taking responsibility for their own necks, *providing* they don't endanger anyone else.

At first I really struggled to accept this laid back approach and kept asking my friends if they were *sure* that's all there is to it, such was the depth of negativity and censure ingrained at home. Contrast the endless rigmarole to get my new Cricket approved during her fourteen months of construction. Two box files of paperwork stuffed with receipts and certificates for nuts, bolts, washers, aluminium sheet, box sections and tubing, each of which had to be verified by our build inspector and signed off to confirm they met aviation standards. Two box files of paperwork: countless letters back and forth, any minor difference from previous models – perhaps an improved bracket or extra attachment – raised suspicion, invited scrutiny and further query when common sense is all we craved. To me as a British gyronaut, being let loose in France is a veritable feast of opportunity, a banquet of Henry VIII proportions after twenty years on a diet of bread and water. Throw us another chicken leg, s'il vous plâit...

The gyro community were very supportive, rallying round to help us through formalities and complete the transition. Thanks to Eric and Hervé, Delta-J was good to go in her new guise as W31XM, and Gilles had the lettering ready and waiting to apply to her tail when we arrived. In a matter of minutes she was transformed, but the new registration looked most peculiar! She'll always be Delta-J to me. My licence was converted thanks to the tenacity of Jean Michel, who guided me through the paperwork and dealt with legalities on my behalf. Xavier kindly assisted the process by testing my airborne proficiency in the AX05, which I'd briefly flown before, but a full twenty minutes on the controls left me with monumental cramp. The big rotor blades are more than twice the weight of mine and rest heavily on the stick, making it completely different in handling. Xavier makes it look so easy!

In a single day, Delta-J's axles were adapted to fit a pair of slim six-inch aluminium wheels, replacing her dumpy plastic hubs for a better ride over grass. The difference was quite surprising: we still bounce and jolt painfully along the runway (only a time-consuming major restructure can cure that), but the new wheels were a marked improvement. The next priority was to turn her into a *real* French gyroplane by attaching a tail plane, and expert advice agreed that the best solution for my particularly petite machine was to place it flat along the keel. Thierry generously donated a piece of laminated honeycomb from which Jean Marie would cut a basic tail plane for us to play with, but before we could do all that, my time had run out again and it was off up north to catch the ferry. Back at home I sketched several ideas, tweaking them to scale on graph paper until I had something workable to suit Delta-J's dimensions. I've always felt that the Cricket tail is too small to maintain rudder authority should the engine fail in flight. I'm no expert by any means, it just feels like there's too much frontal area for the rudder to overcome without prop wash over the tail - I'll find out one day when the engine stops! Anyhow, we had just enough material to make a small pair of winglets, theoretically adding a little more in the way of directional stability ready for when the elastic snaps.

Six months later on my return to Bois de la Pierre, our new horizontal tail plane was ready to assemble and test fit, after which I would take it all home for refining and finishing. Jean Marie had done a nice job and while I much appreciated his efforts, this was my first experience of bolting materials from the local hardware shop onto my precious flying machine. I was a little apprehensive, it all looked so disturbingly minimal. Each winglet had a single bracket of thin aluminium angle to attach it to the tail plane with commercial screws. The tail plane would be braced against the fin by a pair of narrow aluminium tubes, crushed flat at either end and strengthened with a small piece of steel riveted inside, and the whole assembly fixed to the keel with more commercial screws. I wasn't at all convinced. Jean Marie is a well-respected veteran gyronaut with decades of experience, but all I had ever known were a few sturdy British-approved gyroplanes, designed and built like the proverbial brick outhouse. Situated close to the propeller, barely inches away from the full blast of prop wash trying to wrench it from the keel, I doubted this tail assembly would survive. Consequently, neither would me and Delta-J.

There was a growing sense of unease when a large Frenchman advanced upon my gyroplane wielding an angle grinder. Like I said, they just get on with it! I was quietly having kittens as the sparks flew, tensed in anticipation of an accidental gouge that would condemn the keel tube and cause a major rebuild, but somehow nothing vital came off except for the line of rivets he was aiming at. But if that was bad in the stress department, what followed was way worse! The feline population increased dramatically as Jean Marie casually forced a 10 mm drill straight down through the eight rivet holes now exposed on top of the keel tube. That's a two-inch box section keel tube, through which he rammed the drill bit top to bottom – no rivet-sized pilot holes – straight down with the 10 mm guesstimated by eyeball. I was horrified! Boring holes through airframes is always done with the utmost caution, normally involving drill jigs and pilot holes to ensure accuracy and prevent scoring of the inner wall so as not to create weak points. Oh God...

There was no going back, the damage was done and I had to trust that Jean Marie's guesstimates were considerably more accurate than my own (not difficult, to be fair). We secured the tail plane to the keel tube with a little persuasion and realignment. The long cap screws were reluctant to pass cleanly through angle brackets, tail plane and slightly butchered keel tube, so there was more nail biting in store as the drill bit wiggled out the holes to fit. In twenty-three years of autorotating at home, nothing had prepared me for this! Perhaps it wasn't as bad as it looked... Jean Marie plonked the fin back in place and hooked up the rudder, while I attached winglets and bracing struts to the final assembly. I could tell he was perturbed by my lack of enthusiasm, and I tried to explain that my doubts had nothing to do with his engineering skills (well maybe just a tad!) and everything to do with British gyronaut conditioning. I really meant no disrespect. The other Club members didn't see any problem with our new tail feathers and rightly pointed out that some of the machines are held together with even less.

The annual gyroplane meeting was upon us and time was of the essence with so much work waiting to be done at the airfield. I had to man up. We were almost French and this was a fitting induction to the new regime. Taking to the air held together by ordinary high street hardware would be a worthy test, but first I wanted to see how the tail would fare in the prop wash before subjecting it to a full blast. I wasn't *quite* French yet. With Delta-J idling on the grass we scrutinised her hind quarters for potential failure, followed by a sustained burst of 4,500 rpm. No one saw any cause for concern, but I couldn't help but think of all the paperwork – properly drawn plans, exact angles and dimensions, stress analysis etc – required to attempt such a venture at home. Months would evaporate before any sign of permission to proceed, yet here we were ready to go in a matter of days with not a certificate of conformity to be seen. Leaving the engine to cool, I closely inspected every inch of the tail, thoroughly rechecked and checked it again for good measure, finding no particular reason to chicken out. Jean Marie was impatient to see us fly and it was crunch time (probably not the best turn of phrase in the circumstances).

With my action-cam pointing back at the tail, we saddled up and headed out to the runway, Jean Marie and Hervé watching intently by the fence. Not being completely assimilated just yet, I began with a couple of cautious low passes, but when nothing important fell off we went for it on the next run with a conservative 6,000 rpm and up into the circuit. I was still nervous: the entire tail assembly was attached by nothing more than those skinny commercial cap screws rammed through the keel tube, but the improvement in handling was immediately apparent. My Cricket was transformed! Normally twitchy in pitch, she was rock steady as we made tentative S turns along the downwind leg. The thought of blasting along the runway five feet above the grass never entered my head, but she felt so solid as we swung round on final approach that that's exactly what happened – I'm no hot dog by any means but that just felt *so* right! I was amazed how this basic mocked-up tail plane had made such a difference.

A combination of sensitive rotor blades and a reduced offset in the rotor head would trigger a nodding pitch oscillation that required a delicate touch on the controls above 60 mph, or in gusty weather (great fun in a gyroplane). Further experiments later in the week gradually increased my confidence as Delta-J behaved impeccably, cruising comfortably at 80 mph and more. One hot thermally day found us at 800 feet where it was quite blustery despite there being little wind on the ground, so I let go of the stick to see what would happen. At 60 mph she merely nodded gently through the thermals, the tail following through as if in slow motion, rising up to level the keel and stopping the oscillation without me having to catch it. Coming back into wind was markedly different and we were on the roller coaster again although nowhere near as bad as before, more like balancing on a beach ball rather than a marble.

Back home for summer, and three months in which to modify Delta-J's tail feathers and beef them up for peace of mind. The in-flight footage showed the winglets had a tendency to flutter, which wasn't really surprising being minimally restrained as they were in the full blast of prop wash. There was a bit of reshaping to do first, the tail plane being quite angular compared to the curvaceous form of my drawing. The winglets should've mirrored the shape of the tail fin but that was now impossible, all I could do was round them off a bit before taking it all to the paint shop – and that didn't go to plan either! My carefully drawn and painstakingly measured pattern being casually slapped on by hand, several inches adrift. The requested hi-viz dayglo orange came out as a low-viz burnt orange, but of course I said that's great and thank you very much, as it's far better than anything I could have achieved, so it's all a compromise.

I replaced all the skinny angle brackets, doubling them in both size and number so that winglets and tail plane are now bonded and screwed together inside a rigid aluminium sandwich. The bracing struts bent a little too easily for my liking, so I made another pair out of a heavier gauge tube and got them TIG welded for good measure. It was well worth the effort, the whole assembly now being sufficiently sturdy for an anxious aviator. I keep a close eye on it with a very thorough pre-flight each time, a seed of doubt remaining over the commercial high street hardware that *secures* the entire back end of my gyroplane, but as duly noted, some French flying machines have even less holding them together!

Six years later and I'm still adjusting to the French approach. There's some play in the rotor head thanks to the awful twist it takes when the pre-rotator engages, this tangible slop being what my mentor of old would've termed 'slack as a yak', is now appraised as 'normal' by my squadron mates. Concern over carbon build-up on a piston crown was also casually brushed aside - 'The motor is turning so there is no problem!' I await my first engine failure with interest.

Coming of Age

I wrote this after an idyllic afternoon with my gyroplane on a special day, putting pen to paper to mark the occasion. It was only meant as a private musing at the time, but it feels appropriate to place it here in tribute to those who made it possible.

*

G-BVDJ is twenty-one years old today. It was exactly twenty-one years ago on a Sunday afternoon at St Merryn, when Chris Julian took her into the air for the very first time. The pile of metal we had carefully cut, shaped and bolted together now transformed, the process of creation hadn't been in vain. I still remember the elation - how pretty she looked in scarlet silhouette against the sky - how impossibly tiny. There were teething troubles naturally, but now I owned a real flying machine. How cool was that!

Never in my wildest dreams did I imagine that twenty-one years later (29 May 2015, to be exact) we would be in the south of France, stirring the air together under the imperious gaze of the Pyrenees. Back then I had rarely left British shores and had never ventured abroad by myself. To drive alone, some 600 miles on the wrong side of the road in a foreign tongue - not to mention towing the most important part of my life behind on a vulnerable trailer - *nah,* don't be daft! Yet here we are.

Twenty-one years. That little red flying machine changed my life. With the encouragement of the late great Wing Commander Ken Wallis, I left home and moved 200 miles to be near our treasured airfield at St Merryn, where a small group of veteran gyronauts patiently kept me the right way up as they shared their wisdom with the neophyte. 'She won't fly' sneered the critics, 'Girls don't fly gyroplanes.' 'She flies,' affirmed my mentors, 'like a bit of silk.' And thanks to them and the gyro-glider, I did exactly that. They're all gone now, the gurus whose autorotational roots traced back to the 1960s, but the memories we made together and the skill they gave me to survive lives on, encapsulated in Delta-J. The little red rotorcraft that they helped me to create and to master exists because of Chris Julian and Tony Philpotts, along with Bob Partridge and Les Cload; their knowledge and friendship remains a vital part of the fabric that made me a gyronaut.

As does the man who has done more for the ordinary British gyronaut than any other: the unassuming and unsung hero that is Tony Melody. He took this gyro-glider fledgling and defied expectations by moulding me into a gyroplane pilot. Who says girls don't fly gyroplanes? And not forgetting Mark Hayward, who in his yellow Montgomerie Bensen led us on many adventures, helping to build this new gyronaut's confidence in straying from the local patch. Tony and Mark, to share your experience and great sense of fun has been both an honour and a pleasure.

People don't notice you when you're shy. Normally I'm invisible, but Delta-J defines me. When we're together I become someone and people want to talk: *'What is it? How does it work? Do you fly it?'* What's more extraordinary is that *I* can talk – the barriers dissolve and words flow with unaccustomed ease – such is my passion for the wondrous art of autorotation. Since taking my first step into the gyroplane world in 1990, all the friends I have are a direct result of becoming a gyronaut. It's my superpower.

The pioneering spirit that infused St Merryn barely survives in Britain these days. Any sign of enthusiasm for the homebuilt gyroplane is crushed by the ignorant, and with it dies the innovation and curiosity to evolve. My veterans would be saddened by what we've become. Even the basic skills are gone, the essential now re-labelled 'old fashioned' by those with no clue of which they speak. But across the English Channel, a whole new world of possibility opens up, and it's here that Delta-J and I have rediscovered what we thought irretrievably lost. Twenty-one years of memories, the strong roots that hold us firm as we begin our new incarnation with the friends who have become as important to me today as those of old. On this quiet little airfield of Bois de la Pierre, the Gyro Club Toulouse has embraced our lost soul and given it new purpose. The positive attitude does wonders, and a mutual passion for autorotational flight binds us in a strong community that's an honour to be part of.

So it's nicely fitting that my gyroplane should commemorate her twenty-first birthday with a flight from Bois de la Pierre today: the wide canvas of endless countryside and a colossal barrier of snow-capped mountains to the south, a very different landscape to that from whence we came. It was an emotive flight through an overcast sky as we celebrated her coming of age and remembered all those who made it possible. Delta-J is much more to me than just a machine, you see. Her very existence personifies the twenty-five year journey that began in 1990 with Ken and *Little Nellie*, a time capsule of memories from the best years of my life. As our new chapter begins with new friends far from home, even if it all ends tomorrow I thank my lucky stars for Delta-J and every moment that we've shared. So onwards and upwards to the next twenty-one years!

A Certain *Je Ne Sais Quoi*

It was the weekend after Whitsun in 2016, another cloudless and blisteringly hot day when I was invited to join Eric, Armand and Jean Marie on an outing to nearby Muret for an air show. Muret-Lherm is similar in size to Blackbushe with a single asphalt runway, and it's an impressive event for a provincial aerodrome. I'd been there six years earlier when the new Airbus A380 popped across the road from Blagnac to perform an astonishingly agile low-level display. The close proximity of such an infeasibly large and unwieldy-looking aircraft with its oddly truncated fuselage was most extraordinary, and I couldn't imagine the CAA granting permission for such a spectacle at home. Only in France!

The Pyrenees loomed large on the horizon, adding to the exotic vibe of the unfamiliar aircraft on display. We started at Air Copter's factory unit, where Pierre Chauvin gave us a somewhat melancholy tour after the recent loss of his business partner, veteran Gyro Club member, Jean Pierre Doleac. It was sad to see the stack of unfinished rotor blades and other projects that Jean Pierre had been working on before the illness took him. Back outside in the blazing sunshine and naturally the lads were going to eat first, having been invited to a hangar meal by the resident flying club, a gesture also extended for me with typically generous hospitality. Unfortunately I couldn't cope with the airless heat inside the confines of the hangar, enduring it through an aperitif before making my escape as soon as manners would permit.

At home in Cornwall, the Atlantic breeze tempers summer's heat so it's not as oppressive in the sun – not that the mercury reaches levels attained in southern France! Calm summer days are distressingly common on the flat plain south of Toulouse, and any shade is at a premium. The trouble with airfields in general is they require a lot of flat open ground with minimal obstructions to arrest the progress of a passing aircraft. This includes trees. Exposed to the full strength of the sun on an open expanse of ground makes me feel like an insect beneath a magnifying glass, and I wither beneath its glare. Suffice to say there was no shade to be found among the array of stalls and exhibition stands, and hardly a breath of wind to ease the relentless heat. The Pyrenees shimmered in the haze, their snow-capped peaks seeming impossibly at odds with the furnace of the airfield and I longed for the fresh mountain air.

By now my stomach was becoming quite insistent with its prompts for sustenance, although I didn't feel particularly hungry, the gurgles intensified in both frequency and volume. Scouting round the catering area for something small and simple, the variety of food on offer was a far cry from your typical British event with its stale hot dogs and grease burgers. There was nothing small and simple apart from me, but at last I discovered a stall willing to provide a plain serving of chips without any meats, salads, cheeses, gooey dressings, sticky sauces and other such potentially messy additions. However, I wasn't prepared for the mountain of chips that arrived, piled high on a shallow polystyrene tray. No such thing as a small portion in France, I should have known! Happily there were no seagulls in the vicinity as I carefully manoeuvred through the crowds looking for somewhere to sit. Try doing that in Cornwall...

Turning in search of a place to rest on the tinder dry grass, I almost trod on a little lad whose chin came exactly level with the tray I was holding. His eyes widened in surprise at the pile of chips that had suddenly appeared beneath his nose, and he looked up at me with a smile before dropping his gaze back to my lunch. What could I do but invite him to indulge, there was more than enough for dinner and tea as well! The smile widened as he politely selected a single chip, beaming as I encouraged him to dig in, which he did with enthusiasm after looking to his dad for approval. What a little charmer.

Later reunited with my squadron mates, all full of plumptiousness after a good feed, we took a stroll around the exhibits to watch the flying display begin. Apart from the familiar warbirds (Spitfire, FW190, Mustang, etc) there was a nice variety of the unusual like a tiny twin-engine Cri-Cri; the quirky yet versatile Bronco, and an aerobatic glider that performed an elegant aerial ballet to music. Some of the aircraft I didn't recognise at all. A flock of geese performed obediently behind their 'mother', a flexwing microlight which led them back and forth over the runway in perfect vic formation much to everyone's delight, something else we'd be highly unlikely to see at home.

Speaking of which: a squadron of Piper Cubs (six in number) put on a low level act of *crazy flying,* reminiscent of the barnstorming era of the twenties and thirties. Accompanied by a running commentary over the loud speakers, a 'student' pilot took off without his 'instructor', performing some wild manoeuvres quite close to the ground as the alleged instructor ran along behind, waving his arms in apparent distress. The remaining Cubs then took off in pursuit of the pretend pupil who was actually an excellent pilot, leading the swarm around in front of the crowd with some skilful wobbly wing drops, bunts and dives from barely a couple of hundred feet. It was all very entertaining and I couldn't imagine the CAA allowing that either!

We took our leave early to go back to the Gyro Club for what was left of the afternoon, getting ahead of the inevitable tangle of traffic when the show came to an end, but there was a final treat to be had. The Patrouille de France were due to perform, so Armand drove us a short distance away from the airfield and parked in a small residential area under the approach path. It felt somewhat incongruous to be standing in a quiet cul-de-sac with Alpha Jets roaring in low above our heads, staining the sky with plumes of coloured diesel (with all the current furore about emissions, I find it strange that no one mentions aerobatic displays). It was a great spot to catch the action as the team split in varying directions to come thundering over in ones, twos and threes with each formation change, heading back towards the main display line. We could almost have reached up and grabbed one. Only in France.

EATING HABITS

Driving down through France I never fail to be impressed by just how big it is (again this is from a British perspective: Americans and Australians for example, wouldn't be quite as impressed!). There's so much open space in comparison to home, you can literally go for miles and not see a soul. Tiny deserted communities appear without warning: silent narrow streets tightly bordered by higgledy-piggledy houses, wooden-shuttered windows firmly closed to the outside world. And everywhere you look there's food, the countryside a rich palette of colours packed full with nature's bounty. Endless swathes of ripening cereal ripple gently in the breeze, subtly accentuated by the bright scarlet of wild poppies in timeless memorial to centuries of battle. The rolling contours of vine-covered slopes display every shade of green, and the vibrant yellow of flowering rapeseed adds a joyous touch against a wide canvas of ever changing blue.

Vast acres of forest and woodland shelter rabbits, pheasants, and more elusive game like deer and wild boar. Trees and hedges offer fruit, nuts and berries, and the lakes and beautifully clean rivers teem with fish – food almost comes up and taps you on the shoulder. It's no wonder that the French take such pleasure from dining. How different to my tiny sceptred isle, bursting at the seams with a population it can no longer sustain. It's said that any society is only a few meals away from anarchy, but while the proud and volatile French never shy away from protesting their rights, they have no fear of starvation in this bountiful land. So when a scrawny 48 kilo Anglaise arrives in their midst, chaos naturally ensues.

It's like being a child again when you first venture on to foreign shores. Everything is new and different and even the most mundane of things can be fascinating because they're - well - *different*. Supermarkets are much the same as at home apart from being much bigger, yet I like to browse the unfamiliar labels that somehow make ordinary household items seem exotic and exciting. The language remains a mystery so reading and writing reverts to primary school level, and being unable to communicate properly means that you're never entirely sure of what's going on. Kind people tend to take you under their wing and you placidly follow along, putting your trust in the grown-ups. It's all very pleasant if slightly regressive.

It's been fun to discover and negotiate around the little foibles between our two countries. Having been invited to stay with new friends Thierry and Chantal, I was asked in all seriousness if I'd like a full English breakfast every morning. They genuinely believed the crazy British start the day with a huge fry-up, as in sausages, bacon, eggs, beans, mushrooms, fried bread etc. Back in the mists of time, a *full English* was the traditional fare of lorry drivers at greasy-spoon transport cafés, and maybe an occasional treat for Joe Public on a weekend, but to indulge in a daily plateful of cholesterol is really hard on the arteries, as it were. Nor would I dream of being such an imposition on my hosts, but was very touched by their kind effort to make me feel at home with what they perceived to be typical British fare.

Milk is another great divide. Tea and coffee in France are taken black in the main, whereas we British prefer to stir in a splash of milk or cream with our beverage. I'm not really a coffee person at home but I love it in France, gurgling black and fresh from the percolator, although some blends can be lethal. One such memorable brew was served to John and me late one evening while strolling round Amboise, on the banks of the river Loire. John was in need of a rest so we stopped at a nearby café to partake of a couple of coffees, perking us up ready for the walk back to the campsite. The dainty thimble-sized cups that arrived belied the potent liquid within - it was like rocket fuel! Several sugars were added to tone it down, making for a syrupy mixture that we swallowed with some difficulty and considered ourselves most definitely perked. It blew our socks off.

French supermarket shelves are stuffed with an eye-watering variety of breakfast cereals, which remain something of an enigma to my friends in the Haute Garonne. Milk is an ingredient for making pastries, cakes and sauces, not to be consumed straight from the carton. It was 2012 when Jean Marie and Claudine first began to adopt me on a permanent basis, and they had no idea what to expect of this strange foreigner from the island in the far North. They have a beautiful home sheltered halfway up the side of a steep hill overlooking the village of Montesquieu Volvestre, with a panoramic view of the Pyrenees. Jean Marie has a fantastic man-cave under the house, the majority of the ground floor being taken up by his garage/workshop/office with all the appropriate toys. An extensive garden provides them with fruit, nuts and vegetables all selected fresh for the table.

Poor Claudine was very concerned about what she should feed me, and most anxious not to cause affront, despite repeated assurances that I'm very easy going and was nothing but indebted by their kindness. But no, they would take me shopping to select the appropriate foodstuffs to my liking. What can you do? So we went on what would become a regular occurrence in the next few years, a special trip to the outskirts of Toulouse and one of those enormous hypermarkets that always leave my brain reeling in disbelief at the sheer scale of goods on offer. Jean Marie invariably parts company, taking off towards the cameras, laptops and other interesting technological gadgetry, leaving the females to deal with domestic stuff. I'd much rather go with him!

Claudine led me round the different food sections, up and down endless aisles pointing out various products, and did I like such and such. Then we arrived at the breakfast cereals, something she was clearly unfamiliar with. Did I eat cereal? Normally yes, but when abroad I like to partake of local customs different to that at home. *When in Rome,* and all that... Frowning, she picked up a packet of muesli – did I like it? Well, yes but... Into the trolley it went, along with all the other food she really didn't need to buy especially for me. Come next morning, there was the packet of muesli waiting on the kitchen table. I was perfectly content with black coffee and piece of bread and jam like they have but didn't want to appear ungrateful, the problem being there was no milk, and munching on a mouthful of dry muesli wasn't hugely appealing. Luckily morning coffee is served in a cereal bowl. There was nothing else for it. Claudine watched with interest as I poured a small helping of muesli into the coffee and stirred it up – actually it's not so bad.

To be fair, she and Jean Marie always insist that I ask them for anything I might need no matter what, but my introverted nature dictates that I adapt and overcome rather than be an inconvenience to anyone. So it's inevitable that we gently skirt round in circles, one side in genuine effort to please and the other just trying not to be a pest. This has gone on for years now and although we've naturally become close, I still pour the muesli into my coffee at breakfast time.

*

It struck me right from the start that my French friends are quite strictly regimented when it comes to meal times, and I'm afraid I didn't take it too seriously at first. Not being programmed to eat multiple-course meals at set times, I didn't realise the implications of failing to eat at a specific hour. Left to my own devices I eat when prompted by a demanding stomach, never have a starter and very rarely indulge in dessert. Another factor is the climate because for no particular reason I tend to eat less when it's hot, and for someone who lives on the Atlantic coast – being hundreds of miles deep in the landmass of France – it's usually hot! So there we are: not hungry, don't eat. This causes total bewilderment to my friends (and I love them dearly), but when time is limited I'd rather not waste it sitting around eating, especially when I'm still full from the previous meal. This is actual heresy, there's no such thing as a quick snack.

One such Saturday during a Whitsun weekend, I was twice rounded up from photographing the flight line and herded protesting to the dining table. Five courses halfway through the day when temperatures were hovering around the high end of the twenties was more than I could – er – stomach.

Consequently, when corralled for the evening meal, I couldn't eat another morsel. Quelle horreur! This was beyond all comprehension, bless them, they just didn't understand. Was I ill? Did I not like the food? Could they make something else for me instead? Some cheese, then? Perhaps some apple tart? I know they meant well but it was relentless!

Whether this specific time to dine is typically French in general, or just among the older generations I don't know, my experience is very limited. That said, however, my friends in Thénac seem more relaxed and are not adverse to taking a drink or a snack between meals. Certainly the whole country stops for lunch: the shutters come down, streets empty and traffic thins as everyone disappears to eat. Presumably their industry allows a more generous allotment of time than the average thirty minutes for a British lunch break.

So I'm afraid this scheduled eating has led to some mild friction a time or two. The Gyro Club's homely grass airfield is particularly pleasant as the heat of the day subsides in to evening and I love to stay and absorb the peaceful colours of dusk, sometimes taking to the air to watch the sunset paint the mountains in pastel shades. It's too gorgeous to waste. But 20:00 is dinnertime, which means having Delta-J packed away and hangars locked up by 19:30 ready for the thirty minute drive to Montesquieu. Jean Marie is constantly checking his watch. To be fair, I'm occasionally allowed a little leeway (sometimes 20:30!), but even though I tell them not to wait and to go ahead and eat, I know they won't. Inevitably I feel guilty for keeping them from their meal and curtail my activities accordingly. I hate being late, it's rude to keep people waiting no matter how casual the arrangements. I was once informed that this is *classic shy behaviour*. I thought it was just good manners.

*

One year, the last day of my stay coincided with a family function, an inevitable feast to which I was also generously invited. Not wishing to intrude and having been under their feet for two weeks already, I thought to slip away early and leave them in peace, thus gaining as much precious time as possible with my gyroplane. Caught in the act of escape that morning, I was pursued down the length of the driveway by a frowning countenance, scolding me not only for missing breakfast but declining to take half the contents of the fridge with me for lunch! Munching a snack while engaging in something more useful at the same time is an alien concept to my friends, and I (their only experience of a captive Anglaise) am disturbingly alien at times.

*

It's well over a decade since I first landed in their midst, making it increasingly hard to find any different gifts to take each time, and even more so since Britain left the European Union. It took a marathon trawl through post Brexit regulations to discover what can and can't be taken into France (mainly can't) since we parted trading company. No fruit, no vegetables, no dairy, no meat, no cereal etc, which considerably narrows not only the choice of gifts but my range of camping provisions as well. Incidentally, another pointless piece of bureaucracy was replacing our traditional **GB** vehicle marking with *UK*. Everyone knows that **GB** stands for Grand Bretagne but now as Claudine pointed out, we appear to originate from the Ukraine, so rot in hell, Mr Putin.

I freely admit defeat where alcohol is concerned, my attempts at giving wine or spirits haven't gone down well at all (so to speak). It's such an integral part of everyday French life that the average Brit cannot hope to comprehend, especially one who doesn't drink. I have not the foggiest notion of what may constitute a quality vintage, and my criterion of choice relies purely on the visual - a pleasing tint or shapely bottle - which has only gone to prove that you really shouldn't judge a book by its cover! The intrinsic national interest (dare I say *obsession*) with even the most ordinary of foodstuffs leaves me floundering, my ignorance of nutrients exceeded only by my ignorance of alcohol. The gift of an innocuous pot of jam dressed in twee rural English packaging was received with great interest. *Is it a local recipe? How is it made? Is it a speciality of the region?* No, it's just a reasonably pleasant pot of mass-produced jam decorated with a particularly English-afternoon-tea kind of vibe! Happily they're used to me now and regard my helpless ignorance with charitable amusement. Apparently it's part of my charm...

Christine once made a point of taking me to a small shop in Lombez that specialised in English food, catering for the needs of the many ex-pats employed by Airbus, just up the motorway in Toulouse. It seemed like an abomination to me. With the exception of a proper roast dinner or a plate of fish and chips, why would anyone still in possession of all their faculties choose English food over French? Christine was genuinely intrigued as she perused the shelves, closely inspecting various alien products and enquiring as to the purpose of the more obscure. Then she arrived at some jars of Marmite. *What is this?* I was stumped. I struggle to describe Marmite in English, never mind French. *Is it edible?* Yes, but some would refute that! *Is it a sauce or confiture? Is it served with meat or fish? How is it prepared?* I managed to convey with some difficulty that a thin layer of the savoury spread is merely applied to buttered bread or toast, which did nothing to convince her that the English are anything other than bonkers. I'm rather partial to a Marmite sandwich.

*

Another big difference between our countries comes with regard to alcohol. While many Brits imbibe gallons purely to detach themselves from rational thought, the French are far more civilised, as they are about most things to be fair. I fail to see the attraction of getting drunk: gulping large quantities of alcohol in search of momentary oblivion, no doubt making a complete fool of yourself into the bargain. Retribution quickly follows as your poor abused system rids itself of the contaminants so thoughtlessly ingested and extracts its revenge with a pounding headache. Why would you do that? Neither do I understand how people can slurp multiple pints of beer in an evening, distended stomachs awash with fermented grain sloshing around inside. How can that be pleasurable? It takes me all day to finish a pint of water.

Personally, I don't touch alcohol: not for any prohibitionist tendencies, far from it, it simply doesn't agree with me. I don't know why. As a teen growing up in Devon, our Saturday lunchtime treat would be a fresh pasty and half a mug of cider, which I thoroughly enjoyed. It may be coincidence but following an incident from my fixed-wing days, even a small amount of alcohol goes straight to my knees with disturbing affect, after which I succumb to a very deep sleep. It's quite unnerving.

At the very end of my training as a student pilot, one late afternoon my ground school lesson was interrupted by everyone packing up and clearing off to the pub for my instructor's leaving do. Peter (my assigned fixed-wing guru and subject of said festivities) naturally felt this was a more attractive prospect than coaching me through the innards of Lycoming engines, and decided we should likewise adjourn to the pub. Given a choice I would have much preferred to go home, but it was his party so I duly hopped on my moped and followed their tail lights through the chill of a November evening. Some kind soul furnished me with a cola while I perched on a stool at the edge of the celebrations, feeling very out of place and wondering how soon it would be polite to leave. Ground school was clearly over for the day!

Then Terry arrived, one of the senior instructors normally to be found at the business end of a Lockheed Tristar. Seeing me huddled on the bar stool after the short but frosty ride from the airport, he mistook my discomfort for cold and became genuinely concerned. Despite my protests he took my glass and added a brandy to warm me up. He was a nice guy with the best intentions so I sipped it to please him, but it tasted awful and there was far too much to drink. Later in desperation I furtively left it on the bar as everyone moved through to the dining area, but Hamish found it and thoughtfully retrieved it for me. However (as I found out next day), thinking it was just a plain glass of cola, he added a shot of Martini to warm me up. It was vile! I managed to sip about half of it under duress, the consequence being a most horrible and disconcerting sensation as if my limbs were shutting down. I could feel my core consciousness retracting from extremities inch by inch and shrinking to the size of a golf ball. Trees do something similar with chlorophyll as winter approaches. I have vague recollection of being poured into a taxi and taken home, much to the amusement of my family who never imagined they'd see *me* rolling in drunk!

Surprisingly there were no adverse affects when I finally awoke later the following day, and sheepishly returned to Blackbushe to take my airframes and engines exam. Somehow I managed to pass. Cheers, Peter.

One Man's Meat...

One evening while staying at Thierry's house, he decided to further my culinary education after hearing that I hadn't experienced steak tartare – and an experience is exactly what it turned out to be. I'm not a great meat-eater although by no means vegetarian, but I'm wary of meat dishes served in France as pretty much everything goes in. During one hangar meal on an early visit to the Gyro Club, one of our fellow Brits remarked on a particularly chewy morsel that he was having difficulty with. Delving further into his generous portion of cassoulet, our British sensibilities recoiled in horror when he fished out an entire pig's ear! Personally, it's the pinkly oozing cuts of meat bleeding into the gravy that turns my stomach. Meat in France is invariably served *rare*, which to British minds is practically raw. Inversely, the frowned upon request for *bien cuit* (well done) in carnivorous terms is regarded by the French as burnt. So when Thierry decided to introduce me to this gastronomic wonder of steak tartare, I was quite apprehensive, expecting a bloody slice of some unfortunate creature with all the fat and gristly bits still attached and flash-fried for the briefest of brownings. I couldn't have been more wrong.

The kitchen was a hive of activity later that afternoon with great preparations afoot, much to my dismay. They were taking so much trouble to do something nice for me – how could I get through this without causing offence? The table was set in front of the wide-open hearth where a pile of logs burned merrily in its maw. It was witching hour. The four of us took our places in the warm glow of the firelight, three French diners relaxed over aperitifs in genial anticipation of a good meal, and one cowardly English gripping a fruit juice in a state of mild terror!

Well the melon for starters was lovely and I would've happily called it quits right there. Imagination had been working overtime and I had no idea what was coming, so when Thierry proudly arrived with plates bearing a carefully crafted mound of raw mince and onion, each crowned with the golden yolk of a raw egg, I sensed a practical joke in the offing. But no... My companions set about their mounds with a flurry of seasoning and sauces, which they proceeded to mash in to a pink and sticky mess. Seeing my confusion, Thierry explained that the blend of onions, sauces and seasoning would 'cook' the egg and mince, so rendering it fit for consumption. *Okaaay?* I applied the salt and pepper to my unappetising mound as instructed, passing on the fiery selection of chillies and pimentos, and mashed everything into a pink and sticky mess of my own. It didn't look any better. After a few minutes pause, presumably to allow the process to do its thing (wouldn't want to overcook it, heaven forbid!), my friends tucked in appreciatively.

I didn't want to be rude after all the effort made on my behalf, yet I couldn't help but think of salmonella and other such unsavoury microbes associated with raw meat and eggs – or maybe that's what the chillies were for – to nuke the bugs in to submission. I sent my mind out for a stroll around the block to distract it from what I was about to do, and scooped a blob of pink goo on to my fork. Admittedly it wasn't as repulsive as expected in a raw egg and mince kind of vibe, but 'delicious' is not a word that I could truthfully apply, unlike my friends who were evidently in gastronomic heaven. I managed to swallow a few mouthfuls before they took pity on the callow Anglaise and graciously polished off the rest, while Thierry very kindly rustled up some fried eggs for me instead. France 1, England 0.

*

Snails. Why would anyone eat snails? No one eats slugs as far as I'm aware, so what's the difference? Slugs presumably return home at night after a hard day in the vegetable patch, whereas snails are the Caravan Club of the mollusc world, parking up wherever the fancy takes them. In comestible terms, snails are in the same pointless category as oysters - and are those poor creatures still alive when they get swallowed? Doesn't bear thinking about.

'You have never had snails!' came the cry of disbelief. Oddly it was Thierry again. 'Cover them in garlic butter, *mmm* delicious!' he enthused. Right, so garlic butter provides the flavour, distracting the diner from chewing on a garden mollusc about as appetising as a pencil rubber. Can we dispense with the snail and I'll just have some garlic butter, please? 'But you must try them, they are a delicacy!' Oh God. I don't deserve these good people. Thierry and Chantal disappeared that afternoon on a special mission to provide a banquet of l'escargots for my delectation. I was mortified. If the steak tartare had me worried, the thought of chewing on a snail filled me with horror. How could I swallow it without throwing up! Now I have no problem at all with snails in ordinary every day life. I pluck them from harm's way lest an inattentive shoe or tyre shatter their leisurely progress, and cringe in genuine remorse at the crackle of a hidden shell in the grass beneath my feet. I'm fine with snails. Just don't want them on my plate, is all.

Thierry and Chantal were gone for several hours, leaving me to stew queasily over the impending rubbery treat. I really wasn't happy, but thankfully salvation was at hand. My kind-hearted friends returned empty handed, lamenting the lack of suitably fresh molluscs with which to widen my dining experience, although frozen specimens were readily available (the mind boggles) they just didn't cut the mustard. I hid my relief with some difficulty, that really wouldn't have ended well! I'm not sure Thierry was being completely honest, though. I reckon he couldn't catch them.

*

I have to admit partaking of another stereotypical French delicacy; frog's legs. John and I were staying with Marie and Martial at their peaceful farmhouse set among the vineyards of the Dordogne, when the conversation turned (as it so frequently does) to the topic of food - and frog's legs in particular.

Learning that neither of us had previously indulged, it was immediately decided that amphibians were on the menu that evening. I didn't feel quite as apprehensive as when threatened with snails, after all, there couldn't be much fat on a frog, and at least I had a fellow neophyte for moral support. Now I'm a cowardly carnivore: if I had to kill my own meat I would either starve or turn vegetarian, no two ways about it. Likewise I'm squeamish with any meat that still resembles its original form. How people can choose a living fish or crustacean from the restaurant tank to be dispatched and served up for their consumption is beyond me. I'd put them all in a bucket and take them back to the sea.

So when Marie presented us each with a plate bearing the lower half of a dozen or so tiny corpses, chopped off at the waist, legs akimbo, I felt an overwhelming sadness. It looked so brutal, a scene of froggy mass murder. I really don't know what I'd been expecting, to be honest, but not these tragically unmistakable remains. Even the longest leg was barely the size of my little finger. Picking a sliver of meat from the tiny thigh bone as demonstrated by our hosts, while not unpleasant, I could detect no discernible flavour apart from the seasoning of lemon juice and black pepper. Divesting the remaining limbs of their sparse flesh, I felt a terrible sense of guilt. Why should so many little creatures have to die just to sacrifice a spoonful of meat – a teaspoon at that – there was no need. It felt like a wake as we collected the plates and gathered up a sad pile of diminutive bones, still disturbingly recognisable as their former selves. The evening chorus of hidden amphibians croaked accusingly into life as the sun dipped below the horizon in a blaze of pink and gold. *We know what you did...*

*

What crazy adventurous soul discovered that artichokes are edible, and how on earth did it even occur to them to try! An eccentric looking vegetable with an equally bizarre method of consumption, it resembles a large thistle with its spiky punk-rock bloom crowning a tight fist of green and purple scales, like a cross between pine cone and hand grenade. Needless to say, my friends love them. I have an over-developed sense of the ridiculous, which added to my natural off-kilter perspective of the world often loses something in translation, especially where the very important subject of food is concerned.

Presented for the first time with a large pile of steamed artichokes, I had not the faintest idea of what to do, and certainly would never have guessed! Jean Marie and Claudine demonstrated the art by peeling off an outer scale to show me the edible bit (a thumbnail of pale green pulp nestling at its base), scoop a dribble of oily dressing on to the pulp and scrape it off with your teeth. Discard and repeat. This was clearly a labour intensive process. I selected a grenade from the pile and worked my way around it as instructed. Pluck a scale, dip in sauce, ingest slightly bitter pulp, discard and repeat until all that remained was a naked and slightly squidgy green centre, topped by a parasol arrangement of strange fibres. Pinch the top of this parasol and it comes away like a hat, leaving the heart (the squidgy green bit) to be consumed – this is the best bit, apparently. The majority of each grenade goes in the bin.

I do my best to show willing when a heap of giant explosive thistles appears on the table, but my friends have accepted defeat with good grace where this uncivilised Anglaise is concerned, and it's become a regular joke to threaten me with artichokes. I just wonder what the origins are as it's not exactly an attractive vegetable that cries out to be consumed, in fact its spiky armoured demeanour suggests anything but. They're an acquired taste, but it's all good fun and life's too short to take it seriously.

BONHOMIE

While I greatly appreciate my French friends, their generosity overwhelms me at times, leaving me somewhat embarrassed that I can't reciprocate to the same extent - not that they expect it. Inviting them round to my house really isn't practical even if I *could* cook! Seven hundred miles is hell of a way to go for fish and chips. They do amuse me though, and no doubt I in turn am as equally entertaining to them...

*

French drink/driving laws are very strict, so a breathalyser is kept behind the bar in the clubhouse just in case the conviviality surpasses itself of an evening. It's not unusual to be waiting around sipping coffee until alcohol levels sufficiently subside. Jean Marie was among those who failed the test late one evening after the monthly meal, although no one was remotely tipsy nor the slightest bit impaired. Half an hour of black coffee failed to give him a green light and it was now past midnight, so he handed me his keys. The fact that I'm not used to a left-hand drive vehicle and possessed no insurance with which to drive it was of little consequence - I could beat the breathalyser and that's all that mattered. Despite being half asleep and repeatedly trying to change gear with the door handle, we eventually made it home at a snail's pace. The prowling gendarmes missed a prize catch that night, they would've been delighted with me! A sober yet completely illegal Anglaise was more of a liability than the lightly marinated Frenchman, but I had to admit his logic was exquisite.

We actually did get stopped going home separately from the airfield one night, when the gendarmes had set up shop at the motorway junction just outside Carbonne. Jean Marie was a few minutes behind having stayed to lock up the hangars, so I was first to fall into the net. Two glasses of fruit juice saw me safely in the green, no fun to be had there and I was tersely waved away without further ado. I wondered how Jean Marie would fare but there was no time to warn him. Arriving later back at the house, he had indeed been caught in the red, yet somehow managed to talk his way out of trouble in a *responsible-club-president-carefully-going-home-on-quiet-back-road-after-aperitifs-with-his-pilots* kind of style, and duly escaped with a warning. The big joke at the airfield next day was *me* getting breathalysed! It's powerful stuff, that fruit juice.

*

Camille lives on the side of a small mountain (or an extremely large hill, whichever you prefer) accessed by a very steep and narrow twisting track that overlooks the valley of Soueix-Oust on the edge of the Pyrenees. His family have lived there for generations and he has a born instinct for the terrain and its weather patterns. The pique-nique has become another ritual of my every visit to the Gyro Club. Early one morning just as the sun is rising, Jean Marie, Claudine and I (sometimes accompanied by our friend, Jeannine) load up the car with rucksacks, woollies and waterproofs, sturdy boots and stout sticks – and most important of all – an enormous quantity of food. After an hour's drive we rendezvous at Camille's charmingly rustic home and prepare to hike through stunning vistas for a high altitude lunch somewhere along the line, which usually involves an avalanche zone.

Jean Marie always defers to Camille to pick the day of our excursion, based on the weather forecast and his innate sense of actualities. He has never been wrong. There are some seriously tall peaks peering over the shoulders of the lower slopes surrounding the isolated homestead at Paloumère. We arrive around 08.30, the sun yet to appear above the distant crags and burn off the early morning mist that drifts languidly through the valleys, adding an icy chill to the clean mountain air. It's always a little brisk up there first thing, like a cool refreshing shower before the heat of the day. The house, its fields and outbuildings are home to an ever-changing menagerie of feathered and four-legged friends that wander in and out at will. It's not unusual to hear exasperated shrieks as Lys repels an invasion of feral kittens, or ejects a confused sheep from her kitchen.

So now the comedy begins with a mad scramble to change footwear and transfer supplies to Camille's little Suzuki *quatre-quatre* (4x4, pronounced *cat-cat),* a minimally-padded Spam can with a wheel at each corner. Like most utility vehicles in rural areas, the poor machine has had a hard life and seen better days, but it'll be driven until it drops. It rattles like a bag of spanners accompanied by a worrying smell of burnt rubber, which doesn't bother Camille in the slightest. The worn canvas roof and sagging vinyl windows provide welcome ventilation in the sun's glare, but conditions change and temperatures drop with startling rapidity in the mountains, blasting jets of frigid air through the gaps. It's a vehicle with character, taking us to places that those ridiculous Chelsea tractors and macho muscle wagons posing on the high street would never reach.

It's a snug fit for four of us, but when Jeannine joins the expedition we three in the back are crammed in like sardines. Claudine and I take opposite corners, perching on the bare metal of a wheel arch with Jeannine straddling the transmission shaft, squashed in between. Marion with her school bag climbs in on top, and we all hang on to each other as the gallant little cat-cat lurches its way down the track to the valley floor. Marion is untangled and safely despatched to class, and we continue on to the village bakery for the all-important daily bread. The bakery stands part way down an ancient narrow street which Camille nonchalantly blocks by bailing out on the adjacent corner, leaving us and the cat-cat to the rancour of obstructed drivers.

And so on to our destination, which (if we have taken the cat-cat) is certain to begin from some improbable goat track clinging to the side of a mountain. It's remarkable how the poor overloaded vehicle manages to get to where it does, and to look at the little tin can you wouldn't believe the places we've been. The best one was the day we trekked up to see 800 feet of spectacular waterfall, the Cascade d'Ars. Rising up from the back of beyond, a single tarmac lane fizzled out into an overgrown track that grew steeper, narrower and rockier the further up we went, teetering on the edge of a sharp drop that followed the course of a gushing mountain stream far below. It looked impossible: surely we can't go any further?

The hapless cat-cat ground its way painfully upwards, lurching from side to side as wheels bounced from rock to rut with ominous twangs from the suspension. It was like being in a tumble dryer. We were thrown around like rag dolls, hanging on for dear life, only too aware that the thin metal sides and canvas roof offered no protection whatsoever as we tilted precariously along the edge of the drop. The engine howled in protest, Camille studiously ignoring the glowing warning light on the dashboard and increasingly pungent smell of burning clutch as he hammered the little vehicle up the track, which finally petered out in a leafy glade. We untangled ourselves from the back and bailed out with difficulty, battered and bruised and giggling in relief. It's tougher than it looks, that little cat-cat.

Now for me, a picnic consists of a couple of supermarket sandwiches and a bottle of juice, unless I'm feeling particularly devilish and throw in a bag of crisps as well. I'm still amazed by the amount of food we routinely hike up a Pyrenee. It seems absurd to my culinary uncultured English mind to haul the weight of a large loaf, boiled eggs, lettuce, shredded carrot, tins of sardines, cheeses, tomatoes, ham, sausages, cake, pots of yoghurt or crème dessert – and don't forget the two bottles of wine, flask of coffee and two bottles of water! Condiments, cups, plates and cutlery are crammed into any remaining space and lugged up a mountain for an average three hour trek. The first time that I helped them to pack for a pique-nique, I honestly thought they were joking. Like I said, I love these guys! Scrambling up a Pyrenee, aching in every limb to feast beside a thundering waterfall of pure melted snow – in an avalanche zone with several hundred tons of rock poised above – it really puts life in to perspective. I wouldn't miss it for the world.

*

I love the marvellous ability of the French to create a party out of anything. John and I were again staying with Marie and Martial, when they invited us to join them for a lively event in the nearby village of Sigoulès. Every Friday evening during July and August, this typically small rural community holds a miniature food festival in the village car park. Catering vans (*food trucks* in French parlance) lined the perimeter, surrounding long rows of trestle tables arranged down the middle. A sturdy wooden pole formed the apex of what looked like giant Hawaiian garlands hung across the street in a wide parasol of colour. Popular tunes played by a mobile disco added to the party vibe as people from the local area gathered to socialise, to eat and drink and dance the night away. The aromas alone were enough to whet the appetite: spicy curries, Oriental and Mediterranean cuisines, along with more traditional French fare, all freshly prepared on site and lubricated with a wide selection of beers, wines and spirits. The cheerful ambience put even a foreign introvert like me at ease, and John was well away after a few glasses of the local red, taking to the dance floor to boogie on down in joyful abandon much to the delight of the crowd.

Evening darkened into night, wrapping the scene in a warm glow of coloured lights as temperate as the summer air. I was dispatched with Marie to collect ice cream just as the disco pumped up the volume with an obviously popular melody, a slow burner that swelled into an immediately catchy chorus and the whole gathering responded enthusiastically by thumping the tables in spontaneous accompaniment. Waiting at the counter to collect our desserts, Marie joined the impromptu percussion by slapping the side of the ice cream van – it was brilliant! – everyone united in harmony by this gleefully spirited song. It wasn't until a few months later that I was able to identify it, thanks to Claudine who recognised it from a short video filmed at the time. Ironically, *Les Lacs du Connemara* sung by Michel Sardou, is actually an Irish song with anti-British sentiments! Regardless, it remains a favourite on my play list, bringing with it with the happy memories of that genial summer evening with my friends in the depths of rural France.

*

It was the weekend of Jean Marie's birthday when I arranged to meet them during a Gyro Club excursion, converging on Claudine's parental home in the village of La Roque-Gageac on the banks of the river Dordogne. The plan had been to tow their gyroplanes up for a celebratory weekend of flying based at the hilltop airfield of Sarlat-Domme, but a poor weather forecast had thrown it in to serious doubt. I'd been unable to contact Jean Marie since driving down from Roscoff the previous day, so I arrived at the airfield not knowing if the rendezvous was still happening and a little disconcerted to see no one else around. It was a lovely late September day, spoiled only by a strong blustery wind that rendered any prospect of autorotational action highly unlikely. Sitting in the van pondering over circumstances, I knew that if anything was going to happen it would be around lunchtime, so if no one appeared by two o'clock I'd assume the trip had been cancelled and make my way on down to Bois de la Pierre.

After about twenty minutes there was a crunch of tyres and a car pulled in alongside. Lost in my reverie, a horn beeped and I looked up to see Eric and Mathilde beaming at me through the window, a small convoy of cars arriving behind. Lunchtime – I *knew* it! The impending bad weather had dissuaded several of the usual participants from joining the jaunt but there was still a good turnout for Jean Marie's special day. The cars were all laden with provisions which I now helped to fetch and carry for the ladies, busily arranging a feast at tables overlooking the deserted runway. As Eric remarked with a grin 'This is France – first we eat!'

The four stalwarts of Hervé, Pierre de Raigniac, Eric and Jean Marie had brought their gyroplanes with them, but there was no chance of any flying thanks to the boisterous wind that was playing havoc along the tables as we sat down to lunch, and tomorrow's forecast was even worse. Never mind: we can't fly but we have the next best thing, so a convivial couple of hours were spent *à table* just happy to be together. Later we all crammed into three cars and went to look around Montpazier, an attractive little fortified town nearby, after which a stroll around the grounds of a local château worked up an appetite ready for the party in the evening, and a good time was had by all.

Unfortunately, the weather behaved exactly as predicted, Sunday dawning beneath a heavy curtain of mist that leaked a persistent drizzle in dismal prelude for the monsoon to come. After breakfast we took a moist amble through the village which threads along the foot of a massive vertical rock face, tracing the course of the river. Driving rain thwarted our attempt to eat alfresco by the restaurant cabin on the riverbank, so we dashed back to the house where an assortment of tables and chairs were quickly gathered up and arranged inside a rustic garage. The restaurateur at the water's edge threw everything into his van (china, glasses, cutlery, sauce boats, condiments - the lot) and delivered each course piping hot from across the road. He even brought the coffee. How splendidly surreal to be surrounded by my friends on plastic garden chairs in an old brick garage, enjoying a five course meal with all the proper restaurant accoutrements as the rain poured down in the open doorway. It was absolutely brilliant! The French are in a class of their own when it comes to dining, nothing will spoil the party.

Neither Fish nor Fowl

Surprisingly there are advantages to being ugly, shy and verbally challenged, which are defects enough without having inherited my dad's body odour as well. There are far worse afflictions: so the bodywork's rough and the chassis starting to sag, but the engine is sound and I'm most grateful for that. It wasn't until my fifth decade that I began to discover and appreciate the positives after years of dejection, enduring snide remarks from so-called *friends* who were always ready to put the boot in once I'd served my purpose. Being an outsider grants a different perspective, opening up a whole new world to which most are oblivious, being heavily occupied with their pursuit of the normal. Change the way that you look at things and the things you look at change. Somehow I've always known that I'll be alone, and I'm cool with it. As a nine-year-old, I asked my mum if she would mind me not having children. Two years later in secondary school, when our teacher asked each of the class how many offspring we might produce in the future, without hesitation I replied 'None.' Motherhood has never been for me, but how can I have known and been so definite in my conviction – a child with no notion of the mechanics of life.

Spared from Nature's prompting to pair up and prolong the species is wonderfully liberating. Unfettered by the need to breed, I lack the primeval nesting instinct to attract a mate, which as I've grown to appreciate fits perfectly with my inherent shyness and complete lack of physical attraction (unless you're a mosquito, then I'm highly desirable, damn it). Children are tolerable in small and preferably quiet doses, but the thought of producing one of my own has always filled me with horror. I was once accosted in town by an alleged gypsy who was most insistent on telling my fortune, so I crossed her palm with silver just to get away. Grasping my hand, she gazed at it for a couple of seconds before confidently declaring that I could expect two beautiful grandchildren, no doubt the standard safe bet that would prove applicable to most, but in this case - epic fail! There are far too many people in the world, and we're of no benefit to this wonderful planet whatsoever. Sorry, did I say that out loud...

The vast majority of the uninhibited have no concept of how debilitating it is to be shy: *she won't talk, she doesn't mix,* ergo, she's aloof, snobby, not interested, blah blah blah. My own father didn't understand how stressful social situations can be and could always be relied upon to come out with the predictable quip of 'She's anti-social!' I actually hated him for it and wanted to retort 'I'm SHY, for gawd's sake!' Of course I only yelled in the confines of my own head, shrinking up against a wall and staring at the floor. I was born when the apple trees were in bloom, and my parents had planned to name me Blossom (and how enormously glad I am that they didn't!), but perhaps *Violet* would've been more appropriate.

I remember one time when my mum came down to stay at the Chalet. Chris was enthusing to her over my handling of the gyro-glider, when suddenly he paused and said in a quizzical tone, 'She dun't never say nuthen.' Not missing a beat, Mum replied 'That's all right, she doesn't talk to me either!' which Chris thought was hilarious (a tale he would repeat many a time). But it came as a complete surprise when Mum added 'She doesn't do small talk.' She was absolutely right. Endless superficial prattle, talking for the sake of it without actually *saying* anything - it's just noise - yet until that day, I didn't realise that I don't do small talk.

Unable to emulate the casual insouciance of the extrovert and sail confidently into the midst of social gatherings, life is solitary in the main. Reluctant to inflict myself on company thanks to my dad's malodorous genes, I can never assume that I'm welcome, hovering uncomfortably on the fringe (preferably in a corner with back to the wall) while others move easily between babbles of conversation. I'm always surprised when people seem to like me, so becoming part of the Gyro Club family has been a wonderful journey. However, with the best will in the world, I know that I'd make a poor compatriot.

I'm a pathetic carnivore: squeamish of bloody gravy, unable to consume fat or gristle without gagging, and am invariably saddened by any expired remains still identifiable as its original form (frog's legs!). I can't cook and have little interest in doing so with only myself to feed. A microwave oven and small halogen grill are perfectly adequate for the needs of an undomesticated goddess who struggles to finish a two-course meal. I'm clueless about wine (a deadly transgression in the land of the sacred vine) and I don't touch alcohol as it puts me to sleep. I guess the other stereotypical aspect of French expertise is *l'amour,* but having been single all my life with no inclination to be otherwise, I'm a dead loss in that respect as well!

That said, I'm not your typical *rosbif* either. My French friends don't realise that even on my native shores I'm regarded as somewhat 'different'. Conventional social patterns bore me: the mundane conversations about kids, work, television, sports results, who said what on Farcebook, or the latest brainless video on ThikTok. Normality leaves me cold – possibly because I don't fit in the accepted 'norms' myself. So whether in Britain or France, I'm neither fish nor fowl. Yes I drink tea with milk, and turn a startling pink when exposed to the sun. I wait patiently in queues while the locals surge to the front, but don't like to complain or make a fuss. I suffer from a surfeit of English reserve and apologise repeatedly for no apparent reason. Some things you just can't escape.

*

I don't know why Nature and the elements have such an effect on me, but maybe this connection lays deep within in us all. Swamped in the frenetic pace of the human race, it gets drowned out like a badly tuned radio. Clouds blossom and swirl in poetic motion across the sky yet so few will see their beauty. I spend hours out on the cliffs bewitched by the ceaseless movement of tides, powerful waves racing in to slam against a wall of rock, the very edifice of my island home. Sunset fills me with peace. A mystical moment and perhaps a primeval calling to the fleeting fusion of fire, water, earth and air as they meet in a mirage of flame. I love the sense of the Earth's rotation as it turns away from our life-giving star, a brief perception of the enormity beyond our world. Dusk descends with the haunting brilliance of moon and stars and all the infinity of space, such wonders are timeless and I'm helpless in their presence.

Sunset is my favourite time to fly. It's been my privilege to hang on the wind over the Cornish coast for a grandstand view of the illusion as the elements converge, setting the ocean ablaze. Now hundreds of miles away down south, the sun disappears behind the curvaceous hills of the Gers, accentuating the lone heights of the Pic du Midi on the skyline. Should the mood take them, the Pyrenees soften in pastel silhouette across the horizon, sometimes demure behind silvery veils of mist or cloaked in dark fury by towering storm clouds spiked with lightning. Nature is peerless, and with Delta-J I have the best seat in the house.

*

The formidable bulk of the Pyrenees combined with the baking heat radiating off the flat plain of the Garonne gives rise to some epic storms. Clouds boil to impressive heights among the distant peaks, a voluptuous mass of billowing energy gathering for the onslaught to come. One particular Whit Saturday, we left the hangar late at night after the evening meal and immediately dashed for cover through heavy rain, the air fizzing dangerously with static. Storm cells packed the sky for miles around like a fleet of galleons locked in furious battle. Lightning flared in every direction, a constant stream of illumination exposing the swollen bellies of the clouds, scarcely 300 feet above. Incredibly, there was very little thunder, but when it came it sounded like the sky had been cleaved open, shaking the ground in apocalyptic manner as if Thor himself was in a terrible rage. It was nearly midnight, yet the scene was bright as day. I've never seen such rapid and continuous lightning, shooting through the solid mass of cloud like a thousand flash bulbs all firing at once.

Drenched to the skin and deafened by rain battering against the van, I sat dripping in the cab, unable to tear myself away from the magnificent fury raging through the windscreen, an insignificant speck beneath the most powerful force on Earth. That was indeed, truly awesome. (And we're supposed to believe that humans can stop global warming!)

LANGUAGE BARRIERS

As I write this, it's been fifteen years since my first visit to France. Well, strictly speaking it was the second: the first being in 1986 when I couldn't believe my luck to be invited for a back seat ride to Le Touquet by my flying instructor, who was doing a cross-Channel check ride with another pilot in a Grumman Tiger. That was the first time my feet actually touched foreign soil, or at least the tarmac of Le Touquet airport. It doesn't really count as we were barely there long enough for a coffee in the café before heading back to Biggin Hill, and required zero linguistical effort on my part. The six-day road trip of 2005 involved limited Anglo/French interaction from me and my fellow Brit, travelling as we were with two super-fluent Belgians who handled the majority of conversation. Even so, I was surprised at how many words I could recognise from the residue of school French that remained tucked away somewhere between my ears.

I always hated French lessons at school and couldn't wait to drop the subject in Third year. No one we knew travelled abroad back in the Seventies, and crossing the English Channel was about as likely as visiting the moon. The evening news was filled with reports of French fishermen attacking British trawlers, or scenes of appalling cruelty as French farmers deliberately set fire to British lorries containing flocks of terrified sheep. It was heartbreaking, an indelible stain of depravity – who would want to go to such a barbaric country? I'm afraid my opinion of France wasn't exactly favourable at the time. I still detest the mob mentality that flares up even to this day with its callous penchant for arson. Lord knows, Britain has more than its fair share of mindless idiots, yet we have not sunk so low as to burn defenceless animals.

So this was not the most conducive of backgrounds for learning French: I hated the country and dreaded the lesson! Reading aloud was torture for me in any subject but trying to do it in French was a whole other level of sadism. Worse was to come when we were herded from the classroom into the clinical detachment of the Language Lab. Isolated in our own little booths, penned in with a malevolent microphone and clunky reel-to-reel tape recorder, we were left bewildered to repeat unintelligible phrases fed in to our headphones from the central control desk. Traumatised is too strong a term to describe my dread of that room, yet may possibly explain why I struggle so badly to communicate in French all these years later. The strong regional accent doesn't help matters either. The many audio courses that I've invested in over the years all use Northern or Parisian French, which can seriously confuse a stupid person arriving in the South!

Down there, they don't use the standard 'an' sound at the end of words such as pain (bread), or demain (tomorrow), instead pronouncing it 'eng' as in *peng* and *demeng*, which caused me a few complications to begin with, but I'm not the sharpest couteau in the box. Such was the time when Pierre proffered a bulging paper bag and asked if I ate mice. *Er...?* Correctly sensing a translation error, he opened the bag to reveal a wealth of crimson cherries plucked fresh from his garden, and not a handful of small rodents. To me it sounded like *souris,* when he was actually saying *cerises.* It's a minefield! The boot was firmly on the other foot one evening when two pals dissolved into giggles after asking why I was outside on my own in the dark. I was sure I replied correctly that I was watching the bats (chauve-souris; literally bald-mice), but what they heard was *chaud-souris* – hot mice! It's all good fun.

Listening-wise I find things work a lot better when not trying too hard. Very occasionally when not paying any particular attention to a background conversation, without realising, I've heard the words in English. Being able to see the person speaking and read their expressions and gestures is an enormous help in understanding, which of course makes any telephone conversation an impossibility and I suffer an immediate brain freeze when put on the spot. Language skills improve slightly by around the third week of my stay, but as soon as I'm back across the Channel all the hard won progress leaks out of my ears and it's back to square one. It baffles me how lyrics to long-forgotten songs and childhood rhymes can come back instantly and with almost total recall at the sound of a familiar tune. How can they be stored for decades in the attic of my brain when the French language defies all attempts to adhere it to memory?

A major difficulty for me (and for many Brits) is the use of gender for inanimate objects, which are somehow classed as masculine or feminine and therefore different in spelling and pronunciation. In English we have *he, she* and *it:* if something isn't male or female, it's an *it.* Simple, or at least it was until the gender benders began to butcher the language. In French for example, morning is male yet night is female: aeroplanes and bicycles are male, but houses and cars are female – it confuses the hell out of me. I can never remember which is what: is it *le* or *la, ma* or *mon, un* or *une?* If there's no E on the end it's a male and therefore don't pronounce the last letter. Sheesh.

Somewhat less of a bewilderment, which I've pretty much managed to master most of the time, is *You.* Again in English very simple: one word, applicable to one person or to many, to a friend or a stranger, to adults and children alike. Easy. The French have two versions covering a multitude of sins to perplex the non-native speaker. For family, friends or children use *tu,* but only for one person: several people require the use of *vous,* for plural. Vous also applies to either one or several people that you don't know very well. My audio lessons only covered vous, which is fine until acquaintances become friends and expect the use of the informal *tu.* I've had several gentle reprimands for getting my vous and tu's in a twist.

The flip side to the vous and tu's generally happens on the way home. After several wonderful weeks immersed in rural French life, I've become so ingrained with the use of informal tenses with my friends that I forget to revert to the formal (and polite!) *vous,* becoming unintentionally over-familiar with strangers en route. No one has slapped me yet... So I've more or less conquered the *tu* form thanks to online language sites and the vast improvement in WiFi connection. Happily, the Internet is now readily accessible, unlike ten years ago when I was hanging out of the bedroom window trying to intercept a single bar of itinerant signal with a dongle. Only with a crescent moon and an L in the month would it make a connection, otherwise I had to drive twenty-five miles to Truro to get a signal, hoping that the battery would last long enough to read my emails. Kids these days have no idea!

*

Sometimes words fail me – usually French ones. Attempting to speak in French means that my brain has be three or four steps ahead of my mouth, because somewhere along the line I'm going to get stuck and will need an alternative way to express the same thing. Experience has proved that any effort to assemble a reasonably coherent sentence will inevitably hit a roadblock, therefore my verbal contributions remain minimal and in pidgin French at best. It's so frustrating. I don't say much at home but at least I can make a sentence!

Camping at the airfield one evening, I was enjoying a pleasant amble along the runway when suddenly a large stocky bird flapped on to an adjoining field and landed about forty feet from where I stood. Daylight was almost gone and it was difficult to see clearly, but judging by the size, shape and what little colour I could discern of this magnificent bird, I'm pretty sure it was an eagle owl out on an early hunt. After barely a minute's pause it launched itself back into the air with a hurried beating of wings and vanished in the dusk. I was chuffed to bits to see an eagle owl in the wild, a rare privilege indeed.

Pierre was out for his usual morning stroll the following day and seeing me in residence, stopped by for a chat. I tried to tell him about the owl, but the appropriate word chose that moment to scuttle into the closet for a game of Hide and Seek. Scrabbling frantically around in my head for an alternative, all I could manage to articulate was 'a big bird of the night' which my irreverent brain immediately linked to that classic British comedy, *'Allo 'Allo*. Poor Pierre listened in polite confusion as

I fought a losing battle to stifle the giggles and complete a coherent sentence, sabotaged by visions of a hapless René Artois confronted in his café by a large lady of the night! All because I couldn't remember the French word for owl. I swear my psyche has got it in for me.

*

Now this amuses my tiny mind. I don't know how or why us Brits came to use the phrase 'Pardon my French' as an apology for cursing, but I catch myself saying it repeatedly (in French) when attempting to communicate across the English Channel – and I really *do* mean pardon my French!

WE'RE NOT IN KANSAS ANYMORE

Flying in a foreign language brings its own challenges. My friends credit me with far more intelligence than I really possess, believing I understand their every word when it's usually guesswork and I'm quite literally winging it. Using the radio has always been a struggle for me. The jargon poses no problem, it's more the mental block to get the words out and broadcast to one and all across the frequency, a hang-up deeply rooted in my general failure to communicate. I'm sure I was a mouse in a previous life (still got the teeth!), preferring to remain hidden and not draw attention to myself, *anony-mouse* as it were. Trying to transmit in French is highly likely to cause confusion, and my British radio licence isn't valid anyway. Instead I rely heavily on my squadron mates and observational skills to keep out of trouble. It limits our range somewhat when flying alone, avoiding other airfields and sticking to areas we've previously explored en masse, but just to be in the air and feel the wind through the rotors is pleasure enough.

During the week, the aerial prerogative over the plain belongs to the Armée de l'Air. I'm not too comfortable flying on a weekday! Many a time the peace has been shattered by an unearthly roar and dark shapes ripping through the circuit, sometimes a fleeting glimpse of fiery jet pipe barely 200 feet above. And they're always in pairs, unless it's the Patrouille de France who blast through with their nine Alpha Jets at minimal height. A hapless gyronaut would be chewed up and spat out before they even knew what hit them, the wake turbulence alone would be enough to ruin your day. Climb high enough to avoid being ingested by a passing Mirage, and you could well encounter one of the large military transports that habitually traverse the plain. While these are considerably more leisurely than the fighter jets (and much easier to spot!) they're certainly not to be tangled with. Having been encouraged to aviate one pleasant Thursday evening by Jean Marie, who casually refuted my nervous query that nothing fast and dangerous was likely to spoil the moment, I was alarmed to spot the dark bulk of an A400M sliding across the landscape below and heading straight towards our circuit. True, it wasn't as fast as an Alpha Jet but it sure would've spoiled the moment.

It reminded me of a near miss I once had many moons ago as a student on a navigation exercise, when a twin-engine Dash 8 inbound to St Mawgan skimmed the top off the Bodmin zone. Luckily the only traffic in the normally busy circuit was one tiny gyroplane and its rookie occupant on climb out. I happened to glance back over my shoulder and was startled to see the distinctive T tail of the turbo-prop sailing away at an acute angle that was rather too close for comfort. They weren't on frequency and we were at the same level – a few seconds earlier and that angle would have converged. They never saw us, it didn't even twitch. But guess where the blame would have fallen had they mowed us down from behind: a professional airline crew on a scheduled commercial flight, or a student pilot in one of those 'dangerous' home-made gyroplane contraptions? My guardian spirits are exceptionally good.

So back at the Gyro Club, we have Mirages, Rafales, Alpha Jets and their ilk from 200 feet, the transports slightly higher, and above them a whole host of heavy metal heading in and out of Toulouse Blagnac, a mere fifty kilometres away as the A380 flies. Toulouse of course is the home of Airbus, and we're basically in their back yard. Stir in a smattering of light aircraft, helicopters and ULMs from the many surrounding aero clubs and we can have just a little too much excitement for my liking. *Don't go too high*, my friends warn after persuading me to partake of the weekday sky. They habitually fly around at 400–500 feet, which seems like hedge skimming as I look down from the relative safety of 800 feet. My flying opportunities are very limited and confidence levels diminish accordingly with lack of hours. I like to have a decent chunk of altitude beneath us, a few extra seconds of safety margin to compensate for my lack of practice should there be any hiccups in the horsepower department.

Although we use the same engine as other single-seat machines at the Club, theirs are uniquely configured to accommodate bigger propellers and rotor blades. My little bird only has room to wear a petite 52-inch propeller, which coupled with our lightweight 22 feet of rotor span cannot hope to match the performance of the French. Consequently, they don't understand my reluctance to fly in temperatures over 20°C and the zero wind conditions that persist from May onwards - we just don't have the oomph! On squadron fly-outs, the others casually sail past and disappear into the distance leaving us to flounder in their wake, my poor engine screaming in protest with temperature gauge nudging the red zone as we struggle for a morsel of lift.

A couple of years ago, we had a narrow squeak that was the closest I've yet come to a forced landing. It was the last weekend before packing away for the summer and it'd been roasting all day. Wow, it was hot! We waited patiently in the shade of the hangar, Delta-J and me, willing the temperature to drop so that we too might partake of some autorotation. My pals had no worries, stirring the air with their big rotors all afternoon and clearly puzzled as to why I wasn't indulging with them. Evening drew in and the mercury held fast at 28°C, the windsock hanging limp from its pole, dead to the world. This was our last chance until September. The others had flown with no apparent difficulty - let's see what we can do.

I do not like using the pre-rotator. A few brief nudges at first just to get the blades moving, then a dreadful snatch as the Bendix engages, twisting the whole rotor head in shock. The push rods vibrate horribly, transmitting their convulsions through the control stick and knocking hell out of my poor machine. I hate it, but on a hot day with no wind, brute force is what it takes to rouse a lazy pair of Dragon Wings. They've shown a whole new side to their personality since we've been flying in France. On the Cornish peninsula surrounded by ocean, there's rarely a day without any breeze and a nice bit of lift to play with. Now it's a whole new ball game!

Taking off from grass with six-inch wheels and no suspension doesn't do either of us any good – we get hammered. Dragon Wings are particularly sensitive and it's all too easy to set them flapping, and you *really* don't want that. Erring on the cautious side, I tend to use a longer take off run than we probably need, because it's the lesser of two evils. So we finally struggled into the air with a very muted performance having used half the runway to unstick, and clawed our way slowly up to 1,100 feet. Our normal 5,000 rpm cruise couldn't maintain altitude and the engine worked extra hard, but things felt more comfortable after the scramble to get up there. Despite the sluggish conditions it was a perfect evening with great visibility. The plump hills of the Gers curved away to the west, forming a border replicated by the eastern range across the river Garonne. Barely a ripple disturbed the quiet waters. Lakes shone like glass embedded in the plain, and a pale haze softened the forbidding ramparts of the Pyrenees in lilac silhouette. To think we almost missed this.

We lingered over the western side for a while then headed across to the river, idly tracking its sinuous course and chasing our reflection towards the eastern hills. But something wasn't right as we neared the rising ground: I sensed a curious change in the rotors, although everything appeared to be running normally, it just didn't *feel* right. A thickening haze squatted heavily on the horizon and smudges of smoke hung motionless above distant bonfires. The air felt weirdly lifeless. It was quite disconcerting, so I made an executive decision to cut short our excursion and head for home. Dropping off the edge of the hills to slide back over the plain as we have done so many times before, I could feel the lift evaporating from the rotor disc and nudged on some power to compensate as the altimeter began to unwind. We often lose lift in that area and I wasn't too concerned, expecting it to pick up as it usually does once we've crossed the motorway. But this time it didn't...

Already running at 5,600 rpm, I threw in another 200 for good measure with no discernible gain, ramping it up to a more determined 6,000 rpm as we trickled increasingly lower.

Normally I'd turn into wind and climb back up, yet on this particular evening the air was completely dead - there *was* no wind. This was novel! I could see the airfield ahead, teasing, creeping painfully closer as I tried to stretch our descent. It was going to be tight. Full throttle now: the engine roared its heart out with nothing left to give and the altimeter continued to unwind. Somehow, at 85 mph, nose down in mid-air, we were caught on the back of the power curve and I was out of options. Incredible, there wasn't a single molecule of lift for the rotors to get hold of! It felt very uncomfortable with such a tenuous grip on the air, as if the rotors were slipping through olive oil instead of the usual syrup.

It was pure luck that got us home. Had we been any further away I would've had to force land as she was coming down and I could do nothing to stop it. There are many suitable places to land along the route so it wouldn't have been a problem to put down, but somehow we scraped back to the aerodrome for a straight in approach with nothing left in the bank for a go-around. Clearing the trees over the threshold, I throttled back a little and we dropped like a stone. Happily the engine didn't miss a beat and caught us in time to prevent a heavy arrival - I thank my lucky stars for that one! Now if we venture up on a hot day with light winds, I make sure to stay downwind of the airfield and not stray too far, theoretically allowing us to pick up some lift on return. It's not a good feeling when your rotors have nothing to bite.

*

Wind shear is another interesting phenomenon thanks to our proximity to the mountains and those wonderful rolling hills that border opposite sides of the plain. The windsock by the runway is no indication of what's happening aloft (although that's generally the case anywhere), yet here it seems amplified. It's not unusual to be teased by the wind coming at us from varying quarters, suddenly losing lift on the nose only to be booted up the rudder by an impatient gust from behind. One particular day it came out of nowhere and soon became very uncomfortable.

We had flown for about twenty-five minutes in clear calm conditions with not the slightest indication of what was in store, when a couple of sharp gusts came out of nowhere and slapped us round the chops. Suddenly we were being battered from all sides. It felt so abnormal that I thought something had come adrift and immediately slowed down to assess what was going on. The rudder seemed to be flapping yet the pedals held firm against my feet: the rotor disc responded to my questioning touch, and the engine gauges said all was tickety-boo at the back. Mechanically speaking we appeared to be fine, yet altimeter and airspeed indicator were both fluctuating wildly. This was not the pleasant thermally bounce that we often enjoy over the sun-baked plain – this was a rough and random pummelling that hit us from all sides and there was nothing pleasant about it at all. Somewhat reassured that Delta-J wasn't coming apart at the seams, I slowly turned her nose for home and crept away from the clutches of this wild bronco ride. When at last we arrived at the airfield, the windsock was drifting casually at its pole with not a hint of the turmoil above. We skimmed overhead and settled gratefully on the grass beneath a deceitful sky that appeared calm and inviting with not a cloud to mar the innocent blue. That was nasty. Jean Marie was surprised to see us back so soon and seemed quite sceptical to hear of the physical assault we'd just endured, but looking up at that perfect sky – I wouldn't have believed me either.

*

While I would love to evolve more autorotationally (and in France many things are possible), the reality is the short amount of time that I get to spend with my gyroplane precludes any major surgery, not to mention a very tight budget. Flying with my friends and their powerful four-stroke engines is so effortless compared to Delta-J's screaming two-stroke as we struggle for a morsel of lift. Suspension would be marvellous: imagine gliding across the grass like the others do instead of crawling along being shaken to bits! Of course I'd love a bigger fuel tank, longer range and the economical cruise of four-stroke reliability. Heavier rotors with better inertia would be nice, no more to endure the horrible slipping sensation of losing traction on the air, flogging all the horses and still coming down. It'd be great to keep pace with the gang on squadron fly-outs and not feel that I'm holding them back.

Hailing from a heavily regulated gyroplane scene where very little is allowed, I've seen the possibilities and tasted forbidden fruit in this marvellous parallel dimension in the skies of France. So why not buy a French gyroplane instead? That would mean the unthinkable. I can't afford to have two machines and parting with Delta-J would be like selling my soul. She embodies all our years of incomparable experience and those dear departed veterans who made it possible. I couldn't betray their memory by letting her go. So be gone green-eyed monster! Be grateful for what we have.

SURVIVAL INSTINCT

Late one evening, an unexpected visitor arrived at the house. A persistent high-pitched yowling had us puzzled as we relaxed over coffee after another epic dinner party. Claudine opened the door to investigate the strange commotion outside, and a streak of silver fur shot through the gap and disappeared under the table. A restless tabby kitten invited herself to supper, announcing her presence with determined squawks as she rapidly patrolled the dining room, a slippery little customer scooting behind the furniture to evade capture. It was funny. With Claudine in hot pursuit, the errant feline paused in mid-flight to wrap herself around Jean Marie's ankles, smudging affectionately at his shins and peering up at him, mewing loudly. His face was a picture! It took a plate of langoustine scraps to eventually lure her back outside, which she wolfed down in an instant while our guests made their escape through the downstairs garage, Jean Marie quickly shutting up shop to thwart further feline invasion. She was still yelling in the darkness outside as we cleared away and went to bed, generating a lot of noise for one so small.

Woken next day by sunlight blazing through the window, I had to smile at the sound of Jean Marie's footsteps being greeted by a familiar mewling as he went downstairs for his morning exercise. She was still here! Later as we sat down in the kitchen, a cute furry face appeared at the patio door and loudly demanded attention. Claudine relented and took out a dish of water and some cuts of ham, but the kitten slipped through the door behind her and joined us for breakfast. She was a proper handful, constantly on the move and squirming away from

Claudine's captive embrace, fidgeting like a hyperactive toddler and equally as vocal. She was about three months old: a pretty little thing with black stripes marking short silver fur, and a tawny smudge on her nose. We had no idea where she may have come from, but her survival instincts were excellent. She found some friendly humans and decided they belonged to her.

She followed us everywhere, chattering constantly in feline French so we couldn't fail to notice her. The house is built part way up a steep hill that continues to rise for over a hundred feet behind. I love to climb to the top, a short but lung-busting hike rewarded by a magnificent view of the mountains to the south, and the flat plain of the Garonne stretching across to the distant contours of the Gers. It's a great spot for butterflies. Some unusually large and colourful varieties appear as the sun warms the slope, flitting through the long grass to alight briefly and drink from the wild flowers, a teasing pause in which to snatch a photo. Having tracked a target and crept close enough for a shot, trying to keep it in focus as the delicate stalks sway in the breeze, it's in the lap of the gods whether I manage to press the shutter before my subject takes wing. Butterfly tracking is tricky enough without the determined assistance of a cheeky kitten.

She latched on to me as I collected my camera and scrambled up the bank and over the fence into the field beyond. The wild grass stood knee high but she gamely tagged along in leaps and bounds like a miniature tiger, sometimes completely engulfed in vegetation with just the black tip of a tail to be seen. I suspect that real tigers would starve if they made as much noise on the prowl, she sure had a lot to say. After a few minutes of hard climb, we reached the top and flopped on the wet grass to catch our breath. My chatty companion clambered sociably into my lap and made herself at home as I sat back to admire the scenery. A deep contented purring rumbled through the lithe little body, a pleasant change from her usual insistent yowl, but the exertion of the climb had taken its toll in the warmth of the sun, and soon she surrendered to sleep. Well, it was a perfect spot with a wonderful panorama to gorge on, so I didn't mind being used as a mattress. It made a change from being a doormat.

Butterflies began to appear as the temperature rose

steadily, delicate flickers of colour darting on the breeze above the grass, but I waited a while in deference to the damp bundle of fur snoozing peacefully in my lap. I couldn't help but be impressed by her tenacity, that climb was no mean feat for a kitten - it was a struggle for me! She knew what she wanted and she wouldn't give in. The dew was soaking further in to my jeans but they would soon dry on the warm hillside, it was cramp that was causing the trouble. I wriggled complaining limbs in a vain attempt to restore circulation without disturbing my guest, but a pair of sleepy golden eyes stared up at me and she mewed loudly as if in reproach. It was nice while it lasted! Batteries were sufficiently recharged and she was off again, bounding through the grass, shouting as she went. Photography was out of the question. Patiently stalking butterflies and quietly homing in as they settled on a bloom, just as everything was lining up nicely - *MEOW!* - she sprang into shot scattering my subjects to the wind. Every time! The wonderful thing about tiggers.

Back at the house, I was dismantling a spare Rotax engine and soon acquired a helpmate. Working on the garage floor made me an easy target as she came trotting in after a busy morning squawking at Claudine. Having made a thorough inspection of all the tools and components, she scrambled up my leg and curled comfortably in to my lap, purring like a diesel and promptly fell asleep. Well come in, sit down, make yourself at home! Folded up on the hard concrete floor, my legs were soon protesting as I tried to manoeuvre around her and continue attacking the engine. Later in the afternoon, Jean Marie came down to help remove a particularly stubborn bolt that was fighting back (there's always one). Crouching over to steady the engine block as he applied the wrench, disturbed my furry friend, who roused herself and promptly climbed up my back to settle on my head. Maybe she just wanted a better view - I was helpless with laughter! She wasn't going to move either, even when it was time to clear up and get ready for dinner, I did so with my fur hat on. What a character.

Enquiries around the village failed to find anyone missing a kitten, and although we enjoyed her visit (an engaging little thing when she wasn't yelling at us) we had to find her a permanent home. Consequently, the following weekend saw four grown adults trying to wrestle one small feline into a cardboard box ready to go to her new family. How that tiny scrap of life fought back; she was having none of it! Legs and paws burst out from all angles as we struggled to seal the box, inevitably her head appearing through some impossible gap, ears flattened as she squeezed herself free and shot back into the garage. In the end Jean Marie found a wooden crate in which we finally managed to contain her, wedging it into the boot of Camille's car to keep it shut. I was really worried for her survival as the car suffered from a leaky exhaust, the fumes could be bad enough in the back seats never mind shut in the boot for an hour. But survive she did, arriving safely at Paloumère up in the mountains, where Marion christened her new pet *Tigrine*.

We met again the following year during our regular visit to Camille's for a Pyrenean hike. Although grown up and rounder of face, she was still barely bigger than the little fighter that we had stuffed into that box – and already she had a family of her own. I had to smile. One of her brood was the absolute double of her: an insistent handful of black and silver fur who mewed constantly and followed us everywhere, demanding attention. Déjà vu, it had happened again, but now they all have a safe place to live and Paloumère is delightfully overrun with kittens (eleven at the last count!). But Tigrine remains an inspiration to me. Sometimes when it's been a struggle to stay positive and retain my sense of humour, I think of the tiny silver kitten who invited herself to dinner that night; lost and alone in the world, she refused to give up. Never surrender.

THE GOOD LIFE

La piste d'en Lébé – another beautiful moment

I love the camaraderie of the French microlight world and the hundreds of small grass airstrips dotted throughout the country. It doesn't matter how you choose to leave the ground, you're an aviator and welcomed accordingly. It's been such a pleasure. My accursed shyness makes it all but impossible to make friends, incapable of drawing attention to myself just to go up and greet someone new. The final few years at St Merryn in the company of Grenfell and his partner only enhanced the negativity, bolstering their egos by repeatedly highlighting my defects – as if I'm not already well aware! Wrapped up in their fanciful sense of superiority, they could never resist a snipe. But it's all so different now.

*

Touching down from an enjoyable jaunt around the local area one afternoon, we taxied back to the parking area shortly followed by a three-axis microlight which had appeared unseen behind. A squat low-rider with open cockpit, it was a mass of triangulated tubes and wires topped by a pair of faded rectangular wings, between which a small pusher engine of the Rotax variety wobbled unsteadily on its mountings. It had a real grass roots vibe. The pilot was obviously well known to the Gyro Club, a jovial character wearing industrial safety goggles and plastic ear defenders, he was the perfect match for his flying machine.

The light breeze posed no threat to my rotor blades, so rather than apply the brake I let them slow down in their own time, expending their energy with a whispering swish. I love that sound, it's the sweetest music. Over by the microlight, young Clément was being installed in the passenger seat. A tug of the starter cord brought the quirky contraption to life and as it taxied past us towards the runway, the grinning pilot pointed at me repeatedly, inferring that I was next. They came whirring back in after about twenty minutes with Clément wreathed in smiles, clearly loving the ride. I was indeed sought out by this magnanimous aviator, who handed me a pair of goggles and ear defenders as he buckled me in to the thin plastic seat.

It was even lower to the ground than Delta-J! The few instruments were housed in a small binnacle mounted overhead, and there was nothing out front except our feet on the rudder pedals. The clattering Rotax increased in volume to a tinny two-stroke whine and we were off without further ado, amused to find myself airborne in this extraordinary machine with a total stranger. He gestured for me to take control as we headed out over the plain. It'd been many years since I'd flown with my left hand but the little kite was very light on the controls, my only minor difficulty was judging the attitude, lacking anything out in front to use as reference. It was most entertaining and entirely unexpected! I later learned from my squadron mates that the pilot's name was Guy (the owner of nearby Le

Fousseret airfield), and the marvellous flying birdcage was called a Quicksilver. It's so typical of the community spirit down there: pop across to a neighbouring airstrip and share the gift of flight. Trés gentil.

*

Robert appeared at the airfield one day, an elderly little gent smiling beneath a floppy white hat, who having called out 'Bonjour monsieur' was startled to find that the scruff half-hidden beneath the nose of a gyroplane changing a tyre, was actually *madame*. Now briefly acquainted, he always politely stopped by anytime he saw my van parked at the hangar, so I was more than happy to give him a hand when he requested my assistance with his vintage aeroplane. He has a very nice Druine Turbulent: a single-seat, open cockpit tail dragger with similar dimensions to a single-seat gyroplane. We walked over to the hangar and I guarded the wing tips as he wiggled the little machine out through the door with not a lot to spare, pushed it on to the grass and left him to do his pre-flight checks in peace.

Having done my good deed for the day, I was alarmed when he returned a little later asking me to sit in and help to start the engine. The potential for confusion was a potential for disaster if I got it wrong, but no - *you are a pilot of the Gyro Club - there is no need for concern!* Oh 'eck. Back to the dainty red aeroplane we went. Robert pushed a pair of inadequate looking chocks under the wheels, insisting that I climb up the wing and sit in the cockpit, as he pointed to the throttle and switches that he wanted me to operate. It had no brakes. He wasn't worried but I was! I made him repeat all the open/close, on's and off's to be sure I understood correctly before he disappeared under the nose to prime the engine. I could just see the top of his hat over the cowling as he grasped the propeller blade to suck in fuel. I've seen a variety of aircraft run away in just such a manner over the years, and my feet twitched for the comfort of brake pedals in a long forgotten throwback to my fixed-wing days. I didn't want to be responsible for running him over, wondering if my presence was really necessary and how he would have managed it by himself.

Robert's smiling face reappeared at the wing root having primed the engine to his satisfaction, I set the throttle lever as instructed and switched on the ignition. The floppy hat bobbed in front of the nose, and the propeller spun briefly as the engine coughed and died. A second swing along with a brief nudge of encouragement to the throttle had the desired effect and the engine burst into song, blasting an agreeably cooling breeze back over the cockpit. Thankfully, the little Turbulent showed no inclination to make a break for freedom and remained burbling obediently on the grass. Robert stowed the chocks back under the seat and we changed places - amused to see that he was keeping his hat on! When all was ready I pushed the wing around to line him up with the gap in the fence, and watched the pretty little aeroplane bump away across the grass, Robert smiling cheerfully beneath the floppy hat that was somehow resisting the slipstream to stay on his head. I loved it! No aviator shades and posing swagger for this Top Gun. He was happy doing his thing, and that's all that mattered.

*

One sunny autumn afternoon at the Gyro Club, Hervé, and Pierre de Raigniac invited me to join them on a visit to a private airstrip hidden somewhere among the hills of the Gers. This was undiscovered country for me. Flying in a foreign land without radio communication means I don't land away unless accompanied by a local gyronaut, so to head out over the curvaceous landscape of the neighbouring region was a welcome adventure indeed.

Hervé flew an ELA, a two-seat tandem gyroplane manufactured in Spain. Pierre's tall opened-frame single-seater wears the same engine as mine, but his is attached to an absolute beast of a propeller, which in addition to longer and heavier rotor blades makes his machine considerably more efficient. While my pals carry generous fuel reserves for extended range, Delta-J's modest 30 litre tank limits us to ninety minutes safe airborne time and without a fuel gauge it's crucial to keep track of time before it all goes quiet at the back. Our longest trip without refuelling totalled exactly two hours and included two full power take offs, flying with Mark from Cranfield to Duxford and back. I was so tense on that return flight, ears primed for the first missed beat before a final cough, splutter and silence. Cranfield was getting no discernibly nearer as the ground passed below us at a crawl, the hands of my watch eating up the minutes as fast as I imagined the engine was sucking the fuel tank dry, yet somehow we made it.

So it was typically generous of my two wingmen to burden themselves with a slow, limited-range companion. Hervé assured me that the airstrip of piste d'en Lébé was well within reach of my tiny tank, and the chance to explore a new patch on such a gorgeous afternoon was too good to miss. I would stick with Pierre, keeping station above and to his right so he would know our whereabouts even if he lost visual. We three lined up with Hervé in the lead, his bright yellow machine easy to spot as we climbed above 1,500 feet, much higher than our usual Gyro Club outings. Visibility was perfect in the late afternoon. We cruised over a glorious panorama of undulating hills, farms and hamlets widely scattered among secluded woods and valleys. Hervé was well out in front setting the pace, Pierre slightly below on my left, sunlight glinting on his flickering rotor disc – this is the life! Half an hour en route and all the usual landmarks were behind us, I was lost above an endless spread of rolling countryside. Glancing at my watch, the doubts began to creep in as forty-five minutes elapsed, half of our safe range, but Hervé sailed serenely on. My inner five-year-old began to fidget – *are we nearly there yet?* Fortunately the air was unusually buoyant, giving the rotors plenty of traction and easing the burden on the engine, conserving our fuel.

Another five minutes passed: finally Hervé's machine began to descend and Pierre was dropping away to the left, but where were we going? All I could see were fields. Reducing power and putting her nose down just enough to trickle along behind Pierre, I watched him closely, unwilling to surrender our cushion of altitude until I could properly see the target. It's a little disconcerting sometimes when you can't communicate with your mates in flight! Then far below, a yellow gyroplane settled on to a short grass strip that suddenly materialised between the crops. Crikey, that looks a bit snug. I throttled right back and swung around behind Pierre, touching down nicely in an idyllic setting apparently miles from anywhere. It was a short strip (475 metres as I discovered later) surrounded by tall maize, with an uphill slope for take off. I would worry about that later. Hervé's machine was already parked alongside a trio of Piper Cubs in the shade of some trees next to a large farmhouse. Imagine living here with aircraft on the lawn, falling out of bed in the morning beside your very own airstrip, the stuff of dreams for a grass roots aviator.

The colours were intense. Our gyroplanes bright scarlet and yellow parked on a cushion of green, edged with fields of ripened harvest beneath a sky of pristine blue. It brought to mind another evening excursion many years ago back at home, when I flew from Cranfield to Sywell with Mark and Simon. That too was the end of a lovely summer day and taking to the air was like diving into a blue lagoon. Together we rode the warm breeze through a genial sky dotted with the lazy bulk of hot air balloons. Sywell was a picture: a triangle of neatly trimmed grass runways stood out in a rich contrast of greens, flanked by a lake of molten silver. Settling lightly on to the immaculate lawn, three gyroplanes, one red, one yellow and one blue, made a rainbow on the grass, bathed in the silence of evening sunlight. It was the exact same vibe: a special bond between friends forged by the unique way that we fly.

A yellow Piper Cub whispered in over the maize and settled daintily on the grass, momentum carrying it on up the slope before turning back to join its friends parked by the trees. A delightful oasis hidden in the middle of nowhere, but time was getting on and we had to make tracks for the Gyro Club. Thanking our hosts, we three prepared our mounts while the Cub pilots, families and friends gathered under the trees to watch the show, which did nothing for my rapidly fading confidence. A warm evening, a short uphill take off in zero wind, the least powerful gyroplane in the hands of the least experienced pilot (and a foreign female to boot), what could go wrong! I wished we had a bit more oomph, that maize looks awfully close. On the plus side we were several kilos lighter having burned through half a tank of fuel already, so for the honour of the Gyro Club get on with it and don't embarrass your mates.

Hervé took off easily with his powerful four-stroke, no problem there. As Pierre lined up on the threshold and engaged the pre-rotator, I tucked Delta-J in as close as I could on the narrow strip to catch his prop wash and boost my rotor blades. They lapped it up – it's never failed! As Pierre accelerated, we edged forward to take full advantage of his wake, still feeding the rotors until he was clear. They had such a lovely beat going that it was safe to put the power on almost at once, the nose wheel came up and we were out of there much easier than expected, thanks to Pierre's giant propeller. It was all plain sailing now. With the sun low on the horizon behind us, visibility was perfect as we headed back in loose formation towards the distant bulk of the Pyrenees, and home. What a beautiful ride, made all the more special for sharing it with friends. Moments like that are what it's all about.

A Soupcon of the South

The casual attitude with which my squadron mates handle petrol worries me considerably, particularly in the sultry heat of the Haute Garonne. Pleasantly situated out in the sticks, the Gyro Club is a good twenty minute drive from the nearest fuel source, so when the feast of Whitsun is upon us with visiting gyronauts needing to refill their tanks, typical French ingenuity is called for - and it scares the hell out of me! A dozen or more thin plastic containers that once held twenty litres of such innocuous liquids as vegetable oils, are gathered up and thrown into a van (or a car with trailer attached) and taken to the petrol station at Carbonne. Here the motley collection of flimsy bidons are filled with highly flammable 98 octane and casually hauled back to the airfield, unsecured. One spark would send them all to oblivion, yet they do this every year with no apparent precaution or concern.

Back at the Club, these bulky potential fire-bombs are stowed inside the oven-like heat of the small hangar, often with Delta-J still in residence alongside Jean Marie's machine. Refuelling is carried out with similar nonchalance: the inadequate containers upended and sloshed into a funnel gaping from the mouth of a fuel tank, a shimmering curtain of vapour rising in the heat, nicely primed for a spark of static. Gawd, they worry me! Years of British Health and Safety paranoia tempered with good old-fashioned common sense and cowardice, but apparently there's a different formula for spontaneous combustion over there, and for that I am very grateful.

This Way Up

*

One Monday evening following the traditional Whitsun gathering at the Gyro Club, all the local members had left for home and a well-earned rest after their labours. A tremendous amount of effort and physical hard work goes into that weekend. Charles summed it up brilliantly one year as I helped him load his gyroplane for the long drive back to Paris. Drained of energy and aching in every limb, his tired face turned to me and said in marvellously accented English, 'We eat. We fly. We are broken.' I loved it, the whole Gyro Club experience in a nutshell! So it was the calm after the storm that found me and my van camped on the airfield that Monday evening, along with the two remaining motor homes belonging to friends who would begin their journey home on the morrow.

My neighbours were Raymond and Josiane Lapert, a lively couple in their seventies, and Jean Marie and Nicole Enfissi, regular visitors of many years with their big twin-seat gyroplane, accompanied as always by Atos the little black spaniel. It was another gorgeous evening rich with colour in the softening light, and insects trilling amongst the grass. Beyond the trees rose the imperious peaks of the Pyrenees standing guard on the horizon, starkly outlined against the infinite blue. As usual we were shattered after the crowded exuberance of a successful Gyro Club weekend, the evening silence a welcome balm in which to reflect and soak up the memories.

Another feast was in preparation. The two couples were dining alfresco, setting up an array of picnic tables between the motor homes, and without a second thought, the good-hearted people automatically expected me to join them. It'd been a poignant weekend amid all the merriment and partying. Jean Marie was terminally ill and had been unable to join us the previous year, but somehow he had rallied and brought his gyroplane back to fly with us one last time. We knew we would not be together again, so tonight was the here and now to be remembered and cherished. I helped to fetch and carry for the two ladies who were doing wonders in their compact little kitchens, while Raymond and Jean Marie attended to the wine and aperitifs. The innate ability of the French to turn a simple meal into an occasion, never ceases to amaze.

Pierre Cena came shuffling down the rutted track to join us, and I was summoned to bring my chair from the van as everyone gathered round for aperitifs, Atos patrolling expectantly around our feet. The old friends chatted comfortably between themselves in mellow mood, words flowing in lilting French as evening turned to dusk and darkened softly into night. A surround sound of amphibians began tuning up for their nightly chorus, a mass prelude to the timeless unveiling of stars winking into existence above our heads. Darkness embraced us, we could hardly see each other across the table, not that it mattered at all.

Josiane broke in to snippets of song and Raymond hummed along in accompaniment, *bobob-a-bomming* contentedly somewhere in the moonless night. Jean Marie fetched his accordion and began to play. It was perfect. Nothing could've been more French. My companions paired up to dance, swaying gently under a canopy of stars as Jean Marie filled the air with music. It must have been past midnight, the roads were silent and here and there a solitary light glowed softly from the village. When a bottle of champagne was produced to crown the evening, I declined the offer of a modest glass but Jean Marie requested especially that I drink with him. What else could I do but accept a small measure to toast our friendship, knowing that his time was all too short. It was pitch black when we finally parted company. The two couples both had long journeys ahead and would be leaving early in the morning, so I promised to be ready to see them go. A strange wooziness enveloped my limbs as I stumbled back to my bed, pausing for one last gaze at the infinity of space.

I really shouldn't touch alcohol. It was well past eleven o'clock when I woke next morning, my little van standing alone on the airfield. Jean Marie Enfissi died shortly after, cruelly taken too soon as the good ones generally are. The sound of an accordion always brings him to mind, a fond memory of the obvious pleasure it gave him to play for us that night. Rest in Peace, Jean Marie. And thank you for the music.

One evening I had the house to myself as Jean Marie and Claudine were out visiting friends, not that it stopped Claudine from preparing a meal for me to warm up, along with salad and dessert despite my protests. It amuses me that twice a year I drive the length of France from top to bottom to fly my gyroplane, but am still deemed incapable of feeding myself! So I feel bad for creating more work even though I tell her there's no need, she won't listen. During the course of my stay there are usually a couple of dinner parties at the house – I see more people in three weeks in France than I do all year at home! The small kitchen is a whirlwind of industry, every surface covered by platters of meat and mounds of fruit and vegetables, pots bubbling and pans sizzling as Claudine orchestrates another feast for her guests. It's amazing, I wouldn't know where to start, but French ladies seem to have a natural ability for cuisine. Rarely am I allowed to assist with the stack of washing up after another epic feed. Once after being repeatedly shooed away from the sink, I remarked that she's always working – to which she replied, 'What else would I do?' I found it rather sad.

The world won't cease to exist if dinner isn't ready on the dot, but Jean Marie has a set routine that's ruled by the clock, whereas I go with the flow. Claudine spends hours planning, preparing or shopping for the next meal and seems to thrive on providing for everyone. I guess it's another one of those cultural differences, but looking back at my mum's life (and even myself as a teen in the Seventies) convention dictated that women stayed home to cook and clean while the men went out to work. I'm eternally grateful to Mum for not enforcing the domestic side on me as her strict father had once enforced it upon her. My grandmother was bedridden, paralysed with arthritis, so it was taken for granted that my mum would cook and clean for her parents and two brothers. She didn't have a choice.

Anyway, back at the homestead that late May evening on my own: the temperature was comparable to a Cornish summer's day as darkness fell, ridiculously hot for the comfort of a wimpish Brit. I left the windows open, resigning myself to the rabid attention of French mosquitoes, who find my Anglo-

Saxon blood to be a particularly tasty vintage, or maybe they just enjoy a different flavour. Whatever, the damn things are vicious! It was still too hot to sleep, so I turned off the light and climbed up on the window sill to listen to the sounds of the night.

Somewhere in the trees a bird was singing: I don't know what it was (maybe a nightingale) but the purity was hypnotic. Then in the distance another bird took up the song as if in reply, joining the melody in a perfect duet that flowed long into the night, filling the silence between the stars as if the world had stopped to listen and was holding its breath. I sat there captivated until some time later headlights shone up the driveway, heralding the return of my friends. Jean Marie appeared in the doorway, staring quizzically at my empty bed. I greeted him from the window sill and he laughed as he spotted me in the dark and came over to see what was going on. He thought I had gone to roost in the back of my van when he didn't see there, but no, I was just enjoying a late night concert. Together we listened for a few moments to the exquisite duet, then kissed goodnight as he went to his room. It was only then that I realised he had no trousers on.

A SHALLOW MISCONCEPTION

Whenever we tread the rocky slopes of the Pyrenees, my thoughts turn to the brave Resistance fighters of the nineteen-forties. They risked their lives on these same inhospitable peaks helping desperate people to flee from the tyranny of Nazi occupation. The mountains haven't changed in a mere eighty years and it's a humbling experience to walk those same tracks, but for us it couldn't be more different. Our treks depend on favourable conditions: we're well equipped with sturdy boots, modern weatherproof clothing and of course, plentiful supplies of food and drink. We reach the snow line in bright sunshine with cooling breezes to enjoy a leisurely lunch overlooking stunning vistas, returning safely the same evening to all the comforts of home. It would be so easy to twist an ankle on the steep and rugged terrain. Even a minor injury could cause great difficulty on these remote slopes, meaning a long and painful hobble back to the car park and civilisation, yet it's nothing in comparison.

We're not weakened by wartime deprivations and fleeing in fear of our lives. We don't endure the bitter cold of winter, struggling through ice and snow, blasted by gales and battered by storms. We've never stumbled in silence through the darkness, afraid to betray our presence with a feeble beam of light – hunted by dogs and pursued by the guns of brutality and hatred. There's no possible way we can imagine the hardships faced by those courageous souls eighty years ago on these same mountain tracks.

Several of the evasion routes used to cross into Spain are now commemorated as part of *le Chemin de la Liberté* (the Freedom Trail), which begins at the excellent museum in Saint-Girons. One particularly poignant memorial is found at the base of the Pic de Lampau, honouring the crew of a British Halifax bomber that crashed one night with the loss of all seven lives. Some of the wreckage is still there. We hiked to the plateau beneath this distant peak one pleasant October day. The autumn colours of the trees and tranquil beauty of the surrounding valleys were hard to reconcile with the sudden violent end of seven young men high up on the rocks above us, a lonely place to die in the freezing darkness, many miles from home. But they're not forgotten.

Once on the way back from a hike, we stopped at the museum in Saint-Girons, a town once in the thick of Nazi resistance where many brave souls began the arduous trek across the Pyrenees. We spent several hours in respectful contemplation of the horrors of war, and the stubborn courage of those forced to endure it. Ordinary townsfolk stared back at us from faded photos lining the walls, just a few generations distant from my own friends whose forebears had known them. There's a common misconception by outsiders who believe in the myth of a submissive French surrender, a grave injustice to the many brave men and women who remained defiant and risked everything for their country's freedom. Such ignorance does not belittle their courage.

*

Oradour sur Glane. What can anyone say about Oradour? I found myself on the outskirts of Limoges when taking a different route on the way home one year, and being vaguely aware of the tragedy attached to the name, I couldn't pass it by. Those who crave conflict are fools. Oradour sur Glane is living memory of just one of the countless atrocities committed under the pretext of war. Alongside the thriving modern town rebuilt in its name, the walled remains of the murdered community seems to cower away like a beaten puppy nursing a pain too deep to bear. *Why did they do this to us?* The crumbling walls of gutted buildings remain enduring proof of the cruelty mankind can unleash on fellow human beings. Cars, bicycles, crockery, pots and pans – ordinary possessions of the lost souls lay rusting amongst the rubble, just as they were left on that terrible day when the Nazis came and the clocks were stopped forever.

I wandered the ruins for hours unable to process the horrors suffered by this typical French community, no different to those I passed through every day on my travels. There a bakery, the post office, a school and a church, empty shells turning to dust. Treading the quiet streets where families once gathered and children played, I followed in the footsteps of evil. A whole town wiped out. All that remains is a stunned silence that seems to resonate through the decades. For once I took no photos, and my camera stayed in my pocket: it felt disrespectful, a vulgar intrusion into a grief I could never begin to imagine. But the trees remain clearly in my mind, for they had lived through the horrors of that day.

I remember being drawn to one aged specimen in particular, spreading its branches like a protective shield above the ground near the shattered church. A silent witness, it felt the powerful resonance of misery and fear on the day that the clocks were stopped. Could it somehow have absorbed the echoes of those lives so cruelly taken and kept them safe inside, cherished and soothed by it's own tranquil existence. Are those echoes immortalised perhaps, recorded like a seismograph in the growth rings of its trunk, a living memorial to the innocent? I hope it flourishes for many more decades, along with all the other trees that bore witness and the echoes that they may hold. Resting my forehead on the rough bark, I pressed my palm against its trunk in a helpless expression of regret for the lost souls. Man's inhumanity to man – and still it goes on. Will we never learn? A single word adorns the entrance in both French and English. Souviens-toi: *Remember.*

Lost for Words

August of 2019 saw the 20th anniversary of Thénac aerodrome celebrated with a fun weekend of feasting and flying. Owned and operated by our friends Marie and Martial Lajoux, it was a pleasure to join the festivities despite the relentless heat that flattened both John and me, the only Brits at the party. Scientists declare that perpetual motion is an impossibility – well they haven't met Marie! Energetic isn't the word, she's an absolute dynamo. Plug her in to the national grid and she could probably light up Paris. Struggling in 30°C, we helped with preparations as best we could, fetching and carrying, laden with provisions and trying to keep pace with Marie's tireless organising. Dusting off an assortment of tables from the cavernous wooden hangar, we clustered round to assist in peeling mounds of boiled eggs, onions, potatoes and tomatoes plus a ton of fruit, slicing and dicing to make salads enough for several hundred guests. With no electricity on site and no conveniences like hot water or refrigeration, the local ladies created a feast of ingenuity from the barest of essentials.

I love the French community spirit: everyone pitches in and works together for the greater good, a feeling of belonging that's rarely the same at home. Maybe it's our natural English reserve, or the increasing bureaucratic fun sponge that sucks the joy out of everything with petty regulations for even the smallest of communal efforts. Alongside the hedge, a crate of logs stood next to a giant barbecue, made from an oil drum sliced down its length and laid across a rustic frame. Filled with wood and set ablaze, it belched a steady pall of smoke and flame that rose vertically in the torpid air until the embers subsided into a healthy glow. The sight of Martial tending dozens of steaks sizzling beautifully over the smouldering oil drum, would leave the British Nanny State reeling in horror. No warning signs, no safety barriers, no hygiene certificates, no food allergy or calorie content labels, yet everyone enjoyed it immensely. After lunch a merry game was played with a small compressor firing plastic bottles high into the air for the children to chase, which they managed to do most joyfully without wearing safety goggles, hard hats or ear defenders. How dare people take responsibility for themselves!

The weekend was crowned by a diverse assortment of flying machines arriving for the celebrations. A tropical sky buzzed with a steady procession of weight-shift flexwings, gyroplanes and an eclectic mix of three-axis microlights, as well as a squat little amphibious biplane and several conventional light aircraft. The resident Thénac pilots were constantly busy giving passenger flights, their guests no doubt grateful for a brief respite from the intense summer heat. Evening's calm brought perfect conditions for the paraplane to take wing: a Mad Max-style open chassis with a caged propeller fastened on the back, it swung ponderously into the air suspended beneath a bright canopy of red and yellow.

It was during that weekend that I was treated to the wildest ride I've yet experienced in a gyroplane. Actually I'm not sure it's possible to get any wilder and still keep the machine intact. Ye gods, I enjoyed it thoroughly – afterwards – when my brain had caught up with the rest of me! Wow. Having flown with Patrick at Sainte Foy in 2012, I had a suspicion of what to expect, but that was a walk in the park in comparison. We're complete polar opposites, Patrick being a very skilled and confident gyronaut with an aversion to flying straight and level, he knows his machine inside out and exactly what it's capable of. The fact that he's survived pulling those manoeuvres for all these years is confirmation of his piloting skills, and a real testament to the strength and quality of Italian engineering. Personally though, I'd be happier if he allowed himself a little more of a safety margin – especially when down in the dirt!

The intention had been to let me take the controls in the

front seat, but short-arse couldn't reach the rudder pedals and moving them back proved to be a little more problematic than anticipated. Patrick had been busy giving flights all morning and it was getting close to lunchtime, so I didn't mind taking the back seat and was grateful just to get off the ground. He still insisted on attaching the rear control stick for me to fly with – not that I had it for long! Admittedly there was a quiver of apprehension knowing full well that Patrick would be going all out for my benefit. Snug in the rear of the high-sided pod, clad only in T-shirt, shorts and headset (no crash helmet), I tightened the lap strap to its limit. Well I'd had a good life and what a way to go! Regretfully there wasn't time to grab my action cam, and all that remains of that epic flight are a few snap-shot images in my head, like peering straight down at the ground barely ten feet beyond the blade tips as the rotor disc bisected the horizon at ninety degrees. What a ride!

It was a stifling 32°C with barely a breath of air to tickle the windsock. Delta-J would have struggled horribly in such conditions, but that M16 is a powerful beast and Patrick didn't waste any time. Barely attaining 300 feet on climb out, he stood it on its tail and pivoted the big machine through a 180, powering back in a low pass along the runway to swing up over the field of dried sunflowers at the end. We went up, we went down (mainly down!), fast and fluid, wheels inches above the parched earth as we blasted *between* trees and hills at impossible angles, accompanied by the heavy beat of hard-working rotor blades. No roller coaster could produce such a thrill. Supremely confident and smooth on the controls, Patrick was in his element as he handled the big Magni like a jet fighter, twisting round in his seat to give me a beaming thumbs-up, which I was delighted to return.

Back over the sunflowers again, we roared down the runway at a matter of inches, using the momentum to swing up and stand the machine on its tail for the obligatory hammerhead. Poised in mid-air, nose to the sky, the airframe spun like a compass needle beneath the span of rotor disc to point back from whence we came, floating in for a gentle touch down as the rotors expended their energy in triumphant song. That was gloriously terrifying! Grinning like a loon, I made my way unsteadily back to the hangar where John was waiting for what was left of me, his unbridled laughter confirming that I probably looked exactly like I felt. I couldn't even begin to articulate. Trying to assemble my scattered wits and process what the heck had just happened, I think I may have sworn...

BEFORE THE WORLD WENT MAD

It's a very long drive down through the visual feast of rural France to get to Bois de la Pierre. It seems like the roads get longer with every trip, or maybe it's those pesky 30 kph limits that breed like rabbits in every town and village. I particularly love the landscape of the Gers, the neighbouring department of the Haute Garonne. There's something very pleasing about the graceful fluidity of its rolling hills, and just over yonder, looming large beyond their comely brows, rise the majestic peaks of the Pyrenees. Imperious and forbidding, rooted to the very core of the planet, they stand timeless above the trivial scuttling of humanity. They are awesome.

So back once again my heroic little van and me, thanks to our eccentric satnav which continues to lead us down ever-varying detours from north to south. It'd be so easy to hop on one of the excellent autoroutes and blat down the length of the country from A to B, seeing nothing but tarmac in between, oblivious to all the gorgeousness bypassed along the way. That's no fun. I love the hidden surprises discovered away from the haste of the beaten track. So it's two days down and two days back, every Whitsun to help prepare for the meeting and refresh my soul with the music of free-spinning rotors, a melody no longer heard at home since the symphony of St Merryn was silenced by one man's greed. But on this idyllic little airstrip deep in the south of France, the orchestra is in full swing – and it's magnificent! A marvellous diversity of gyroplanes fill the hangars, and tucked away at the back of this forest of masts and rotor blades is the smallest of them all, my raison d'être. Delta-J, the little red Cinderella who only gets to party twice a year.

It was an unusually late meeting with Whitsun falling on 9 June, so unfortunately for me it was going to be hot. Preparation for the fête had long begun with the heavy steel framework already bolted in place to form an extended canopy over the front of the main hangar. Supplies for the modest bar had been gathered and stowed, with yet more to be purchased on a special excursion across the border to Spain, ready for the hundreds of enthusiasts that will squeeze into the clubhouse over the weekend. There was still much to do, so it was all hands to the pump and everyone mucked in for the honour of our Club.

The old tractor trundled by in endless passes, drivers swapping at intervals in a continuous relay to cut the grass or drag the heavy home-made roller over the runway, flattening the mole hills into submission. A large garden parasol fixed at a rakish angle above the driver's seat provided much-needed shade, comically engulfing the occupant peering out from beneath its fringe. Everyone was tanned nut brown except the adopted Anglaise, my pale limbs now candy striped with glowing pink – *rosbif!* I'm not born to the sun like them, the strength of its rays oppresses me, sapping vitality. I fried gently basted in greasy sun-block, *bien cuit,* sizzling in the heat, sustained by frequent slurps from the bottle of increasingly tepid water by my side.

The gyroplanes were untangled from the main hangar and pushed outside, leaving it exposed in preparation for the next assault. This caused great agitation for a pair of slim thrush-like birds who had built their nest on one of the rotor assemblies, resting on brackets high up on the wall. Unfortunately the rotors were needed for the fête, so the nest was gently removed and placed on top of a small cabinet instead. This was much lower down and positioned just above the sink, bringing the nest into close contact with the noisy humans disrupting the hangar. Matters wouldn't improve for poor little mum and dad, and in due course an insistent high-pitched cheeping announced the successful arrival of their offspring. The chicks grew quickly. Craning our necks from a respectful distance, we could just see a layer of soft grey fluff that erupted with gaping mouths at the approach of a busy parent. Before long, three comically wide yellow beaks and three pairs of tiny black eyes peeped back at us from the rim of the nest. How cute was that!

Soon we had to be very careful where we trod in the vicinity of the sink, stopping frequently to scoop up a diminutive fluttering bundle and pop it back in the nest, as the parents shrieked in alarm. No doubt the chicks were badly disturbed, and kept hopping out of the nest to tumble helplessly off the cabinet. It quickly became habit to do a head count every time we went by, and retrieve any escapees before continuing with the job in hand. Happily they all survived the commotion of Whitsun weekend, and afterwards were still keeping their anxious parents busy as they fluttered randomly about the hangar, proper new feathers already sprouting through the fluff.

*

Leaf blowers are a source of puzzlement to me, a pointless accessory that seems to create more work than it actually achieves, but Jean Marie loves them. The hangar floor was first hosed down to quell the dust, and (like the leaf blower) it had minimal effect. Dark gritty clouds swirled up, agitated by the blower, merely rearranging the dirt which inevitably drifted back in, but it's all part of the ritual. This annual spring clean is a symbolic rebirth that throws off winter's dismal cloak to embrace the coming of summer. Cupboards, closets and clubhouse were thrown open and pulled apart, sending small lizards darting for cover. Anything that doesn't move gets washed, scrubbed and vacuumed, the detritus of the old year swept away to begin anew.

Wooden stakes still in their piles from the last meeting were pulled from the garage and assessed for further use. Discarding those too splintered or rotten, the fit-for-purpose pile was slapped with a new coat of whitewash and quickly sun-baked dry. It doesn't take long. Next in the firing line was the fence bordering the runway. I'm very well acquainted with this fence, and the large community of *l'escargots* that cluster in the precious sliver of shade beneath its rails. At first I tried to paint around them, loath to pluck them from their sanctuary to roast in the sun while I redecorated. It became a source of amusement among the campers over the weekend, as the snails went about their business liberally adorned with go-faster stripes. It may have helped to reflect the heat... But I needn't have worried, these are Olympic class molluscs. Gently detaching the snoozing shells and placing them in the grass, it's a race to cover the portion of fence before they tenaciously ooze their way back up the freshly whitewashed posts to re-adhere themselves beneath the rails. It's a good thing the paint dries so fast.

While I played with the snails, the lads continued with more manly tasks such as arranging metal barriers on the other side of the runway, and cutting back wayward tangles of vegetation sprouting along the drainage ditches. Bundles of newly painted pickets were paced out and hammered in place, and signs of various flavours affixed on the field and along the local routes, pointing the way to gyroplane heaven. Sometime later a short break was signalled, everyone converging on the clubhouse for refreshments before the next part of the ritual began. The ancient farm wagon plays an important role during the festivities, but first it must be unearthed from its nearby resting place and dragged down to the village hall to collect the flagpoles.

Divested of mower, the tractor under its green parasol chugged gaily down the track to Pierre Cena's house, the extraction crew assigned to manhandle the heavy iron trailer trudging along in its wake. Later the rattling convoy returned, the crew now riding in the back of the rusted wagon, jolting along behind the tractor in a cloud of dust. A moment of merriment as Jean Marie towed the procession on to the grass and swung around in a couple of tight circuits, parasol flapping amid cheerful yells from the human cargo flung around in the back. I'm not usually part of this phase but an animated chorus of shouts as tractor and trailer sailed past in a final loop, summoned me to abandon my paint pot and make haste – I was on the wagon!

Willing hands reached down and hauled me onboard into the midst of a carnival vibe. Jean Marie steered across the runway and out on to the road beyond, a happy band of inmates rattling along behind. Like most rural outposts, the streets of Bois de la Pierre are somewhat slender, a reality greatly accentuated when riding on the deck of a heavy farm trailer with the throaty growl of a tractor resonating off the walls in a concussion of sound. It's only a short ride to the town hall, but several ninety degree turns add to fun as we threaded noisily through the deserted village and into the car park. Sheltered from the light breeze in the lee of the hill, the torpid heat intensified, trapped amid the sleepy buildings and radiating off the tarmac.

We bailed out and trooped round to where the pile of patriotically-painted flagpoles are stored. These things are about twenty-five feet long, of which we extracted half a dozen and paired up to shoulder the load back to the trailer – which is barely half their length. With no rope or straps to secure them, we just sat on top of the pile and clung on! The poles greatly overhung both tractor and trailer, almost dragging on the road as we in the back struggled to keep the flexing lengths in place. Navigating the narrow ninety degree turn at the heart of the village caused much hilarity as our extended load barely cleared the walls. I couldn't help but wonder about the structural integrity of that ancient chassis as we chugged back up the hill – and where we might be deposited should it come unhitched! It was best not to look.

Back at the field, we unloaded the hefty wooden poles and laid them on the grass, ready to be heaved upright into their respective slots once the flags were attached. The old wagon was propped up in its usual place, where it would later be transformed into the announcer's podium. Next, two huge tarpaulins had to be hauled in to position over the framework of the hangar extension, always a comedy when the wind snatches the giant covers before they're trapped with lengths of bamboo and endless yards of string. Field ingenuity at its finest. Over the years I've come to enjoy the preparations more than the actual event itself. It's a huge voluntary effort to put on a good show, and for the Club members the weekend of the actual meeting is particularly manic. Time goes by in a heartbeat and before we know it, Monday morning arrives and everything is taken down and packed away again, rather like Christmas with weeks of planning and anticipation for something that's gone in the blink of an eye. Our reward is the hundreds of happy visitors who leave with great memories of yet another safe and successful Gyro Club weekend. *Impeccable.*

RASSEMBLEMENT 2019

Gégé and Alain in the Air Copter

And so to the main event. Graced with perfect conditions there was an excellent attendance over the weekend with around forty gyroplanes on the flight line. The Pyrenees looked amazing decorated with snow against a deep blue sky, and I greatly appreciated the cooling breeze that wafted down from the heights as I guarded the runway crossing in my hi-viz vest. Jokes about the *Gilets Jaunes* protest movement abounded, and all I needed was a placard to complete the rebel image.

Sunday dawned overcast, the cooling breeze noticeably absent and the temperature rose accordingly. This was the day of the traditional Whitsun fly-out to Cazères. I've done this flight four times with Delta-J, and several more as a lucky passenger in the back of a two-seater. In fact, the very first time I took part as a pilot remains one of the highlights of my life, even though it scared the hell out of me! It's not so bad going *into* Cazères as the field is wide open and can swallow several gyroplanes abreast with ease, but coming home to Bois de la Pierre is another matter entirely. The squadron leader of the day (usually Jean Marie) holds a mandatory briefing for all pilots before departure, which is all very well providing everyone plays their part. You might *think* you know what's going on... I don't use radio for reasons previously explained, and Delta-J being the smallest at the Club means we inevitably struggle to keep up.

*

Our last trip to Cazères during Whitsun 2017 was very nearly our last trip anywhere. This group was an exceptionally large one with fifteen machines taking part, and eleven of them were big ones. Being small, vulnerable and mute dictates that we hang back to put everyone else in front where I can see them, unless Jean Marie gives us a specific place in the line. Twice we've been positioned up front alongside him, which isn't so bad although it's hard to keep pace. He also flies non-radio but no one would dare to run *him* down! This particular year though, Jean Marie was being chauffeured in the back seat of an Eclipse instead of leading the pack in his single-seat machine.

I kept us well out of the way while all the big stuff lined up and took off. It looked chaotic with machines going everywhere around the edge of the circuit – we weren't getting mixed up with that lot! Instead we tagged along behind Pierre de Raigniac in his open-frame single-seat, the last two of the line following a swarm of fly-specks towards Cazères. I had to hold back on base leg as a couple of tandem machines were barrelling straight in on a long final, oblivious to the little red gyroplane on their right. Then it was our turn, fluttering down onto the rough grass and joining the others in the parking area with a sigh of relief.

Dismounting for an aperitif and brief mingle around the hangar, everyone piled in for the obligatory group photo (invariably taken by several people at once, so no one ever knows which way to look). With another Gyro Club visit duly recorded for posterity, we crowded round Jean Marie to get instructions for the flight home. The four single-seats were to lead out and fly back direct, being slower than the big boys who would take a longer route and dogleg to form up over the lakes at Peyssies, rejoining behind the little ones for landing. It sounded good in theory. Back to our respective birds as ordered, Charles, Christian, Pierre et moi paired up and jolted our way out to position on the runway, a mass of expensive hardware turning and burning behind.

No wind *again* – and the grass was long and lumpy. Everyone else had the luxury of big wheels and suspension, blissfully unaware of what a challenge it was going to be to rouse a pair of lightweight rotor blades on that rough surface with six-inch wheels, rigid airframe and no wind. They had no idea! Consequently they were already crowding us as I chased my wingmen down the runway, teeth and eyeballs rattling in my head. The big machines sailed by on all sides as we climbed out surrounded by shimmering rotor discs and flashing strobe lights, which rapidly pulled away leaving us four little ones to continue in peace. Now we could relax for a while and enjoy the flying as we tracked towards the distant lakes, a crowd of black dots hanging in the sky to our right. I wasn't looking forward to the next bit.

The airfield at Bois de la Pierre is nowhere near as spaciously accommodating as Cazères, our runway being maybe half the width. During the fête it's forbidden to fly over the camping and exhibition areas on either side of the runway, which makes it even tighter – and this year's fly-out was an exceptionally large swarm of gyroplanes. Already the strobes were catching up fast, and my neck was on permanent swivel as stress levels began to rise. But the four singles were to go in first, leading the parade in the usual photo opportunity low pass down the runway before going round again to land, that's what the boss had said. Pierre was already dropping down, leading us in with Charles on his tail to blast along the runway, as Christian's machine slid beneath my axle to take up position. Acutely aware of a pair of Eclipses lit up like Christmas trees on our right, I reduced power to descend behind Christian as we neared the woods on the threshold, wishing we could land and not have to go round and do it again. The Christmas trees had seen us and were giving us space – the one that nearly got us didn't see us at all. Glancing forward to gauge Christian's proximity in the descent, I was startled to see a big yellow ELA cutting in from the left to curl sharply round behind Christian, filling the space that we were just about to occupy. *Jeeez!!!* Possibly in the excitement of the moment he forgot that there were FOUR single-seats leading in, I don't know. He didn't see us, plain and simple: he wouldn't have done that otherwise and it was far too close for comfort.

*

I don't fly Delta-J to Cazères at Whitsun anymore, as I reply to every enquiry as to whether I'm joining the parade each year. So I have Charles to thank for procuring a back seat ride for me, after asking earlier if was going along. On hearing about our near miss and subsequent chickening-out, he said he would gladly have taken me in his new two-seat homebuilt but was not yet authorised to carry passengers. Instead (and unknown to me) he asked the other participants if they had room for a little one, knowing that I wouldn't ask it for myself. On duty at the runway crossing, watching from afar as the pilots gathered for the preflight briefing, I was puzzled to hear my name come crackling over the PA system. Then Gérard emerged from the throng, waving wildly in my direction to fetch my electric hat and join him in the Air Copter, tout suite. *Yes please!* He too had enquired earlier if I was going with them, but (as he later explained) understood my reply of it being 'too dangerous' to mean that I didn't want to go at all. For my part, I thought he was asking if I was flying my machine to Cazères (not did I want a lift!), hence my reply that it was too dangerous, being slow, small and mute.

Gégé is an excellent pilot. I first flew with him years ago in his three-axis Coyote microlight – he handled it like a gyroplane! Now he owned a two-seat Air Copter, a machine that intrigues me having flown it with him on our frequent excursions to the neighbouring airfield of Sabonnères. Despite its apparent size and large rotor diameter, this Air Copter is remarkably light on the stick (even more so than Delta-J), quite a challenge to get the feel of. It's an enigma to me. I abandoned my post and fled back to the van to collect my jacket and helmet, forgetting in my haste to grab the action cam as well.

Visibility was on the hazy side after several days of high pressure: a dusky contour smudged the horizon betraying the presence of the lower slopes, while distant snowy peaks were lost in the murk beyond. A ragged line of black dots hung in the sky ahead and several gyroplanes flanked us nearby, rotor discs shimmering in the sunshine. Gégé was in radio contact and he had an extra pair of eyes in the back, so I felt considerably safer than I did alone with Delta-J. He seemed very calm as the group strung out and arranged itself in landing order, yet he told me later that he was nervous amongst all the other machines. If that was nervous, I would've been a dribbling wreck! Despite some minor confusion on final approach as we had two Gérards in the flight, everyone landed safely on the ample grass runway and decamped for refreshments with our hosts, who were waiting to greet us by the hangar.

It was even hotter than yesterday with no cooling breeze coming from the mountains. Delta-J would have struggled horribly in those temperatures, but the big Air Copter had plenty to spare - even with all the extra weight in the back. Suspension makes a world of difference to ground handling: it was pure luxury as we sailed rapidly through the rough grass to line up on the runway, riding the bumps with ease instead of being shaken to pieces. We were in the air in no time, following the swarm in the usual climb out right across the middle of the lake. They have far more faith in their engines than I have in mine! We flew back at around 600 feet, Gégé pointing out orchards of kiwi fruit and imparting other titbits of local knowledge along the route. I was loving the ride, so effortless compared to my poor screaming two-stroke.

The leading gyroplanes began to align themselves for the homecoming pass as we approached Peyssies, circling the slimy looking waters like bees round a honey pot as everyone slotted in. Gégé banked tightly to follow the aerial conga line, taking seventh position as we circled repeatedly for everyone to catch up. I wondered what the fishermen below were thinking as the air throbbed to the beat of a dozen pairs of hard-working rotor blades. It felt too low for my liking as we skimmed the trees over the threshold in a fixed-wing-esque approach, scanning all round for conflicting traffic with visions of my previous near miss all too vivid. This was the part that always freaked me out when flying myself. It looks too narrow and congested to absorb such a large mass of rotorcraft, but Gégé had it all under control and we streamed along the runway in line astern for the watching crowd, a spectacular sight from the ground. Accelerating into a downwind turn we swung back around for final approach, six machines in front landing long at the far end and hustling to clear the way for those inbound behind. Happily, everyone kept to the plan and we all landed safely without incident.

What a bonus, I hadn't expected to take part at all but thanks to Charles and Gégé, I had another great memory to keep. Now thirteen months later that memory has become very precious. It's unbearably hard to relate that Gérard Chierotti was killed on 5 July 2020, during a Gyro Club weekend excursion. He was happy, flying formation with his friends as they had done so many times before. As pilots we accept the inherent risk in whatever form we choose to defy gravity, and do our best to minimise the possibility of accidents. We'd be daft not to. Thankfully worst case scenarios are rare but that doesn't make it any easier. A bientôt Gégé. You are greatly missed.

*

The marvellous weekend of gyroplane flying culminated as usual with the Sunday night feast, followed by the genial chaos of the tombola. Sadly from 2017, failing health meant that Pierre Cena rarely participated at the Club and he could no longer play his part at the fête. Xavier still presided over the microphone and Jean Marie chose the order of prizes, but new blood in the form of Eric, Hervé, Vincent, and Pierre de Raigniac gradually play a bigger part each year in a passing of the baton to the next generation. Eric and Pierre are the Club jokers, but put these four together and you've got trouble – in a fun way!

2018 saw the debut of the Coco Girls, which enlivened proceedings no end. Unexpected and total lunacy it was just too funny. Adorned in wigs and copious amounts of lipstick, the quartet took it in turns to deliver the prizes, each lucky winner being engulfed in hair and exaggerated kisses leaving them smothered in rouge. A few particular recipients were singled out for 'special' treatment, being set upon by all four in a mad swarm of camp comedy. It was my fate to be one of these targets. Several visiting Brits leaving before the weekend's finale had entrusted me with their large pile of tickets, which were very successful – unfortunately for me! Every time they scored a prize I was pounced on with glee, buried under a flurry of wigs and generously plastered in lipstick. Everyone was in tears of laughter and it was very funny to watch when not in the midst. This year they added leotards and chiffon tutus to their wardrobe leaving a few poor souls scarred for life, including Jean Marie who came very close to losing his trousers.

Somehow over the years it's become a running joke for everyone to sing 'Happy Birthday' to me at various Club gatherings, once in English and again in French for good measure. I have more birthdays than the Queen. It's spread to the annual meeting, and Eric (inevitably Eric!) has invented a new tradition where he gets the entire hangar full of people – most of whom don't have a clue who I am or what's going on – to celebrate yet another of my many imaginary birthdays. And every time the lights fuse, a spontaneous rendering of *Happy Birthday to you, Shirley* fills the night. Once during a fête we were plunged in to darkness six times and each blackout triggered yet another rousing chorus. I don't know how this became a thing, but that's our Eric!

He took it to a whole new level in 2019, which was quite alarming. Not only was I serenaded multiple times, he then invited people to come up for 'les bisous' – kisses. This was well out of my comfort zone. I'm a mouse shrinking from the spotlight, but there I was caught in the full glare being clapped and cheered by a couple of hundred revellers as Eric led the charge, queuing up to give me birthday kisses. To be fair, it was funny – *afterwards!* You just have to roll with it. A couple of minutes later, when things had calmed down again, Xavier sidled up to me with a big smile on his face and said innocently 'Fais les bises?' which got a huge laugh as I had to stand up and get kissed again. He timed it beautifully. Sadly as with all social gatherings around the world, the 2020 and 2021 meetings had to be cancelled because of this damn virus, otherwise I dread to think what heights they might've taken it to next. Actually, credit where it's due, it was Eric who gave me ideas for this book. I'd given copies of *Spinning on the Wind* to the few English speakers at the Club, and having received his with apparent surprise and pleasure, Eric exclaimed 'Now you will write about us!' So you can blame him.

Tipping the Balance

As I watched my elderly father grow increasingly frail, it occurred to me how much his world was shrinking with him. The circle of life was coming to a close as the hands of time crept round towards midnight. Limited from birth by ability and mobility, our horizons expand as we learn to walk and then run, progressing from tricycle to bicycle and roaming further afield until old enough to become motorised, a teenager's humble moped the first step towards adult independence. The world is our oyster to wander at will, but time takes its toll and boundaries cease to expand once we reach our own personal peak. At some unknown moment the balance subtly tips, setting us on the downward slope, blissfully unaware of shrinking horizons as capabilities quietly begin to fade.

A day trip becomes a short drive to town, which in turn becomes a walk to the village until that too is beyond physical endurance. Approaching his eighties after a lifetime on the road, my ex-heavy goods haulage father suddenly gave up driving, completely out of the blue. So every Saturday morning for a couple of years after, he walked the half a mile to the local shop to get his newspaper until failing health made the effort too much. His world contracted to the limits of house and garden as the onset of Parkinson's Disease confined him even further to his bedsit downstairs, unsafe to venture forth beyond walking frame and grab rails to mostly keep him upright.

Now well in to the second year of adapting to life with Covid-19 restrictions and lockdowns, I wonder if I too have reached my peak and begun the gentle coast down the other side. Will I get back to France and see my friends again to share the joys of autorotational flight? Jeez, I hope so, I'm not ready to hang up my wings just yet! I was a late comer to international travel and it wasn't until the mid-eighties that I spent any time on foreign soil, courtesy of my ever-generous boss, Paul Mitchell. Concerned that I was overdoing the overtime in attempt to keep pace with British Airways' voracious appetite for uniform badges, unbeknown to me, he arranged with my mum to send us away for an all expenses paid week in Austria. The scenery was stunning - Salzburg, Vienna, Innsbruck - the first time that I'd seen real mountains. My head rotated like an owl's, gaping through the coach windows in amazement as we left the airport and drove towards the craggy silhouette of the Wilder Kaiser range. We roamed lush alpine slopes several thousand feet above sea level, struggling to reconcile the solid ground beneath my feet with an altitude normally only achieved with the aid of a Grumman Cheetah.

That brief taste of foreign travel failed to ignite a wanderlust beyond the boundaries of my island home, although we did return for another week in Austria the following year. The embers were definitely smouldering though, a long slow burn that wouldn't set ablaze until that first road trip to Bois de la Pierre. Gyroplanes have been the driving force in my existence since 1990, and likewise the reason behind the life-changing expedition of 2005. I loved the whole journey: every mile, every turn of the wheel increased the sense of distance, a feeling lost by the time shrinking directness of air travel. To experience the changing landscape as we drove down was far more interesting than being plucked from Point A to be deposited at Point B after a couple of hours spent in limbo, like a sandwich with no filling. It's the bit in the middle that made all the difference, which is exactly like life itself. If birth is akin to take off, then death is as inevitable as landing - it has to happen sometime - it's what we do with the bit in the middle that makes all the difference.

Pierre est un Super Bon Pilot!

Happy gyronauts. Pierre and me

Well here we are at the end of 2022 after a long and tentative return to something like pre-pandemic life. I did indeed make it back to the Gyro Club, delighted to be reunited with everyone, especially my poor Delta-J, who despite not seeing daylight for two years was still in better condition than her pilot. Flying activity has been much reduced, our ranks sadly depleted by the loss of Pierre Cena, Jean Francois Comb and Gérard Chierotti, but there was great hope for the future thanks to Pierre de Raigniac, who was training to be an instructor. Every weekend new faces appeared at the Club, inspired by Pierre to sample the delights of autorotation. His cheerful optimism reminded me very much of Keith Balch, they shared the same positive energy and boundless enthusiasm for our special way of flying. Had Keith only recognised his own limitations and not tried to do too much too soon, he too would've made a fine instructor, just like Pierre.

How delicious it was to feel the wind through the rotors and hear their song once again – I missed it so much! We made up for lost time with some memorable flights, including two unexpected and most enjoyable excursions courtesy of back seat rides with Eric and Pierre, the highlight being a spectacular flight through the mountains to Bagnères-de-Luchon. I was with Pierre in his open-frame Air Copter, a very different ride to Eric's Rolls Royce of a beautifully refurbished M22. Along with Eric, and Gérard Castaing in their respective Magnis, and accompanied by Alain (a skilled pilot who flies his three-axis microlight in formation with the gyroplanes), we set course to the south-west under a grey overcast that didn't look too promising. It was quite brisk in the back of the Air Copter. The wind ballooned into my jacket, pushing it off my shoulders with a manic flapping that repeatedly forced open the zip. It was a constant fight just to stay dressed! Pierre sitting out in front took the full blast with no protection at all, and we must have generated quite some drag between us. I tried to photograph our wingmen but the wind's incessant battering made it nigh on impossible to steady the camera, and all I could do was point and shoot and hope for the best.

The low cloud base decapitated the foothills with a feathery grey line drawn across the landscape, yet visibility was good and conditions slowly improved as we approached the valley that would lead us to town. Patches of pale blue showed through a thinning mist above, allowing shafts of watery sunlight to filter through. The rounded hills had grown considerably in stature becoming rugged and muscular, their heavily forested shoulders rising high on either side. This was awesome! I glanced back to see Alain's sporty little aeroplane surfing the wooded peaks several hundred feet above us, wisely keeping plenty of altitude as he followed our slower-paced rotorcraft. Forced landing options down below were quite limited for an aircraft not blessed with a rotary-winged drag chute, and I didn't fancy being over this kind of terrain in anything other than an ultra-nimble gyroplane.

The sun was really breaking through now, burning off the morning mist to reveal a different world from the drab greyness hanging over the plain. Eric was leading, just a small dot out in front suspended between the slopes. Gérard's red machine beneath its shimmering white rotor disc showed up beautifully against the greens of fields and forest, early patches of autumnal colour adorning the leaves. The view became increasingly spectacular as the last pockets of cloud evaporated from the surrounding valleys, as if Nature was slowly drawing back the curtains and saving the best for last. Vast folds of rock created by unimaginable violence, aeons of turmoil set in stone, a mighty monument to the growing pains of a young planet. What an incredible privilege this was.

Up ahead the burgeoning heights crowded closer, merging their footprints on the valley floor and squeezing a narrow road even tighter as it disappeared into hidden depths, threaded between the intertwining giants. There were few patches of level ground to be seen as we funnelled through the pass – not somewhere I'd want to put my two-stroke reliability to the test! I'm too much of a coward to fly this close to the mountains with tiny Delta-J, so it was such a treat to have been invited along with the bigger boys. Safely through the pass, the surrounding slopes opened up to reveal a sheltered valley bathed in sunshine and there cradled at the foot of the mountains lay Luchon, a rocky silhouette of Pyrenean peaks guarding the horizon high above the town. Eric led us down in line astern to land on an immaculate grass aerodrome, a perfect touchdown in a perfect setting. Another one of those *pinch me* moments.

*

That memorable flight to Luchon took place on 9 October 2021. We could never have believed what would happen exactly a year later.

*

I had taken a print of this manuscript down with me to make

corrections, and was so engaged one Saturday afternoon while waiting for the lads to arrive at the airfield. Later larking around in the clubhouse while Eric prepared the coffee, I warned him to behave or else it would go in the book, pointing to some examples on the page. When Pierre came in shortly after, Eric told him that I was writing about them and pushed the manuscript across the counter for him to see. Expressing his pleasure at the news, Pierre picked it up and 'read' loudly with a broad grin 'Pierre est un super bon pilot!' He really was.

Thwarted by the calm and ridiculously hot October day, there was no point in knocking the stuffing out of Delta-J trying to get her airborne so I resigned myself to watching from the ground. Pierre had taken Jean Luc off on a local trip and Xavier was out to play in the AX05, casually zooming around inside the airfield boundary with his customary flair. Later the open-framed Air Copter returned high above for Pierre's habitual vertical descent approach, the big rotor blades making a lovely whopping sound as they gently drifted down to land. Back in the parking area, he spotted me perched in the back of Jean Marie's van and called out in English 'Shirley! You want to fly? – *With me!* flapping his arms as he did so. Yes please! So typical of him, his machine was hardly back on the ground before he found someone else to share it with.

For a gyroplane blessed with suspension, big rotor blades and a powerful pre-rotator, it was a perfect day to fly: the high temperature and complete lack of wind didn't bother it at all. Visibility was good with a few scattered clouds and the higher peaks of the Pyrenees lost in a misty haze. Barely a ripple disturbed the dark waters of the Garonne as we flew over to Montesquieu, circling Jean Marie's house then back across the fields to the lake at St. Elix, where we swooped down in tight spirals chasing the jet skis that carved through the water below. It reminded me of chasing speedboats on the river Camel and how much Keith had wanted to do it too. They had so much in common. Regaining height, we arrived overhead the airfield for a delicious vertical descent – my favourite thing! A great way to end an enjoyable jaunt with a good friend.

Sunday brought with it a lovely bit of wind for my Dragon Wings to get hold of, so at last I was able to coax Delta-J into the air without rattling down the entire length of the runway. Later as we came back in to land, Pierre was taxiing out with a young microlight pilot onboard, embarking on his first ever gyroplane flight. They circled overhead just long enough for me to grab my camera for a quick snapshot, then headed out of the circuit beyond the trees and that was the last time that we saw them. Those joyful swooping spirals above the lake were perfectly safe manoeuvres for a gyroplane in the hands of a capable pilot like Pierre. Tragically, to someone only accustomed to fixed-wing flight – it would have seemed very different.

*

Losing Pierre is like losing Keith all over again, but giving up is not an option. It's the inescapable fate of every single one of us to grieve, for death is just a heartbeat away and life will end for us all.

Flying is a gift, but gyroplanes are a drug: nothing thrills me like playing on the wind with the song of the rotors in my ears.

Becoming a gyronaut has inspired me to do things that I didn't think possible. It pushed my limits and expanded my horizons, bringing me so much joy that I can't leave this tale on a sad note! If it wasn't for gyroplanes, I wouldn't have met all these lovely people and shared those memorable adventures – I can't imagine life without them! Gyroplanes have made me who I am, and without Delta-J, I wouldn't be me.

So should it happen one day that I take off and don't return – just know that I was happy, doing what I love – coz I'm a gyronaut and proud of it.

Other titles by BLKDOG Publishing for your consideration:

Britannia: The Wall
By Richard Denham & M. J. Trow

THE END OF ROMAN BRITAIN BEGINS.

The story opens in 367 AD. Four soldiers - Justinus, Paternus, Leocadius and Vitalis - are out hunting for food supplies at an outpost of Hadrian's Wall, when the Wall comes under attack.

The four find their fort destroyed, their comrades killed, and Paternus is unable to find his wife and son. As they run south to Eboracum, they realize that this is no ordinary border raid. Ranged against the Romans at the edge of the world are four different peoples, and they have banded together under a mysterious leader who wears a silver mask and uses the name Valentinus - man of Valentia, the turbulent area north of the Wall.

Faced with questions they are hard-pressed to answer, Leocadius blurts out a story that makes the men Heroes of the Wall. Their lives change not only when Valentinus begins his lethal sweep across Britannia but as soon as Leo's lie is out in the world, growing and changing as it goes.

**Goblin Market
By Maryanne Coleman**

Have you ever wondered what happened to the faeries you used to believe in? They lived at the bottom of the garden and left rings in the grass and sparkling glamour in the air to remind you where they were. But that was then - now you might find them in places you might not think to look. They might be stacking shelves, delivering milk or weighing babies at the clinic. Open your eyes and keep your wits about you and you might see them.

But no one is looking any more and that is hard for a Faerie Queen to bear and Titania has had enough. When Titania stamps her foot, everyone in Faerieland jumps; publicity is what they need. Television, magazines. But that sort of thing is much more the remit of the bad boys of the Unseelie Court, the ones who weave a new kind of magic; the World Wide Web. Here is Puck re-learning how to fly; Leanne the agent who really is a vampire; Oberon's Boys playing cards behind the wainscoting; Black Annis, the bag-lady from Hainault, all gathered in a Restoration comedy that is strictly twenty-first century.

**Fade
By Bethan White**

There is nothing extraordinary about Chris Rowan. Each day he wakes to the same faces, has the same breakfast, the same commute, the same sort of homes he tries to rent out to unsuspecting tenants.

There is nothing extraordinary about Chris Rowan. That is apart from the black dog that haunts his nightmares and an unexpected encounter with a long forgotten demon from his past. A nudge that will send Chris on his own downward spiral, from which there may be no escape.

There is nothing extraordinary about Chris Rowan...

www.blkdogpublishing.com

www.ingramcontent.com/pod-product-compliance
Lightning Source LLC
Chambersburg PA
CBHW032059090426
42743CB00007B/177